SLICK as a MITTEN
Ezra Meeker's Klondike Enterprise

Dennis M. Larsen

Washington State University Press
Pullman, Washington

Washington State University Press
PO Box 645910
Pullman, Washington 99164-5910
Phone: 800-354-7360
Fax: 509-335-8568
E-mail: wsupress@wsu.edu
Web site: wsupress.wsu.edu

Library of Congress Cataloging-in-Publication Data

Larsen, Dennis.
  Slick as a mitten : Ezra Meeker's Klondike enterprise / Dennis M. Larsen.
     p. cm.
  Includes bibliographical references and index.
  ISBN 978-0-87422-302-6 (acid-free paper)
  1. Meeker, Ezra, 1830-1928. 2. Klondike River Valley (Yukon)--Gold discoveries. 3. Merchants--Yukon--Dawson--
Biography. 4. Frontier and pioneer life--Yukon--Klondike River Valley. 5. Dawson (Yukon)--History--19th century. I. Title.

  F1095.K5L36 2009
  971.9´1--dc22

Fine Quality Books from the Pacific Northwest

CONTENTS

Dedicated to Ken Keigley

ACKNOWLEDGMENTS

Following the compass north from my home in Olympia, Washington, to Dawson City, Yukon Territory, I wish to thank the people who helped make *Slick as a Mitten* possible.

To my wife, Pat, who supports my passion for all things "Meeker." She readily accompanied me to the Klondike as we researched the people, places, and events that Meeker described. Several years ago, we hiked the Chilkoot Trail from Dyea to Lake Bennett in most miserable weather, 100 years too late for the gold rush, but with Ezra in spirit.

To the Washington State Historical Society Research Center, Tacoma, the repository of the Meeker Papers—Joy Werlink and Elaine Miller were immensely helpful throughout years of research.

To the Ezra Meeker Historical Society, Puyallup—indefatigable Meeker enthusiasts and keepers of his legacy.

To Ken Keigley, Ezra's great-nephew now approaching his 98th year, who has done such exhaustive work on "the Meeker genealogy" and family history. Ken has been my partner in research from the beginning of this project, and to him I am much indebted.

To Karl Gurcke, historian of the Klondike Gold Rush National Historical Park, who filled in many of the missing pieces of the Skagway to Chilkoot Pass part of the story.

And to the research and resource librarians at the Yukon Archives in Whitehorse and the Dawson City Museum—as I puzzled together details of the Meeker story, they provided answers to many questions and gave me a couple of surprises in the process.

Thank you one and all.

Dennis M. Larsen
Olympia, Washington
May 2009

PREFACE

For all practical purposes, the documentation is complete. The memoirs are written, the diaries unearthed and filed, the personal papers catalogued. There will be few if any further personal books about the Klondike gold rush.—Pierre Berton, The Klondike Fever: The Life and Death of the Last Great Gold Rush (1958)

In the years since historian Pierre Berton prematurely wrote these words, other personal accounts of the great Yukon gold rush have indeed appeared, now including the Ezra Meeker story. Most of the Klondike letters in the Meeker collection were written on a cheap grade of 5" X 7" inch paper—all are now well over a century old. From their neatly filed appearance, it seems the letters were looked at only a few times, if at all, since archivist Frank Green and his aides cataloged them in 1969, placing them in an archival box labeled "Box 4, Folders 18 and 19 of the Ezra Meeker Papers." The box sits today in the Meeker collection at the Washington State Historical Society Research Center in Tacoma, Washington.

The letters tell a remarkable story. In 1898, a horde of adventurers set out for the Klondike gold fields and Dawson City in the quest for quick wealth. Among them was 67-year-old Ezra Meeker, the very same Ezra Meeker who later made such a mark on the nation's consciousness through efforts, beginning in 1906, to preserve the Oregon Trail. But this is a different tale. It is the story of a man, whom some would call elderly, embarking on a quest that defeated many others who tried, including men often decades younger. Of the 100,000 who started for the north in the spring of 1898, only 30,000 arrived in the Klondike. Meeker was one of them. And he did it twice that year!

Meeker's grand plan was to sell, of all things, soup vegetables, plus other produce, to the gold seekers and frontier merchants. He climbed to the summit of Chilkoot Pass several times in March and April 1898. He missed by only a couple days of being caught in the April 3 avalanche that killed more than 50 miners, and wrote of its aftermath. He had a boat built at Lake Bennett and floated down the Yukon River in June. According to historian Pierre Berton, Meeker's vessel was one of 7,124 setting out when the ice broke. He shot through Whitehorse Rapids and arrived at Dawson City on June 29.

After a short stay—selling nine tons of vegetables— he returned toward home with an estimated $3,000 to $4,000 in gold dust. His route out to the coast was over the Dalton Trail to Pyramid Harbor, near present-day Haines, Alaska. From there, he proceeded by steamer back to Puget Sound. Quickly, in September 1898, he returned north again, this time hauling freight over both Chilkoot and White passes.

More than three years of Meeker's life were devoted to his Yukon enterprise. He made multiple trips over Klondike trails, opened the Log Cabin Grocery in Dawson City, and operated a gold mine on Little Skookum gulch. He celebrated his 70th birthday in the north, welcomed a grandchild to the Yukon, and buried a son there. He chronicled it all in a series of detailed and informative letters to his wife, Eliza Jane, and others back home in Puyallup, Washington. That the letters have survived all these years we owe to Eliza Jane. Ezra found them in her effects after her death in 1909.

Meeker is a well-known historical figure for a number of reasons, and his Yukon trips were no secret. He wrote of them in his book, *The Busy Life of Eighty-Five Years of Ezra Meeker* (1916), though devoting only three pages to the subject. Many researchers over the years have accessed the Meeker Papers but the letters in Folders 18 and 19 and the adventures they tell seem to have escaped notice among the 50,000 or so items in the collection.

I have transcribed these letters and through them feel privileged to tell the story of Ezra Meeker's Klondike years. I have presented the letters as originally written over a century ago. The grammar and spelling remains unchanged; Ezra tells the story in his own words. For the aid of the reader, however, I have occasionally added pertinent annotations to clarify or explain in more detail a subject, person, or event discussed in the letters.

Meeker family portrait taken on the occasion of Olive Meeker and Roderick McDonald's wedding, October 5, 1890.
Ezra Meeker Historical Society, Puyallup

1

BEGINNINGS, 1890-1897

Ezra Meeker had a photograph taken of his family on October 5, 1890, on the porch of their newly built mansion in Puyallup, Washington. The occasion was the marriage of Olive, youngest daughter of Ezra and Eliza Jane, to Roderick McDonald. The young couple stands before the mansion's main doors. Roderick, a Scot who immigrated to the United States in 1888, had been employed for the last year as bookkeeper for Meeker's hop business. He soon became Ezra's business partner as well. (Eight years later, in the fall of 1898, Roderick would find himself in the Yukon Territory of Canada. Olive would join him there in 1900 with their infant son.)[1]

Down the line of family members, second and third from the far right, stands Fred Meeker, the youngest son; his wife Clara is beside him. (They would be the first of the family to head north in 1898. Clara later returned a widow.)

Standing next to his mother Eliza Jane, with a baby in his arms, is Marion Meeker, the oldest son. (He too joined the family migration to Dawson City, in 1901.)

Of the 25 family members in the wedding portrait, only one of the grandchildren is smiling. Though a serious face was the photographic convention of the day, one is tempted to foresee in those faces the grimness that was to come, but on that October day there was no hint of it. The turns of fate and fortune that overtook the Meeker clan and sent them north into the tumult of the Klondike gold rush were still in the future.

The Meeker fortune was built around the hop industry that Ezra and his father pioneered in the Puyallup valley. Growing and brokering hops made Ezra one of the wealthiest men in Washington, and at the time of Olive's wedding he was at the height of prosperity. The good times, however, soon ended. The 1890s would prove to be a difficult and challenging decade for the Meeker clan.

The troubles started around 1891 when aphids, or lice, spread like wildfire through the West Coast hop industry. European hop growers had dealt with the scourge over the years, but it was new to the Puget Sound area. It was a crop-killing bug, and Ezra labored mightily

Ezra and Eliza Jane Meeker, ca. 1901.
Ezra Meeker Historical Society, Puyallup

to fight it. He sent his son Fred to London to research methods that the English used to combat the pest. Locally, Charles Hood and Albert G. Provine (friends, neighbors, and business partners of Ezra's) invented spraying equipment to douse the underside of hop leaves with a solution of oil soap and quassia chips. They learned they could beat the lice. But the costs were enormous, and the pesticides reduced the quality of the hops and the price they garnered.

Crops were so damaged that in 1892 yields were reduced to half of normal.[2] The boom times ended. Ezra had advanced money to farmers all over the valley to be repaid when hops were harvested. Under these circumstances he knew no one could repay, so he wrote off $100,000 in IOUs and saved many a neighbor from losing their farm. At the time it seemed he could afford such generosity.

Then in 1893 a national depression added to Puyallup's woes. Practically everything closed down and commerce dried up. The Puyallup Electric Light Company, owned by Meeker, shut its doors along with almost every other business in town. Construction of the Park Hotel, in which Ezra had invested $1,000 a month, came to a halt. The project eventually was abandoned and thousands of more dollars were lost.

The Meeker hop kilns about 1880.
From Meeker, Hop Culture in the United States *(1883).*

The final blow came in 1895. Ezra had invested $10,000 in the Puyallup First National Bank. His generosity got him a seat on the board of directors but he paid little attention to its affairs. Puyallup needed a bank and Ezra had willingly helped out financially to get one started. Beyond that he had little interest. Unfortunately, the directors proved to be bad stewards of the money entrusted to them.

Meeker later said they "loaned to their cousins and their aunts, to themselves indirectly, and to others indiscreetly, until matters looked shaky. Suddenly 'business' called these parties to other more attractive fields and lo, and behold, I became a bank president."

Ezra found himself at the head of a bank heading for insolvency. He realized his friends and neighbors' deposits were at risk. If the bank shut its doors, the secured creditors would have first crack at any remaining assets. Meeker's Puyallup neighbors would go to the end of the line and be lucky to get back pennies on a dollar.

Ezra would not let this happen. On October 16, 1895, he went to the London & San Francisco Bank in Tacoma and mortgaged his hop farms. With this infusion of cash and the money yet remaining in the Puyallup bank vault, he had enough to make good on the deposits.

An attorney for one of the bank's secured creditors, however, got wind of Meeker's plan and tried to stop him. Thinking Ezra carried the money on him, the attorney physically tackled him. Clothes were torn and buttons popped off in the scuffle, but it was to no avail; Ezra outsmarted him. The money went out the door earlier with Ezra's attorney, Albert R. Heilig, with instructions to pay off the depositors.

Throughout the night while carrying guns, attorney Heilig, bank teller George Macklin, friend and associate Charles Hood, and the bank's cashier, the prominent Tacoma attorney John Hartman Jr., knocked on doors all over town, handing over cash to surprised depositors. By morning only $900 remained, owed to four unlucky souls not at home the previous evening. Eventually the bank closed without litigation, with only the furniture and charter remaining. Gone was the bank's capital, and soon most of Meeker's remaining fortune as well when the Tacoma bank foreclosed on the Meeker hop farms.[3] It had been a rough ride.

Meeker decided that if farming had quit him, he would become a miner instead—sort of! On November 25, 1896, Ezra proposed forming a stock company to buy and sell mining claims on commission. He never fully explained why he chose this path.

THE MEEKER FAMILY

Ezra Manning Meeker (1830–1928) — **Eliza Jane Sumner Meeker** (1834–1909)
Married 1851

Marion Jasper Meeker (1852–1929)
Spouse: Mary Liena Weller (1858–1918)
Married 1874
Offspring: Ray Weller Meeker (1878–1908)
          Thomas Sumner Meeker (1881–1882)
          Ezra Blaine Meeker (1884–1966)
          Marion Grace Meeker (1889–1960)
          Mary Anna Meeker (1894–1975)

Ella Antoinette Meeker (1854–1943)
Spouse: William Alford Templeton (1845–1916)
Married 1872
Offspring: Frederick Meeker Templeton (1873–1911)
          Harry Sumner Templeton (1874–1934)
          William Clarence Templeton (1875–1957)
          Charles Lane Templeton (1877–1962)
          Bertha Rowena Templeton (1879–1969)
          Joseph Holt Templeton (1882–1931)
          Frank Oliver Templeton (1882–1933)
          Lloyd Templeton (1885–1975)

Thomas A. Meeker (1857–1858)

Caroline "Carrie" "Caddie" Meeker (1859–1947)
Spouse: Eben Sumner Osborne (1856–1922)
Married 1879
Offspring: Cora Osborne (1882–1952)
          Olive Osborne (1885–1966)
          Eben Sumner Osborne (1887–1951)
          Ezra Meeker Osborne (1892–1952)

Fred Sumner Meeker (1862–1901)
Spouse: Clara E. Misamore (1858–1922)
Married 1886
No children

Olive "Olie" Grace Meeker (1869–1936)
Spouse: Roderick McDonald (1863–1943)
Married 1890
Son: Wilfred Gordon McDonald (1899–1991)

Earlier, in May 1896, however, he had become editor of the agricultural section in the *Tacoma Ledger* at a time when the newspaper ran sensational stories about gold strikes at Cook Inlet, Alaska, and East Kootenay, British Columbia. The month before, sons Marion and Fred had made an excursion on the steamer *Lakme* to Cook Inlet, no doubt prompted by the newspaper reports. Prospecting ventures for the ship load of wealth seekers proved short-lived, as little gold was found beyond the initial strike. Fred returned home on August 17 and Marion a bit later.

Perhaps it was the *Ledger*'s stories combined with his sons' enthusiasm that set Ezra on the new course. In the fall, he incorporated the International Mine Development Company, and on December 27, 1896, printed the new company's prospectus in the *Tacoma Ledger*.

In the next year he sold stock locally, while, by that summer, son-in-law Roderick McDonald was in England and Scotland selling stock. Roderick had lived in Glasgow for a time when in his early twenties. His brother William resided there now, with other family members nearby. Family and other connections from his youth, it was hoped, would be the key to gaining investors.

The names of the trustees of the "Office of the International Mine Development Company (Incorporated)," headquartered at 942½ Pacific Avenue, Tacoma, were familiar indeed—

Trustees
E. Meeker   President
J.P. Hartman Jr.   Vice President
A.R. Heilig   Secretary-Treasurer
Wm. H. Pritchard[4]
Roderick McDonald

The problem, of course, was that most of them knew little about mining, which they thought was a small obstacle at the time. On February 24, 1897, Ezra wrote the following to his wife from Three Forks, during a speculative excursion to the Kootenay country in British Columbia: "Marion has gone up on the mountain side to go through a mine with the owner for the second time—his second lesson in mining. I can see the tunnel from the window. Tomorrow we expect to go up the North Fork of Carpenter Creek with Mr. Trenary. He has been up there shoveling snow out of the last mile of the trail to his mine."

Ezra, Marion,[5] and their Puyallup associates were taking a crash course in hard-rock mining from the ground up. Fred Meeker would soon join them as well, as evi-

denced by this March 27, 1897, letter from Marion to his father: "I also had a letter from Fred saying that he would leave Seattle Tuesday morning…It turned cooler last night again and I think from the looks of things it will be colder all day. If so we can go out this afternoon if he gets here. If it's too warm will wait and start at daylight in the morning."

The letters from this time period are full of references to mines with interesting names—the Jo John or Jo Jo, the Holton Chief, the OK, and the Cordelia. All were near Kootenay Lake, north of present-day Creston in southeast British Columbia. All were located up mountain sides, covered much of the year with snow and difficult to reach.

An April 10, 1897, letter describes a trip up to the mines and the physical effort Ezra could handle when in his mid-60s: "Fred & I have had our experience coming up the mountain with our little sled & 145 pounds of freight. We tugged away for 5 hours and made three miles and gave up the sled and started on, each with a light pack and in about a mile met Marion & [John B.] McIntosh[6] coming down the mountain to meet us and help us up. The first thing to do was to go to the creek near by and spread our lunch on the snow and hide it away in our stomachs. We had plenty for all and I tell you we all enjoyed it, Fred and I in particular who had gotten up at 4 O'clock for an early start. Marion took the anvil, McIntosh the bellows, Fred a pack of sundries, while I brought up the rear with what I called my 'two bit pack' weight 25 pounds, and so we trouped single file up the mountain but making frequent stops to rest. We arrived in camp at 5 O'clock and found no cook at home, but plenty of dry wood, a sheet iron stove, so it did not take long to 'cook water' and have a bounteous spread of beans & bacon and <u>such</u> coffee that Kate isn't in it *[perhaps a popular expression of the day; it appears in other Meeker letters]*."

On June 3, Marion recorded claim No. 79202 to the OK No. 2 Fractional, under the provisions of the 1896 British Columbia Mineral Act. On July 7, Fred filed his claim. The hop farmers were becoming hard-rock miners, though they were wealth seekers desperately short of money. They convinced themselves that the Kootenay mines were well worth owning, but they needed investors with deep pockets to supply the capital to purchase and develop the holdings.

One potential wealthy investor was Alfred Williams, the owner of the Atlantic Transportation Line and the National Steamship Line based in London. Ezra had dealt with him during the hop industry's good years. Now he hoped to convince Williams to invest heavily in

ALASKA GOLD AND HOMING PIGEONS

MEEKER BOYS GET THEIR FEET WET AT COOK INLET, 1896

A gold boomlet of sorts stirred up West Coast residents in 1896 and propelled around 3,000 to creeks in Cook Inlet, near present-day Anchorage, Alaska. Like most gold rushes, there was much hype and little gold resulting from the Cook Inlet rush.

A small strike occurring at Cook Inlet in July 1895 was widely reported in the press; these stories filtered back to some Boston moneymen who sent out a scout named A. Pennock to look over the ground. He reported favorably, and over the winter an expedition consisting of some 75 hired miners and tons of equipment was organized. In early March, the miners and gear were put aboard the steamer *Excelsior*, which sailed out of San Francisco Bay with as little notice as possible. The organizers attempted to keep a low profile, but, when the *Excelsior* docked in Tacoma on March 8, the *Tacoma Ledger* found the secrecy surrounding the expedition a great lead for a story. Two days later, the newspaper printed all it could discern. The rush was on.

By late March, the steamers *Utopia* and *Lakme,* and the schooner *Ella Johnson,* were preparing to leave Seattle in pursuit of the *Excelsior.* All had a full compliment of passengers. In the spring, ship after ship arrived at Cook Inlet disgorging wealth seekers. By fall, most returned home, experienced in the doings of a gold rush but with empty pockets.

The *Lakme* had been chartered by Seattle folk, who sold tickets to their friends and acquaintances, garnering some $3,000. A group from Puyallup found the lure too difficult to resist; 12 signed up and 11 departed (1 dropped out before leaving town due to illness.) Among the 11 were Marion and Fred Meeker.

Ezra had spent the winter in London trying to salvage his hop business. He returned to Puyallup in March amid the Cook Inlet frenzy to find his sons preparing to leave for Alaska. They promised to keep in touch in an unusual way—by homing pigeon. Fred Meeker had trained pigeons for years, having them return successfully from releases as far away as Salem, Oregon. (Fred's pigeons had been so reliable that he tried to start a news service, flying in stories from Portland for printing in Puget Sound papers the same day they appeared in the Portland press. Despite the novelty, Fred could not compete with the telegraph; the business died before getting off its feet.)

For the upcoming trip to Alaska, Fred practiced setting pigeons loose from steamers sailing to Victoria. Messages were rolled into a quill and attached to a bird's tail feathers by a thin wire. Each pigeon had a numbered leg band.

Ten were taken aboard the *Lakme* and released periodically as the steamer traveled north. On April 6, carrier pigeon No. 134 arrived in Puyallup with a message, which the *Ledger* published the next day.

One pigeon took a bit of a detour. It landed on a ship at sea bound for San Francisco and was captured by the crew. They took it to San Francisco where the story appeared in a local newspaper.

The *Lakme* reached the entrance to Cook Inlet on April 12 but was forced back by thick ice. After several fruitless attempts to enter, the Meekers and the other passengers unloaded at a point near the entrance to the inlet on April 25. Here they found the stranded passengers of the *Excelsior* also waiting for the ice to go out. Not until May 11 were they able to arrive at Six-Mile Creek, the site of the gold strike. (The *Utopia* stayed at the inlet and eventually transported stranded passengers to their final destination.)

After a few days sitting at the mouth of Six-Mile Creek, a general move of miners was made 1½ miles upstream and the "city" of Sunrise was established. Prospecting proved difficult to impossible. Those making the original strike in 1895 had claimed all the "good ground." The newcomers were hampered by snow, permafrost, and high running streams. Travel was extremely difficult. The Puyallup party spent the spring exploring, shooting moose, and generally having a good time. Some of the better claims were offered to the Puyallup party for sums ranging from $6,000 to $75,000. Fred Meeker noted in a letter home: "Of course these figures are out of the question."

James B. Churchill sent out a letter, published on July 15 in the *Tacoma Ledger,* which summed up the situation well. "The experienced placer miners who went in early have sold out their claims on Cook inlet and gone away. This fact is significant. One can find colors anywhere in the sand, but they are so few and so small that there is nothing to be made in searching for them. The colors are mere flake gold, so thin as to be almost imperceptible. The best prospects on the inlet have been worked a number of years and have never paid expenses. I talked with Alexander Matthews, on Six-Mile creek, and he was very enthusiastic over his nine-foot hole in the ground. The Meeker boys and Mr. Briggs of Puyallup had claims close by."

Fred Meeker agreed. In a June 30 letter extolling the flavor of moose meat and explaining how best to cook it, he went on to say: "The Six-Mile district has been boomed for no good reason. There has never been anything taken out of it to warrant even a mild boomlet, let alone the great excitement here that has brought men from nearly every state in the union."

By mid-August, Fred was back home and the others followed shortly. Though they failed to find gold, the "Meeker boys" learned something about placer mining that summer. When their father formed the International Mine Development Company at the end of the year, they faced a new challenge—learning the business of hard-rock mining.

the International Mine Development Company. Williams would be in New York on business and Ezra hoped to meet him there and make the sales pitch of his life. But money was tight: "My Dear—I am coming home again. I want to start for New York next Sunday if we can finance it, to meet Mr. Williams there…We <u>must</u> sell enough stock to carry that property."

Ezra did finance the train trip and met with Williams. "I have had about an hour with Mr. Williams and progressed this far that he does not think it necessary or at present advisable for me to go on across to London. He and Mr. Jacobs [another investor] will each take 100 pounds sterling more of our stock and he thinks he can get another 200 pounds taken so that we may go on and lay out our plans to put two prospecting parties in the field. Harry [Templeton; Ezra's grandson] will go with one of the parties and will leave Williamstown about the 1st of June and go into the Ft. Steel[e] country [in southeast British Columbia]."

On the way home, Ezra took a side trip to Danville, Illinois, to visit relatives. Efforts to get them to invest in the mining company failed, as also occurred during a stop in Minneapolis to solicit contacts. By the end of June and in early July, he was back in the Kootenay country with his sons and Puyallup partner Albert Provine,[7] working their claims.

Then events far away took a dramatic turn, changing everything for the Meekers in a year's time. On August 16, 1896, two thousand miles to the north, George Carmack, Skookum Jim, and Tagish Charlie found gold in the Klondike. Nearly a year later, on July 17, 1897, the *Seattle Post-Intelligencer* broadcast the news to the world with the headline, "Gold Gold Gold." The story began with a sentence that electrified the nation and started a stampede north. "At 3 O'clock this morning the steamer *Portland* from St. Michael for Seattle, passed up the sound with more than a ton of gold aboard."

The Meekers, of course, were not immune to gold fever. They had already committed their future to the mining business, such as it was. The Meekers quickly made new plans. (They would later hear an even more stunning report. On September 10, the steamer *Cleveland* docked in Seattle with 38 miners aboard, fresh from the gold fields, and with a reported $400,000 in their possession. Among them was Milton Misamore of Portland, Oregon, the brother of Fred Meeker's wife Clara. Misamore had gone over Chilkoot Pass to the Klondike in the spring of 1897. He had descended the Yukon River, and now was coming home from St. Michael with $3,000 in gold in his pockets.[8])

Sketch of Milton Misamore, Clara Misamore Meeker's brother. *Morning Oregonian (September 15, 1897)*

About six weeks after the *Post-Intelligencer* first broke the Yukon story, Fred was dispatched north.[9] It appears his aim was to investigate both the Taku Inlet and Stikine River routes into the Klondike gold fields.[10] He traveled into the wild interior of British Columbia as far as Lake Teslin on the British Columbia/Yukon border.

Ezra had sent him off with a list of questions written on August 28; coincidentally the same day that Misamore departed St. Michael on the *Cleveland*.

- Does Taku Inlet freeze up
- Can a sledge road traverse either shore
- How far from mouth of river to steamer landing
- What means of access to river channel by boat; what by land, from landing
- If inlet becomes closed, then about what date and when opened
- When does river close and when open
- Is ice in river smooth or rough
- Can sledges traverse the river channel and along side of it
- What growth of timber
- What cost per mile to open a sledge road and what the nature of the work given in sections for the whole distance

- What depth & width of water in river channel
- What velocity of current
- About riffles, rapids, falls, etc.
- About Indian villages trails, etc.
- Character of soil for summer road; of feed for animals on the way and margin of lake Teslin; what kind of feed
- About a lake landing when open
- Is it practical to run sledges on the lake when frozen
- About snow fall and rain fall
- About material for building relays on the road and at the lake
- About material for boat building on the lake
- What size steamers or barge can navigate the river
- Estimate cost of delivering freight from mouth of river to upper landing = also thence to lake; thence to foot of lake
- About game
- Relative position with the landing on lake from the Stickeene route
- Report on the Stickeen route from best obtainable information, comparative time of opening, cost of transportation, etc.

Ezra seemed quite interested in the Stikine route. He had received an August 23 letter from a family friend, Jean Tolmie, who was a daughter of famed Hudson's Bay Company trader William Fraser Tolmie. She provided much detail and information about the Stikine country and ended by asking Ezra to hire one of her brothers if the International Mine Development Company sent a party north.[11] Others made similar requests.

Paris Packard, son of a family in a party that Ezra guided over the Naches Pass section of the Oregon Trail in 1854, had been exploring the Yukon for the past three years with the intention of laying a railroad into the interior via the Taku route. He returned to Portland on September 23 and gave an interview about his plans and the route, which appeared in the *Oregonian* the next day.[12] Clara Meeker visited him on the morning of September 24, learning that Paris had only briefly seen her husband Fred. She followed up by writing to Ezra with a suggestion: "You better come over & see him if you have a day or two to spare." It is not known if Ezra had spare time to do so.

In regard to the main Chilkoot Pass route to the Klondike gold fields, Ezra had the opportunity to learn all he needed from several sources. On November 11, 1897, the *Tacoma Ledger* printed a detailed description of the much used route. In addition, some time in late

May 1897, Milton Misamore had mailed a letter after reaching Lake Lindeman, describing the journey over Chilkoot Pass. A second letter from Misamore sent July 14 from Circle City, Alaska, on the Yukon River found its way into Meeker's hands.[13] Misamore mailed a third letter, dated Dawson City, July 29, describing his journey down the lakes and rivers, which was published on the front page of the *Oregonian* on September 1, 1897. Clara forwarded to Ezra a copy of the July 29 letter a few days before the *Cleveland* docked in Seattle.

Fred's reports on the Stikine, too, made their way to Puyallup by November 1897. His reporting was quickly and widely circulated to potential investors, and even sent to Scotland that month where Roderick McDonald circulated among Glasgow's moneyed class. A coded cable sent to Roderick said, after its deciphering, "Fred discovered coarse Placer gold near Lake Teslin."

Ezra no doubt hoped the reports, combined with the frenzy in the press, would lure investors. The early plan was to send some mining parties north, financing them with the sale of stock. Clara joined in: "I wish you could send some of his [Milton's] big nuggets to England. It would make them stick out their eyes."[14]

The Scots, however, hesitated to take the bait despite Roderick's best efforts. They wanted to know how much money the Meekers were intending to invest in the Yukon.[15] Of course, the Meekers at this point had little, if any, money to invest. The mining party plan died at birth.

While Fred explored the north country, several other moneymaking schemes were whirling in Meeker's head. He tried unsuccessfully to talk Alfred Williams into leasing him a steamer from Williams' steamship lines to carry passengers and freight from Seattle to Alaska. Ezra also wrote to the Tacoma boat builders, James Ollard & Co., as to the cost of constructing a vessel to carry that trade. The $22,500 quoted in a September 27 reply obviously was much more than Meeker could afford. He wrote his mining stockholders, asking if they were interested in investing in the Yukon. Most were not.

Meanwhile, he continued writing and talking to anyone he could think of who might provide information about conditions in the north. On October 18, Meeker's prominent Tacoma entrepreneurial friend, John Hartman Jr., joined in with a chatty letter proposing a scheme to train and ship sled dogs north. He ended by saying: "I think there is money in dogs when broke to work." Ezra listened, and when he later traveled over Chilkoot Pass on his second trip north in September 1898, indeed he took dogs with him.[16]

KLONDIKE GOLD RUSH TIMELINE

To fully understand the frenzy set off by the Klondike gold rush of 1897–98, one must look at the economic and social tumult affecting the United States in the previous four years. On June 27, 1893, the New York Stock Market had crashed, triggering a major economic depression that quickly spread across the United States. By year's end, over 600 banks, 74 railroads, and 15,000 businesses had failed and a multitude of workers became unemployed.

As the misery of the Panic of 1893 extended into 1894, Jacob Coxey, a Populist in Ohio, began organizing what he hoped would be an "army" of over 100,000 jobless men for a march on Washington, D.C., demanding that Congress take measures to alleviate the economic misery. Coxey's movement spread nationwide.

Ezra Meeker and his wife—recently returned to Puyallup from a several-months-long European trip—found their hometown briefly occupied by a battalion of Coxey's army over a thousand strong. These mostly unemployed workers from Tacoma and Seattle occupied two vacant buildings in Puyallup, including Meeker's unfinished Park Hotel. They hoped to negotiate with the Northern Pacific Railroad for free or reduced passage to Washington, D.C.

As the *Tacoma Daily News* reported, however, 70 marshals, 14 deputy sheriffs, and 4 Puyallup policemen with firearms convinced the "army" to leave town peacefully. They dispersed a few days later. Eventually, some elements of Coxey's army from different parts of the country gathered in the nation's capitol, to an unfriendly and unfruitful reception.

During unrest sparked by the hard times, other cities were not as fortunate as Puyallup. In Chicago, the violent Pullman strike left 13 dead and 53 injured, and with 14,000 troops enforcing civil order at the point of a gun. The depression and political turmoil continued into 1897. Numerous kings of capitalism were taken down, as were many prominent merchants including Meeker himself with the loss of his hop business in 1896.

When the *Portland* and *Excelsior* docked in Seattle and San Francisco in July 1897 with cargos of gold, many people were ready and eager for any lifeline to a better future. Numerous gold rushes had occurred in American history, but not since the days of California's "Forty-Niners" were conditions so ripe to start a stampede. Everyone wanted the hard times to end; the Klondike seemed to offer a way out.

1867—(March 30) United States purchases Alaska from Russia for $7.2 million.

1873—Gold discovered at Dease Lake in northern British Columbia. The Cassiar gold rush draws several hundred prospectors to an area bordering Alaska and the Yukon.

1880—Joe Juneau and Richard Harris make first major gold strike in Alaska near present-day Juneau.

1883—Lieutenant Frederick A. Schwatka of the U.S. Army conducts first complete survey of the Yukon River. The party crosses Chilkoot Pass, builds rafts, and explores the full length of the river, assigning place names (many remain in use today). The Canadian government becomes alarmed by the U.S. military incursion into British territory.

1885—Prospectors moving north from the Cassiar country find small amounts of gold on the Stewart River, a Yukon tributary about 60 miles south of the future site of Dawson City.

1886—Gold discoveries on the upper reaches of Fortymile River prompt the first large rush into the interior and establishment of the town of Forty Mile, at the confluence of the Yukon and Fortymile rivers, about 40 miles downstream from the eventual location of Dawson City.

1887—Canadian government sends George Dawson and William Ogilvie to survey the boundary with Alaska.

1893—Financial panic strikes the United States.

Gold found at Circle City, Alaska, 200 miles down the Yukon River from the future site of Dawson City. By 1896, some 700 people reside in Circle City.

1894—U.S. depression deepens and social unrest grows; "Coxey's army" is formed.

1895—A 20–man contingent of the North-West Mounted Police arrives in the Yukon.

(July) Gold found at Six–Mile Creek on Cook Inlet, Alaska.

(October) Ezra Meeker mortgages his hop farms.

1896—(April) Several thousand prospectors start north from San Francisco and Puget Sound; some to the Yukon and others to Cook Inlet. Fred and Marion Meeker join the Cook Inlet gold rush.

(August 16)—George Carmack, Skookum Jim, and Tagish Charlie discover gold on Bonanza Creek in the Yukon.

(August) Fred Meeker returns from Cook Inlet to Puyallup; Marion arrives later.

(September 1) Dawson City founded when Joe Ladue stakes out town site and begins constructing the first house; 500 more structures built in the next six months.

(October) Ezra Meeker loses hop farms in mortgage foreclosure.

(November)—Meeker forms the International Mine Development Company (IMD).

1897—(February-April) Meeker and his sons in Kootenay, British Columbia, investigating mining claims to purchase.

(May) Ezra Meeker travels to New York to raise funds for the IMD company.

(June) Ezra's son–in–law Roderick McDonald in Scotland promoting the sale of IMD company stock.

(July 14) *Excelsior* arrives in San Francisco with news of the Klondike gold strike.

(July 17) *Portland* reaches Seattle with a "ton of gold" aboard; the Yukon gold rush begins.

(September 10) *Cleveland* docks in Seattle with Fred Meeker's brother-in-law, Milton Misamore, returning from the Yukon River with $3,000 in gold.

(September-November) Fred Meeker explores the Taku Inlet and Stikine River routes into the Yukon.

(December 28) George Cline, an IMD company partner, departs for Skagway with wagons, horses, and supplies.

1898—(January) Fred and Clara Meeker depart for Skagway.

(March 20) Ezra Meeker departs for Skagway with plans to haul 15 tons of vegetables over Chilkoot Pass and down the Yukon River to Dawson City.

(April) Meeker and Cline transport vegetables up the Chilkoot Trail.

(May 28) Construction begins on the 112–mile-long White Pass & Yukon Railway, which will reach Whitehorse on July 29, 1900.

(May 28/29) As ice breaks up at Lake Bennett, 7,124 vessels start down the Yukon River for the Klondike, Ezra Meeker among them.

(June 13) Canada separates the Yukon district from the Northwest Territories to form Yukon Territory.

(June 29) Meeker arrives in Dawson City, selling his remaining vegetables in two weeks.

(July) Meeker starts for Puyallup over the Dalton Trail. Fred Meeker floats down the Yukon River to Dawson City.

(August 13) Ezra Meeker leaves Puyallup on his second trip to Dawson City in 1898.

(September) Meeker and Roderick McDonald sail down the Yukon River to Dawson City, where they establish the Log Cabin Grocery and spend the winter.

(October) Fire burns 26 structures in Dawson City, including the post office and most of Front Street. Rebuilding starts immediately.

(December) Dawson City has an estimated population of between 30,000 and 40,000. By December 1899, the population would fall to approximately 8,000; by 1902, down to 5,000.

1899—In previous months, 110 sternwheelers were built at West Coast ports to be sent north for service on waterways in Alaska and the Yukon. After the spring 1899 breakup, regular steamboat service is established on the upper Yukon River between Lake Bennett and Dawson City.

(March) Ezra Meeker leases a mine.

(April) Dawson City's second major fire consumes most of the business district, with losses estimated at $1 million. Meeker's store apparently survives.

(June 14) A *Klondike Nugget* story announces the gold strike at Nome, Alaska, starting an exodus eventually reducing Dawson City's population by half.

(July) Ezra Meeker returns to Puyallup. Fred Meeker stays behind to work the mine; his wife Clara arrives in Dawson City after working for a year in the Dyea trail area.

(September 2) Ezra Meeker starts north from Puget Sound for his third trip to Dawson City.

(October 8) Meeker arrives back in Puyallup.

1900—(March/April) Roderick McDonald closes the Log Cabin Grocery and relocates to the outlying town of Grand Forks.

(April) Meeker sails for Skagway with daughter Olive and grandson Wilfred McDonald for his fourth and final trip to Dawson City.

(June) The Meeker party reaches Dawson City.

(October 4) Ezra reopens the Log Cabin Grocery on Third Avenue.

1901—Yukon census lists the territorial population as 27,219.

(January) Fred Meeker dies; his wife Clara leaves the Yukon at an unknown date.

(March) Marion Meeker starts for Dawson City.

(April) Ezra Meeker leaves the Yukon for the last time.

1902—Marion Meeker closes up the business and leaves the Yukon.

1904—Roderick McDonald becomes manager of the Dawson City NATT store. Over the next 14 years, he is transferred to Eagle, Alaska, to Forty Mile, Yukon Territory, and back to Dawson City.

1918—The McDonalds leave the Yukon.

Fred and Clara Meeker, March 15, 1886.
Ezra Meeker Historical Society, Puyallup

Reports of looming starvation in the Yukon received much play in the newspapers. Milton Misamore's July 14 letter from Circle City emphasized the danger that miners would face in wintertime due to a lack of supplies. He drove home the point in the interview printed on the *Morning Oregonian*'s front page on September 15. Wintering in the Yukon and Alaska was risky enough without throwing a lack of provisions into the mix. It was the main reason that Misamore came out when he did.

When Ezra read Misamore's Circle City letter, there were two lines that no doubt caught his eye: "A man that knows the wants of this country can make more money bringing in supplies than he can working for wages." And near the end of the letter: "There are no fresh vegetables of any kind here."

Meeker was looking for a plan to tap into the Klondike fever and make some serious money. Misamore

pointed the way. By October 3, with Misamore's help, Meeker was peddling evaporated potatoes and potato meal to would-be miners through the Jones Cash Store in Portland. And, at the end of November, he started running the following advertisement in the *Seattle Daily Times*: "Klondikers, provide against scurvy, ask grocers for Meeker's I.M.D. Company's desiccated vegetables; if not supplied send for samples and price. Address Roderick McDonald, secretary, Puyallup, Wash." Interestingly, Roderick was still in Scotland when the advertisements were running.

It was not in Meeker's constitution to simply supply the Klondikers from Puyallup. He needed to participate in this grand adventure himself. The plan finally settled on was similar to one he had adopted before, in 1858, during the Fraser River gold rush in British Columbia. That year, Ezra loaded cattle and dairy cows on a scow, which was towed north from Steilacoom to Bellingham Bay where he sold milk, butter, and beef to the Fraser bound miners camped on the beach. Rather than grubbing in the dirt, he mined the miners.

He intended to do so again, but on a grander scale. According to one source, Meeker formed yet another enterprise in December 1897, this time in partnership with John Hartman and George Cline.[17] The purpose was to sell soup vegetables, potatoes, and other food stuff directly to miners in the Klondike.[18]

Plans probably were finalized that Christmas. Fred had returned to Puyallup from his reconnaissance of the Stikine River and Clara came up from Portland to join him. With both Misamore and Fred's reports in hand, the Chilkoot route was chosen for their scheme. Ezra, Eliza Jane, Fred, Clara, and Olive celebrated the holiday at the Seattle home of middle daughter Carrie Osborne. No doubt, talk about the Klondike dominated conversation.[19]

Roderick, writing from Scotland, expressed some doubts about the plan, questioning whether if it seemed so potentially lucrative, why were others not doing the same thing. He wondered if the reports of starvation in the Yukon might start a rush of suppliers north, creating too much competition. Roderick also expressed some fear about the Whitehorse Rapids in the southern Yukon: "Going that way there are those dangerous rapids to get over," but he deferred to others in this regard. Little did he know, in the following year he would be passing through those same rapids in a scow with his 67-year-old partner.

On December 16, 1897, Ezra ordered 400 4.75" square by 9" tall cans with threaded tops from the Loyhed Tinware Manufacturing Company in Seattle for use in shipping soup vegetables. That winter, a canning and food-drying operation was set up in the old Puyallup light factory building, located about a block from the Meeker mansion. Eliza Jane, daughter Olive, and anyone else who could be rounded up were put to work drying and canning vegetables. By February, the first portion of what eventually became 15 tons of vegetables was packaged and shipped north. At least two shipments were sent to Skagway before Ezra left home and more followed.

An advance crew led by George Cline and Fred and Clara Meeker arrived in Skagway and Dyea by early 1898 with horses, wagons, tents, and other equipment, preparing the way for the opening of sales. Cline had sailed on December 28, 1897, from Tacoma on the *City of Seattle*.[20] Fred and Clara followed at the end of January 1898.[21]

Upon arriving in Skagway, the Meekers opened a restaurant and left George Cline mainly in charge of the freight hauling and vegetable sales. By February 1898, Cline had set up a business in Dyea, Alaska, on the well used route to Chilkoot Pass. He sold vegetables from Skagway and Dyea to Canyon City, part way up the Chilkoot Trail, and was contracting with miners to haul their freight. As time and storage space permitted, he also moved Ezra's vegetables north. In these initial efforts, the partners hoped the cost of getting the teams and wagons to Alaska could be paid for while they awaited Ezra's arrival.

Meeker departed Seattle early on March 20, 1898, on the steamer *Queen*. To his surprise the ship sailed south to Tacoma. That night he was closer to his home in Puyallup than when he left Elliott Bay. The Yukon venture's letters begin here, aboard ship, with Ezra impatiently waiting to sail north. ※

Notes

1. In 1888, at age 25, Roderick McDonald left his home in Inverness, Scotland, to come to America. He traveled across Canada to Vancouver, British Columbia, via the Canadian Pacific Railroad, and then made his way to the farm of his aunt (Mrs. Samuel Wood) near present day Everett, Washington. After a year of farm life, Roderick became restless and decided to look for more interesting work in Seattle. There he met a man who told him Ezra Meeker was looking for a bookkeeper. Roderick made the trip to Puyallup and was interviewed and obtained the position in 1889.

   (Eventually, after two decades in the Yukon and Alaska, Roderick along with Olive would become orchardists in 1918 near Penticton, British Columbia. Roderick later related his lengthy experiences to the *Penticton Herald*, an account that appeared in the December 17, 1936, issue of the newspaper.)
2. *Tacoma Ledger*, September 10, 1892, page 7.
3. Ken Keigley, a Meeker descendent and researcher, has documented (2005) a drastic drop in the price of hops in 1895–96 that made it virtually impossible for Meeker to meet mortgage payments. Meeker recalled in his book, *Ox Team Days on the Oregon Trail*: "The last crop I raised cost me eleven cents a pound and sold for three under the hammer at sheriff's sale." On October 13, 1896, the London & San Francisco Bank foreclosed the mortgages on Meeker's various hop companies. The industry did recover in time, however, and in 1902 his former Puyallup yards alone earned the bank a gross income of $50,000. For several years, Herman Klaber managed the Puyallup portion of Meeker's former lands for the bank, before purchasing it on November 3, 1902. The *Ledger* reported that the price Klaber paid per acre ($273) was the highest ever for farm property in the State of Washington. See, *Tacoma Ledger*, November 4, 1902, page 3.

   Much of the information for the Meeker story up to this point comes from several of the books that Meeker later published. *Ventures and Adventures of Ezra Meeker* (1909) provides the most thorough telling. Also, E.T. Krefting and Marshall Hunt's "The Story of Ezra Meeker" in the *Puyallup Press*, September 21, 1939, provides more than 16 pages of text based in part on interviews with Meeker family members and others who experienced these events. Krefting and Hunt provided a wealth of new and unfamiliar material. Supplementing these sources are the 1896 and 1897 letters in Box 4, Folder 17, of the Meeker Papers at the Washington State Historical Society Research Center, Tacoma.
4. William H. Pritchard served as a superior court judge in Tacoma. He and Albert Heilig played minor rolls in the mining company's activities. John Hartman Jr., Roderick McDonald, and Fred and Marion Meeker, along with Ezra, were the main players in the firm.
5. Fred and Marion, of course, had learned a little about placer mining (the working of alluvial deposits; initially most familiar as panning for gold in streams) while at Cook Inlet, Alaska, in the summer of 1896. Hard rock mining, however, involved tunneling, blasting, and other various underground mining techniques new to them.
6. John B. McIntosh, another Puyallup denizen whose occupations were listed in various city directories as assayer, miner, and plasterer, also had accompanied Fred and Marion on the 1896 prospecting trip to Cook Inlet, Alaska.
7. In March 1891, Albert Provine, Ezra Meeker, Roderick McDonald, Frank Spinning, and Charles Hood had established the Puyallup Hardware Company. Albert Provine served as vice president. A few years later, Charles Hood bought out the partners and took over sole ownership of the Puyallup firm.
8. Milton Misamore's story is revealed in a series of articles in the *Morning Oregonian* in September 1897. He had left Seattle on April 21, arrived in Dawson City on June 22, was at Circle City on July 10, departed St. Michael on the Bering Sea on August 28, and arrived back in Seattle on September 10 with $3,000 in gold.
9. Fred Meeker's initial journey north is pieced together from various sources. In a letter dated September 7, 1897, his wife Clara said: "I wish Fred could have taken someone with him."
10. The Taku Inlet route began near Juneau, Alaska, whereas the Stikine River route to Lake Teslin started further south near Wrangell. A close reading of the correspondence suggests that

Fred went to Lake Teslin on the Taku route and came out via the Stikine River to Wrangell.

11. British trader William Fraser Tolmie, well known in early Northwest history, had 12 children. Jean Tolmie did not name which of her seven brothers she wanted Ezra to hire, although she did say that William Tolmie Jr. already had departed for Skagway. The youngest, Simon Fraser Tolmie, eventually served as Prime Minister of British Columbia. Ezra became acquainted with the Tolmie family in the 1850s when he lived in Steilacoom; Tolmie was in charge at nearby Fort Nisqually.
12. Paris Packard intended to build a railroad line from the HBC's long abandoned Fort Durham on the Taku River near Juneau to Lake Teslin in the interior. Needless to say, his dream for this rugged, mostly uninhabited area was never realized. Where he met Fred Meeker is unclear, but most likely in Juneau, as both men were there about the same time. See *Morning Oregonian*, September 17, 1897, page 8.
13. Milton Misamore's July 14, 1897, letter is preserved in the Meeker Papers.
14. Clara Meeker letter, September 20, 1897.
15. Reported by Roderick McDonald in his letters from Scotland, fall 1897.
16. John P. Hartman Jr., originally from Nebraska, served for years as a Union Pacific Railroad attorney. After moving to Tacoma in 1891, he became involved in Meeker's business enterprises. In August 1897, Hartman quickly proceeded to Skagway after news of the Klondike strike reached the outside world. He partnered with George A. Brackett and two others in the construction of Brackett's wagon road over White Pass. Shortly thereafter, he also became involved with a group building the White Pass & Yukon Railway. He served for several years as the railway company's general legal counsel, a position that served Meeker's Klondike interests well. In February 1898, Hartman traveled from Skagway to Washington, D.C., to lobby for the White Pass Railway Company. His knowledge of Alaska led to two conferences with President McKinley and several meetings with the Alaska Boundary Commission, which was trying to iron out disputes with Great Britain over Lynn Canal. In addition, that year he drafted the bill that Congress passed creating Mount Rainier National Park. Lloyd S. Spencer and Lancaster Pollard, *A History of the State of Washington, Vol. 3*, (New York: American Historical Society, 1937), 239–41.
17. Historian W.P. Bonney claimed that Meeker formed a new company for the provisioning business. Bonney also provided a brief biography of George Cline; see *History of Pierce County, Washington, Vol. 2*, (Chicago: Pioneer Historical Publishing, 1927), page 426. Cline, a former horse and sheep rancher, had moved from the Yakima locality to Puyallup in 1890. He purchased Ezra Meeker's livery stable, operating it until selling out in December 1897 to join Meeker's Klondike venture. As a contractor, he later built fully one-half of the roads in the Puyallup valley. Cline also helped construct the covered wagon that Ezra made so famous in his commemorative travels over the old Oregon Trail between 1906 and 1912; *Puyallup Press*, September 21, 1939, page 43. Other sources, however, claim Charles Hood as the wagon builder.
18. In early 1898, George Cline set up a business on the southeast corner of 6th and Main in Dyea, and placed advertisements in the *Dyea Trail* by February 18 and perhaps earlier (the three previous editions of the weekly newspaper are missing). The February advertisement stated: "Mr. G.L. Cline is prepared to furnish you with all kinds of evaporated goods. He carries an extensive line of potatoes, onions and soup stock, and sells them at retail and wholesale prices. Mr. Cline is also representing the International Mining Company." In March another advertisement announced: "G.L. Cline…IMD Co…has just received another consignment of evaporated vegetables which he will sell only wholesale to dealers." It remains uncertain if Meeker simply absorbed Cline into the existing International Mine Development Company or formed an entirely new firm to sell vegetables as historian W.P. Bonney later stated. Meeker, however, used IMD Co. stationery when writing some of his Klondike letters. No other company name is identified in any of his correspondence.
19. *Tacoma Ledger*, December 26, 1897, page 10.
20. *Tacoma Ledger*, January 2, 1898, page 10, and the *Tacoma News*, December 28, 1897, page 2. The *Tacoma News* listed George Cline as a Second Class passenger and mentioned that several horses were put aboard in the morning along with 150 tons of freight.
21. *Tacoma Ledger*, January 30, 1898, page 10.

2

OVER THE CHILKOOT TRAIL, 1898

Tacoma *[March]* **20th 98**

My dear, how provoking that we did not know the steamer would not sail until tonight and that it came back to Tacoma.

Well, I feel like I am going to have a good trip and do not now dread it as I have before *[page missing...]* must be of good cheer. I am well and will take care of myself whether I make a success of the venture or not.

Write me often and hereafter always by the mail as things at the P. O. are getting into better shape.

Lover *[Ezra's usual signature was a more formal Husband, EM, or E Meeker.]*

Tacoma
March 22nd, 98

Dear Wife

I was awakened this morning by the lusty cry of "The Tacoma Ledger," and hurriedly opened my room door to call the boy and obtain the latest war news *[the Spanish-American War began shortly, on April 25]*. I <u>do</u> hope and trust there will be no war, not withstanding the war clouds gather.

It is now 9:15, the freight is all on yet no signs of motion or stir about the ship indicate an early start or a start at all. Everybody is apparently happy though except the 40 or 50 dogs on the upper deck that continue their barking and howling and will not be pacified; they want to go home—poor brutes, but are doomed never to see it again. We had a delightful time last evening in social hall. The leader of the Mandolin club is on board bound for Dawson and the whole membership was down with their instruments which they twanged with a vim until midnight to the great delight of themselves and enjoyment of the passengers. I am surprised to see the number of women and children on board, several little tots no older than little Anna *[Ezra's four-year-old granddaughter]*, all seemingly oblivious of the stern trials in store for them.

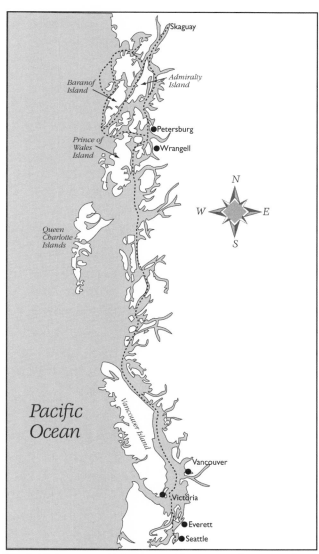

The Inside Passage provided steamers with a measure of protection from the strong winds and stormy seas of the open ocean.
William Shape, *Faith of Fools* (WSU Press, 1998)

When we shall finally sail I know not—am only waiting; have plenty of reading matter now.

EM

On Board Stm *Queen*
March 22nd 1898

Dear Wife

We are just leaving Port Townsend this 4:50 P.M. and by 8 will doubtless be tied up at the dock in Victoria harbor.

I called on Charly Eisenbeis and found he was drying vegetables from his bakery fire when that was not running. *[Charles Eisenbeis moved from Steilacoom to Port Townsend, where he was elected the city's first mayor in 1878. His 30-room "castle" built in 1892 still stands today at 7th and Sheridan. Both Eisenbeis and Meeker lived in Steilacoom for a time.]* He also evaporated eggs, and I arranged for him to send you a can and also took a can with me. You had better test these and also get some of the much advertised La Mont "Crystalized" and see if there is any difference as to quality. Charly says these he puts up are purely the egg product and he told me how he did it. He beat, or broke up the egg "like scrambled eggs" and cooked them enough so he could spread them on a cloth in the drier. He said it "didn't seem to make much difference about the temperature, about a hundred degrees is all right" and "that it was very simple." I did not have time to fully examine his drier but it seemed like a large room in which in the centre was a revolving upright shaft with projecting arms upon which were the arms that held the frames. I think there must have been 8 or ten sets of these arms and when any sets of frames were wanted convenient to examining the shaft was revolved and the frames brought opposite an opening, or door, so he could reach them. In other words, the eggs are dried by spreading on the frames that are placed in a warm room. Our drier at Kent *[, Washington,]* would work to a charm but I think you could easily heat your laundry so they would dry there. I think it is highly important to dry some if you find these of good quality to compare favorably with the La Mont product. Eisenbeis says it takes but 3 dozen eggs to make a pound, not 4 dozen as advertised by La Mont. I have somehow an idea that the raw eggs evaporated would be better than cooked. Charly says though you can make omelet or cakes with his product. You had best try to evaporate some of the raw, as well. I tell you, there is an opportunity to make some money in this if you can strike the right key to make a good article. Everybody wants to take eggs; a couple of young men aboard told me they each took ten pounds. If you succeed, better guard the process closely and not get competition and put the J.M.D. *[When conducting his hop business, Ezra at times used a code in his correspondence. "J.M.D." appears to be a reference to that code.]*

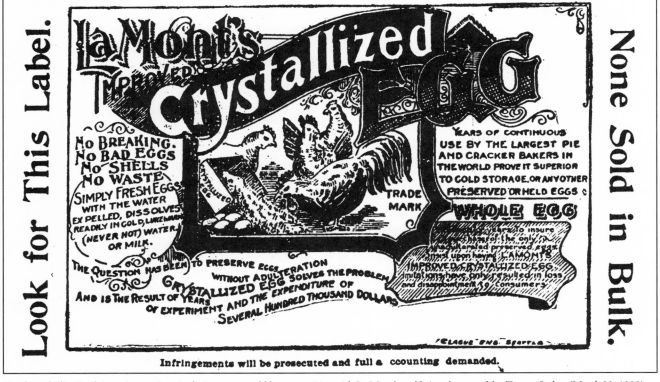

Ezra hoped Eliza Jane's experimentations in drying eggs would be competitive with La Mont's and bring them wealth. *Tacoma Ledger (March 22, 1898)*

Victoria 10 P.M.

I came up town and bought a pound of the La Mont eggs and took the two kinds to a restaurant and had them tested.

The Eisenbeis eggs are not in it and it seems to me has corn meal mixed with it.

The young man that had the test made at the restaurant tells me that an egg once cooked will not make an omelet. The La Mont egg made a splendid omelet and also as good scrambled and in both cases seemingly as good as fresh eggs while those I got of Eisenbeis would not.

March 23, 1898
At Sea

Dear Wife

We at last got started at 5 A.M. this morning leaving the outer dock, Victoria at that hour, but I slept on and on until breakfast call at 7:30. I have eaten two meals today and now at this 4 P.M. am ready for the third when the gong sounds, for the first table at which I was fortunate enough to get my table ticket.

We have not a large crowd aboard—having not quite 250 passengers all told, though there are nearly enough to fill the second table. I have all my big room "by my lone" and opportunity to spread out and have a good time generally.

First let me say send your letters by mail. The special agent of the Post Office Department is aboard, Mr. Linn I think is his name, and in fact I think there are two of them—Mr. Wayland the other. I am well acquainted with Mr. Wayland. Mr. Linn tells me he has full authority to employ whatever help is necessary to raise the blockade *[postal difficulties]* at Skaguay *[an early spelling*

of Skagway] and Dyea and that he will at once have it done, hence I will have a returning confidence in Uncle Samuel's ability to keep us within letter touch of each other. I will, however, if opportunity offers send this from Wrangle *[Wrangell]* by express and my first one from Dyea or until I see that the blockade is raised.

Four little girls are romping boisterously all around about me, the largest about the age of Gracie *[another granddaughter, nine years old]* while the youngest about like Ann. I should say there are about twenty ladies aboard, respectable appearing middle age people with but two as I remember that make an exhibition of their Klondike dress; otherwise one cannot notice there is any difference than with the ordinary passenger lists. In fact, most of the passengers have a sort of sobered demeanor as though they realized the responsibility of their ventures. By this time though the ice is broken and we begin to know each other and I find a dozen or more that know me "from a way back." One of the Gross Brothers is aboard; also one of the Burwells that used to be in the Seattle Hardware Company. We have the Rev. Sheldon Jackson with us, he of the reindeer fame.

[In response to stories of looming famine in the Klondike, Jackson effectively lobbied Congress to provide aid. In December 1897, $200,000 was appropriated to purchase a herd of reindeer to send to the starving miners. After many adventures and misadventures, 114 reindeer finally arrived on January 27, 1899. The whole episode made quite a splash in the newspapers, giving Jackson celebrity status.]

Nobody is sick, though now there is a stiff heavy wind from the north but there is but little "sea."

I must tell you about my cap, that "telescope cap" that when drawn out covers all creation about my head. Well I have gotten *[it]* drawn out like as if I was going to focus for a distant view and I'll be plagued if I can get it back without turning it wrong side out. I mean tomorrow to shut myself up in my room and practice on it which to

---

JACKSON'S REINDEER

Sheldon Jackson, using a Congressional allocation, bought 538 reindeer in Norway, 250 tons of moss for feed, and hired Lap herdsmen. After being shipped across the Atlantic by steamer and hauled by train across the continent, the herd arrived in Seattle. Sent north by sea, the herd was on the Dalton Trail to the Yukon by May 1898, but it took until January 27, 1899, to arrive in Dawson City. One of the Lapp herders had been asked: Do you think there is any hell worse than this one? The response: No, this is all the hell we want!

The irony is that by the time the herd arrived, the need to provision the miners was past. The cavalcade continued down the Yukon to Circle City, Alaska. En route, reindeer got mixed in with a herd of caribou and joined their cousins in the wild. Just a few arrived in Circle City to be given to the local miners. (Archie Satterfield, *Chilkoot Pass, Then and Now*, pages 54–56)

me seems equal to a veritable Chinese puzzle….I am not losing sleep over it, but if I were buying again I would let this particular cap alone. I have not, however, donned any of my Klondike rig except this morning I put on my blue shirt over my white one, and as Uncle Usual would say if he was alive, "its a good one." *[Usual Holford Meeker, 1811–92, resided in Fountain County, Indiana. Ezra quoted him often.]* My white collar and necktie shows so that my dress presents a genteel appearance, and with this on I have no need to wear an overcoat.

**On Board Stm *Queen*
March 24th/98**

This is Thursday and we have been running in smooth water with a channel often not wider than the Columbia river. Last night I awoke with a dread sweat on my brow and knew what might be in store for me though the storm (in my stomach) soon passed with no outward signs from the inner man other than spitting and sputtering—I <u>know</u> this was not imagination.

I am writing again this 4 P.M. after having enjoyed two full meals with every prospect of enjoying a third; but I have enjoyed much more. Having been driven indoors more by the cold wind I sought the library and chanced to pick up a well worn volume which I have now read through*[,]* "A Fair Barbarian," by Mrs. Frances Hodgson Burnett. It is certainly a very delightful little book and I wish you could get it to read. The time has passed pleasantly and strange to say quickly, with no feeling of unrest—in fact it has been as like a vacation which I am enjoying. <u>You</u> would enjoy such a trip I know greatly and I mean to somehow get up some excuses (of business) that will call you up this way.

I was greatly disappointed upon trying those evaporated eggs that I got at Eisenbeis. I took it for granted from what he told me they had the same merit of those on the Seattle market and as he told me frankly how he managed them I had visions of profit springing up which vanished when I found them so unlike those that are having such a run.

I firmly believe though we can learn the art of how to do it. I am convinced the problem lies in drying the egg raw without high enough heat to even partially cooking them while drying and that to do this some way must be devised to stir them continuously. If you can discover how to do it, economically, we can soon have all the money we would need, mind you that.

Would suggest your trying some in your top oven of your cookstove, well beaten and spread out thin on paper first saturated with lard or butter to prevent sticking; be sure though and keep the temperature low. Then again, how would it do to try some in the incubator where you could have the heat regulated with some spread out on paper, some on a plate where you could stir it at intervals and otherwise as might suggest itself. I would suggest you have incubator brought up into the pantry where you can make the thorough trial with convenience. Better ask Roderick to get a pound of La Mont product—make an omelet; try some scrambled, bake a custard & some cake. You will I think find them all right and set a standard of quality to strive for—"If at first you don't succeed, try try again" and again persistently until you do.

[Within a month, Eliza Jane succeeded. Ezra sold her dried eggs in Dawson City that winter, and still was selling them under the brand name "Chechako Eggs" as late as 1901. But they never made the Meekers rich.]

This is an amazing formation, the sea in the mountains with narrow channels, like the Columbia river in the Cascade mountains—Sometimes we are so near shore one could throw a stone to the land.

But the bell will soon ring for supper and I must be promptly on hand or give up my seat on time for the second table.

At 10 O'clock this evening I accidentally learned we would soon be at Mary Island and that mail was to be sent ashore and that the mails were handled there all right, so I entrust this to reach you from there.

We will be at Wrangle about 9 tomorrow morning and I will try to write you from there, or rather, write you on board in the morning and mail from there; the movement of the ship is making me dizzy so I must close with loved as ever

E Meeker

Friday Morning 25th, 1898

Dear Wife

We have just sighted Ft. Wrangle some four miles distant and will soon be tied up at the dock, where we will remain two hours or more discharging freight.

I learn that my letter was not put ashore last night at St. Mary's Island and will be mailed at Wrangle. We have had a delightful trip; the weather has been and

Dyea waterfront, 1898, where Meeker and Cline gathered freight to haul to Canyon City.
Anton Vogee #114, Yukon Archives

still is clear—cold enough though for the wind to make ones ears tingle, yet so bracing that it makes me feel like I would jump a rod at every step. I ought to praise God every moment of my wakeful hours for the great boon of good health that has been vouchsafed to me—and I do, when I think about it.

Well I haven't much time to write just now, but will keep my letter open until we are landed and I have been ashore in far famed Alaska.

Husband

Ft. Wrangle
March 25th 98

Dear Roderick *[Roderick McDonald had returned from Scotland to Puyallup on March 11, 1898.]*

I have had a long talk with *[W.]* Watson, who was up the Stickene with Fred and canvassed the question of going up there for the *[International Mine Development]* company. He would prefer to go and retain privilege of staking one claim for himself on each creek if he prospected more than one creek and in that event would go for $60 per month for 5 months or $150 per month wholly for the company.

It is not a hard trip to get into the creeks only 40 miles packing. I am impressed with Watson as being a thor-

ough prospector and a true man—will write you more about this when I have time as the whistle may blow any time. I could do nothing selling vegetables here—only two established stores here, one stocked, the other say vegetables no good. I have not however had much time. Our steamer sails soon and my next will be from Skaguay tomorrow.

E. Meeker

Skaguay
March 26th 98

Dear Wife

The *Queen* touched the wharf at 6 this evening and I had an opportunity to stop off before the gang plank was put out and soon found Clara and Fred.

Both were rejoiced to see me and Fred evinced more feeling than I have seen in him for many a long year.

He is not drinking. *[Several of Ezra's letters refer to Fred's alcohol affliction. The relationship with his youngest son was complex. Ezra had a deep affection for Fred and made him a full partner in the hop and mining businesses. Over the years, Ezra entrusted him with extremely important tasks and Fred seemed to perform them well as long as he stayed sober, but Fred's alcoholism caused his father much distress. Ezra went so far as to have a secret code made up similar to that used in*

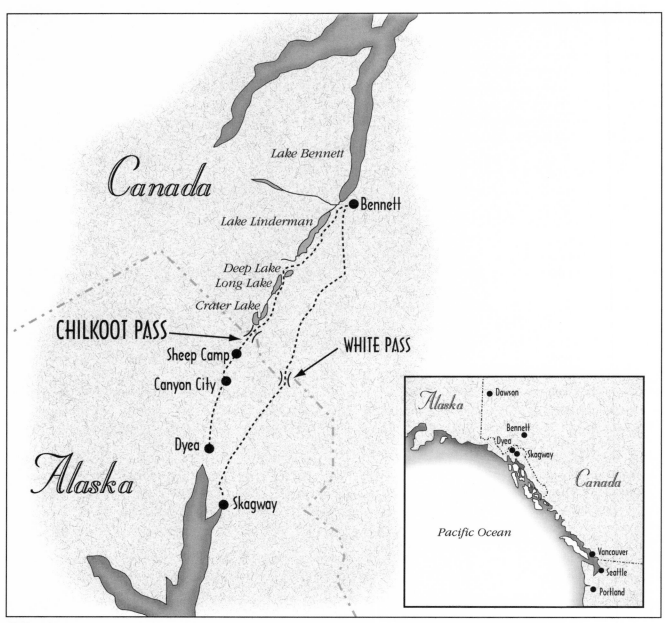

Chilkoot Pass route.
Don McCune, *Trail to the Klondike* (WSU Press, 1997)

the hop business, telling Eliza Jane, *"you can have a copy in the house as I will want to telegraph you some time that I may not want Fred to know."* In an especially bitter letter to Eliza Jane on November 30, 1895, Ezra said Fred was doomed to fill a *"drunkard's grave."* On the docks of Skagway on March 26, 1898, however, Fred was waiting for his father, who was mighty pleased to see him.]

I will have a chance to see this [letter] out by Dr. Corliss of Sumner who sails on the *Utopia* in the morning.

[Canada's North-West Mounted Police (NWMP) employed Dr. John H. Corliss at a Skagway office to conduct physical examinations of recruits arriving after training in Victoria. He cleared them for duty on Canadian soil. After the height of the Klondike gold rush, the North-West Mounted Police was renamed the Royal Northwest Mounted Police in 1904, and incorporated into the Royal Canadian Mounted Police in 1920.]

I find both well; Fred looks the picture of health. If I go over both trails, as I may, I think Fred will go with me as everybody is anxious to have a report made and widely published.

Fred says he thinks *[George]* Cline *[the Meekers' business associate]* has moved up to Canyon City on the Chilcoot trail some ten miles or so from Dyea. He says Will Slyth*[e]* *[of Puyallup]* has sold his outfit after taking it up to the summit and is not going in and that *[Arthur C.]* Dresbach *[also from Puyallup]* is going to or has started a real estate office at Sheep camp. Will Slythe is here at Skaguay but I have not seen him but Fred and I will go and hunt him up as soon as Fred gets through eating supper. I had my supper before the steamer landed.

Clara says there is scarcely any sickness now since the weather has moderated; there is neither ice nor snow nor mud in the streets here though of course the snow is nearby in the mountains that are quite high and pretentious.

I will not get over to Dyea until tomorrow morning and do not know when another chance will occur to send another letter but you may rest assured I will be careful and keep you posted.

I am feeling first rate and <u>so</u> rested that I am eager to get out and have some exercise.

My cap is all right as also my shoes and clothes, which I have worn in earnest for the first time today.

I will write you more before closing as I have to stay here all night and can deliver my letter later to Dr. Corlis*[s]*.

9:30 P.M. Fred and I have been the rounds, saw Will Slythe, Mr. Green & some others I knew. *["Mr. Green" possibly was George S. Green from Seattle who went north in 1898.]* I have not been able to sell anything but think there will in the near future. I will go over to Dyea in the morning and will be guided by circumstances as to my

movements there but Will tells me that Cline was transferring things up to the mouth of the Canion. The *Utopia* is in with the last shipment of potatoes so I will have my hands full for awhile in getting things in shape but will not forget, whatever happens, to write you often.

Things are dull here; most of the passengers are going to Dyea; As to what I will find there, the morrow will disclose; as to this place the gambling hells have the crowds. It is perfectly awful to see the recklessness of the crowds.

E Meeker

Canion City
March 27th 98
[Meeker was inconsistent when spelling place names. Yukon sometimes appears as Yucon, Chilkoot as Chilcoot or Chilcot, and so on. Canyon City most often was written as Canion City and sometimes Canon City. Lake Bennett becomes Lake Bennet. Place names appear here as Meeker wrote them, and are only annotated when his misspelling may confuse the reader.]

Dear Wife
I wrote Roderick hurriedly this morning from Dyea and sent the letter to Skaguay by a local express to be put on the first outgoing steamer. This I will entrust to Tom Wallace to go on their steamer. *[Tom Wallace was the brother of Tacoma's Hugh Wallace, the president and construction superintendent of the Chilkoot Railroad & Transportation Company, which built and operated one of the three tramways at Chilkoot Pass. Meeker seemed to know Hugh and Tom Wallace well; he bypassed a poorly working postal system by entrusting mail to them.]* Cline goes back

---

MEEKER FAMILY MEMBERS PARTICIPATING
IN THE KLONDIKE GOLD RUSH, 1898-1901.

Ezra Meeker

Fred Meeker (Ezra and Eliza Jane's youngest son)

Clara Misamore Meeker (Fred's wife)

Roderick McDonald (son-in-law and business partner)

Olive Meeker McDonald (Ezra and Eliza Jane's youngest daughter)

Wilfred McDonald (Roderick and Olive's son, yet a toddler)

Marion Meeker (Ezra and Eliza Jane's eldest son)

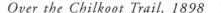

Ezra offered vegetables to this Sheep Camp hotel and numerous other establishments along the Chilkoot Trail.
Anton Vogee #206, Yukon Archives

to Dyea this afternoon. I go at once to Sheep camp. The weather is fine and thousands of men are on the move. There are but few women.

I wrote Roderick to ship us a ton or two of potatoes in the small cans—25 pounds gross and some soup stock, that the product were selling and more would sell; that the teams are doing well, that I hoped to send home some money soon, that Cline had sent $400, that teams were clearing about $100 a day. I want Roderick to have this word at once if you can reach him by telephone.

I will stay at sheep camp to night and see the sights of the scales and summit of the Chilcot pass; hundreds and hundreds are crossing dayly where steps are cut and a rope strung making it perfectly safe; they go up in an hour; I must close now as we have five miles more to make.

While they are changing the team I have a moment more to say that about ⅔ of the two first shipments have been sold at 15 cts for potatoes 30 for soup vegetables: 60 for onions. I believe a good deal will sell.

E Meeker

5 PM arrived at sheep camp am the guest of *[indecipherable]* at headquarters of the telephone here. *[Two telephone companies operated during the gold rush—the Skagway & Dyea Telephone Company and the Sunset Telephone Company. Alva C. Sands of Tacoma, a Meeker acquaintance, was the northwest superintendent of the Sunset Telephone Company and arrived in Skagway by late January 1898 to lay a telephone line along the Chilkoot Trail. Sands seems most likely to have been Meeker's host at Sheep Camp.]*

E*[liza]* J*[ane]* Meeker

I will probably go to Dawson with the vegetables. I went to Lake Bennet to see Major *[J. M.]* Walsh *[commissioner of newly created Yukon Territory]*, to get a permit for the men to go in without taking in the 2000 pounds provisions to the man. I had a long talk with him about the kind of boats to build and the trip down.

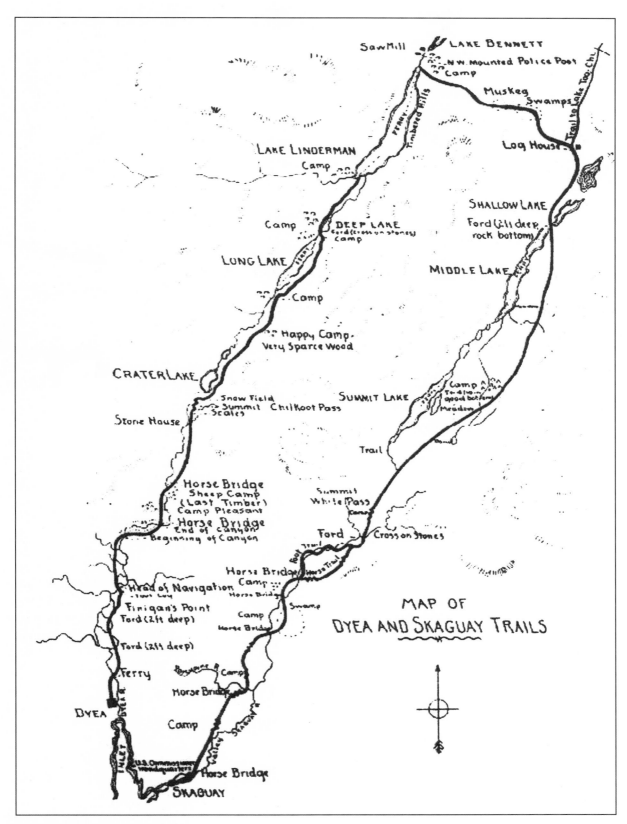

Map of White and Chilkoot Pass Trails.
En Route to the Klondike: A Series of Photographic Views, Part III. People Series (Chicago: W.B. Conkey, 1898)

sheep camp March 28th

summit Chilcoot Pass March 30th

[The Chilkoot trail extended 33 miles from the Dyea waterfront to Yukon River headwaters around Lake Bennett, with the highest point being 3,739-foot Chilcoot Pass, 19 miles in. The Canadian government established a customs station at the summit and required each person entering Canada to bring a year's worth of provisions, arbitrarily calculated at weighing 2,000 pounds. Wealthy stampeders could move freight by wagon over the first seven miles to Canyon City, and by newly built tramways over Chilcoot Pass to Crater Lake on the Canadian side. Here, they hired packers to carry provisions the rest of the way to Lake Bennett. Most would-be miners, however, could not afford this. Instead, they hauled provisions to the summit on their backs in seemingly-endless repeated relays. The effort took on average a month.

Traveling from the pass to Lake Bennett involved another 14 miles of backbreaking hauling. Upon arriving at Lake Bennett, a stampeder next needed to build or acquire a vessel to float down the Yukon River to Dawson City after the ice went out in June. The North-West Mounted Police registered and assigned a number to each vessel, recording the date of inspection and a passenger list.

A series of busy camps and rough towns grew up along the Chilkoot Trail. Canyon City and Sheep Camp were the best known, offering lodging, meals, and even electricity. Meeker paid his way from Dyea to Lake Bennett by selling vegetables to establishments along the way, and by trading food supplies in lieu of cash to the packers hauling his freight over the summit to Lake Bennett. He also paid his custom's bill with vegetables, which probably was rather unique.]

Dyea
April 3rd 1898

I have just returned from my trek over the Chilcoot trail to lake Bennet and return by the Skaguay trail *[usually referred to as the White Pass Trail, not far east of Chilcoot Pass]* to Skaguay. It has been a very interesting jaunt one long to be remembered. I met Milt Logan at the Log Cabin eight miles from lake Bennet.

He has his outfit that far and is well. He was so very kind to me that I feel under many obligations to him in hauling my robe and for over ten miles I rode in his sleigh.

I told him I would write to you to call on his wife and tell her of our meeting and that he was getting along well.

I can not now write you a description of it as it is so late and I must needs be able early in the morning & I ate breakfast at Freds & Claras this morning not exactly with them as I got up too late. They have closed the restaurant as business has dropped off in all lines both in Skaguay and Dyea.

An awful disaster occurred today up on the Chilcoot trail by an avalanche that killed so far as is now known 14 people and injured many others. Many newspaper men are going up to night and will write up the report which will be published. I have been and am still well and have stood the round trip with but little fatigue and not the least exhaustion and have not taken any cold….

Mouth of Canion
April 6th, 1898

Dear Wife
When the great disaster befell the people on the Chilcoot pass, I knew the feeling of uneasiness that would overtake you, first, to know whether or not I was in it and then a continued dread that others might overtake us. I have not yet been up to the scene of the disaster but from eye witnesses learn that the rain fall which was heavy that day, started numerous small slides that kept gathering force from time to time. A heavy snow had just fallen and the people risked more than was prudent in the effort to get to shelter. The snow and rain was so blinding that they were carrying a rope so as not to get lost from one another. The snow has about all come down I am told so that now there does not seem to be danger. Work, however, has not yet been resumed as the search for the dead still goes on; the report has gone out that many were buried 50 feet deep, but the facts are that the snow at the bottom of the slides is not more than 10 feet. About 50 bodies so far has been taken out, but several more—of the Chilcoot Tramway gang—are known to be lost but the bodies are not yet recovered, but how many more is lost, nobody knows and in all human probability never will know.

I closed a contract today with Mr. Woolsey to build a ten ton boat and run it to Dawson City. He has made the trip twice without trouble and thinks there is no danger. I am to pay him $750 for the whole thing, except that we have to furnish 3 men. This gentleman is highly recommended to me by Mr. Sands and after a days contact with him I think he is all right.

[Mr. Woolsey, as Ezra always referred to him, may have been George Woolsey, a 30-year-old Irish immigrant who had made his way to the Yukon from Oakland, California. Records in Dawson City suggest he was in the Klondike in 1896. In September 1897, he filed a claim on a tributary of the Indian River in the far southern end of the Yukon Mining District. If this is Ezra's Mr. Woolsey, it seems that rather than spending the winter in the interior, he came out to Skagway where Alva Sands introduced him to Meeker.

A second possibility for a "Mr. Woolsey" is Fred C. Woolsey of Tacoma. In May 1896, he was hired by the Yukon Transportation Company to haul a 25-foot gasoline powered boat over Chilkoot Pass to be used in carrying mail between Juneau and Circle City, Alaska. No record has been found suggesting that Fred Woolsey carried out this grand scheme or even made it to the Yukon. However, as Alva Sands likewise was from Tacoma, there is a possibility that Sands introduced this "Mr. Woolsey" to Ezra.]

Mr. Woolsey thinks we ought to by all means take in some fresh eggs and some sure enough potatoes and also acids *[likely referring to lemons, pickles, and sauerkraut, all of which were shipped up later]*. I wrote Roderick this morning that now that I had arranged for building the boat, it is more than probable I will come home before long; however, it is difficult to say from day to day or from hour to hour what one will do. Yesterday we were a little slack of freight but today are "covered up" but my presence has resulted in holding it over. Cline is striving to make things go, but he can't be everywhere and so for the present I am looking after this end of the route. We have three tents here one devoted to bunks in which we have a large air tight stove that makes it comfortable. However it is not cold, thawing a little day times and freezing a little at night.

We have two four horse teams at work and have two horses lamed and in the hospital. Freighting has proved quite profitable but not quite so much so as one would at first blush conclude as there unavoidably will be lost time. Yesterday the days work cleaned up about $60.00—while today it will go twice that & so it goes. I have no word from home since leaving; I hope ere this, you will have received several letters from me; if you do not, it will not be my fault for I have written often.

If you will send letters by the *City of Seattle* and steamer of that line, that is, see to it that they are put on board, they will come into the hands of Tom Wallace at Dyea and we will get them.

I have written several times and will again repeat I want all the potatoes, soup vegetables, onions, etc. shipped that Roderick can manage to ship; that we will find sale for them at Dyea, and on the line to lake Bennet and will take in the balance to Dawson. We now have most of the last shipment at Sheep camp and will have all of it that far tomorrow, and would have had a part of it on the summit had it not been for the disaster. All work up this side of the summit to Sheep camp is suspended.

Mr. Woolsey will pass his tools and boat material over the summit in a few days—as soon as all the dead are recovered and the road is open again for travel and will go directly to the foot of lake Bennet and begin work. He has gone this afternoon to Dyea to buy a little additional material for the boat, so that question seems to be settled.

Loved as ever
E Meeker
Saw Dresbach today; he is well.

Camp No 2, *[April 8]* 1898

Dear Wife

If I am right in my reckoning, this is the 8th of April. Time flies; I am busy and so haven't time to be homesick, nevertheless, I often and often think of you. This dreadful catastrophe on the trail ahead of me I know will make you uneasy and unnecessarily so until you come to fully understand the situation. Mr. Woolsey—who is to build our boat was camped in the vicinity and says the danger is past as the fresh snow all came down and brought the old snow fall with it and leaves the mountain bare. The slides occurred after a heavy snow storm that turned to rain which caused the movement. Business has been resumed and everybody is again on the move. I say everybody but must qualify that just a little, as here and there a man falters and sells his outfit and curiously enough there are plenty of buyers at good prices.

I did not get up this morning until seven O'clock and the men had had their breakfast and about hitched up. One of the teams was out late last night and what with some settlements to make I did not get to bed until 11 O'clock so you see I have an excuse for being lazy. Our camp is near the lower end of the canion. There is a little town here of several stores, hotels, restaurants, etc. and a very quiet orderly little town it is for everybody is very busy. The freight is delivered from Dyea here in wagons and at this place is transferred to sledges and which will soon be to pack horses when the ice melts a little more. From about 11 O'clock until 2 or 3 the upper end of the crooked street is crowded with teams and at times becomes so choked up that scarcely anything seems to be moving. But the men as a rule seem to be patient with each other and bye and bye the blockade is raised. Our camp is now a little below where this occurs but as soon as the ice goes out of the canion, then the goods must all be packed on a trail that goes over a low range of hills and which starts out right near our camp and then we will scarcely have room to turn around. Our camp consists of three tents; one, the middle one is what we call the bunk house. I am sitting on one of the upper bunks with my feet on a stick of wood that I have laid across our air tight stove and have turned off the draft so as to make it just comfortable and I tell you it is comfortable to get my shoes off and "bake" the soles of my feet with my shoes off. Then on one side we have our kitchen tent where we cook and eat and on the other the stable tent. Cline has one team at Dyea which we want to sell and is working it on the street—jobbing—watching his opportunity. As soon as the ice breaks we will turn most of our attention to packing from here to sheep camp for then small boats will come up the river within three miles of here. I can't say anything certain about my coming home but my dear you may rest assured that I will take good care of myself and "shirk" when necessary. I will say here, that I am well, eat well, sleep well and can easily stand up to all such work, and roughing it as this has been. Mr. Woolsey has just left our camp to go up to his a mile or so this side of the summit. He will move his camp to the summit as soon as possible—by Monday—and then on down where he will build the boat.

The boat is to be 38 feet long and 12 feet wide and 4½ feet deep. Bunks will be put in on each side and goods stored under them and canvas will be stretched over the bunks at an angle like a tent but not run up very high and will not come together at the middle as Mr. Woolsey says he wants the middle of the boat, fore and aft—clear so he can move freely from the stern to bow an vise versa. Then we will have our stove to cook on so that we will live right in the boat. Mr. Woolsey has made the trip down the river two seasons in succession. He expects to unload a part at the rapids although both times before he ran through fully loaded and thinks it safe to do so again but will be guided by my wish. I need not go through the rapids, but can walk on the bank if I choose. The balance of the river he says is shallow with grainy bottom all the way down; so shallow that he says the boat must not draw more than 12 inches of water. I want to

come home if I can before going but am not certain that I can.

Loved as ever
E Meeker

6:30 P.M. I am "shirking it this P.M." All three of the teams are out and will be until 9 or 10 O'clock. We keep a general utility man—cook, stable man—help to load freight etc. and so I only pitch in when I have to and not then very long at a time, in other words, I am taking the care of my self that I think an elderly gentleman of my age ought to; and yet I am vain enough to think I am of some account in the business without "milking my string of cows."

I feel very much relieved to have the building of the boat off my hands and to have secured a competent man who had twice been over the route to take it to Dawson. I spent the better part of two days with Mr. Woolsey, the gentleman that is to build and run the boat and am thoroughly convinced he understands his business and from him am inspired with confidence in the success of the voyage in safety. I do not of course intend to stay in over the winter, but come back by the first conveyance probably via St. Michael. *[The village was located on the Bering Sea, not far from the Yukon River estuary. Steamboats plied up the Yukon River as early as 1896, but it was expensive, lengthy, and progress was slow in fighting the Yukon's current to Dawson City. Going downstream, on the other hand, was faster and cheaper. It was Milton Misamore's exit route in 1897.]* Mr. Woolsey thinks he can get out in time to make a second trip down the river this year. He advises by all means to take in a large invoice of eggs and also a ton of sure enough potatoes; you know Milt *[Misamore]* said he saw potatoes sell for $100 a sack.

Mr. Woolsey says to pack the eggs in a double weight case, that is, have the case more substantial than the ordinary case; then pack as usual in the paper holders but take nice rolled oats and pack in each layer, being sure to have them well filled around the outside row. He says to have the case tin lined; what would be better would be to solder on a top after filling and make it entirely water proof. He said all the eggs packed that way and kept dry arrived in good order and sold for $4.00 a dozen while those poorly packed or become wet or, I think he said those packed in saw dust or bran did not keep; the rolled oats he says is "springy" and protects the eggs and is salable after having served its purpose in packing. If we receive any we will pack them all the way horseback—and on the men's backs over the summit—to the lakes and not "rattle their bones over the stones" up the wagon road which is a terror indeed for roughness; well supper is about ready and I am ready so far as appetite goes.

EM

[Partial letter]

if we got aground or the bottom is gravely and men can jump out of the boat and wade almost anywhere.

Woolsey says that eggs properly packed is the best property of any and advises us to take in a few sacks of potatoes as raw potatoes are in the greatest demand, sold last year for $1.00 a pound—freight teams arriving; full up for all our teams can do—til midnight.

E. Meeker

April 10th

Dear Wife

I have not until today had a safe conveyance for my letter to Dyea. Mr. *[Andrew]* Crandall *[a Puyallup dentist]* is here and will carry this. To say that I am well and hearty expresses the fact & to say I find plenty to do and am busy is also the fact, yet when I feel like doing so I can go and take a rest and a nap. The teams are hauling freight to sheep camp and some of our men will soon move up there to put our freight to the summit. We expect to move Milts party *[Milt Logan]* in and I hope to make some arrangement to go down together or at least in company. Up to yesterday 54 bodies have been recovered but it is believed there are a few more.

[The envelope for this letter has survived. Written on the outside: "54 bodies recovered April 10 Print most of one of these letters." Ezra apparently wanted Eliza Jane to provide this information to local newspapers, which was unnecessary since the story already was front-page news in the Puget Sound press.]

Camp No 2
April 12th 98

Dear Wife
    This camp is at the little town known as Canon City—the end of the wagon road. Sheep camp is five

miles further up and from there it is three miles to the summit. From here it is 9 miles to Dyea where the goods are landed. I was up to the scales yesterday. This is the last stretch of 1800 feet before the summit is reached. The incline looks at about this angle ╱. A string of men pack up this on their backs and for a regular procession. Then there are surface tramways and arial tramways. One of these passed goods on a cable at least 500 feet above the peoples heads,—so high one could scarcely see the cable but could see the car or box moving slowly in mid air. It was an inspiring sight. I think there must have been 2000 people in sight, some packing on their backs, some tugging away at sleds, some driving a horse or mule or an ox or dog team, all just as busy as they could be. All seemed to have forgotten the disaster that had so recently overtaken so many where 54 were covered by the snow slide and taken out dead and as many were rescued alive. I saw two men that were taken out insensible who have recovered. One of them knew Caddy *[Ezra and Eliza Jane's daughter, Carrie Meeker Osborne, known by the nickname Caddie or Caddy]*; their names were Chas Christadon & J.A. Kunenscraft. They said their sensation was like going to sleep and knew nothing until they awoke while being carried to Sheep camp. The sights there at the Chilcoot pass summit was the most wonderful I ever saw in all my life. I can not find words to express my feelings. I circulated among the busy throng for an hour or more; no one seemed to pay the least attention to others except where they got in each others way or came in contact in business. Every inch of space was occupied—as much so as you ever saw on the Strand or in Broadway. A steady stream of people passed over the summit by both routes and as steady stream came back "coasting"—an hour up, five minutes down. Our goods will be there in a few days to be landed on the summit. I am real well and sleep "hearty." I use my heavy sweater for a night shirt. It is as "warm as wool" and keeps me comfortable. Our bunk tent is comfortable. We have a large air tight stove in it that keeps fire all night, but now, the weather is warm and considerable rain fall at times. I have not received any letters from any one since my arrival though now and then get a hold of a paper by paying 25 cents for it. Cline is well and hearty and ready to pitch right into anything that comes up.

    I was up to Sheep camp yesterday giving out samples of Soup vegetables to hotels and restaurants and will go tomorrow to take orders. I know I will get some and possibly quite a good many. I sell it at 40 cts—a pretty stiff price, but they don't seem to mind the price. I can't now promise you to come home before getting the expedition

NORTHWEST STAMPEDERS

Numerous friends and neighbors of the Meekers and other acquaintances from the Pacific Northwest participated in the Klondike gold rush. Apparently, most did not remain long in the north, and no hints of riches or fortunes followed them home—

Henry Baggs was listed as a logger in the 1897 Puyallup city directory and his parents were longtime Puyallup residents. At the end of November 1897, he sailed for Alaska and was self employed in Skagway and Dyea hauling freight with a horse and small wagon. He also did job work. By 1899, Baggs was in Dawson City with a horse and sled used for his freighting and wood business. As with many stampeders, he seems to have gone in and out of the Yukon more than once. North-West Mounted Police records indicate an "H. Bagg" of Puyallup entering the Klondike on August 10, 1900, in scow No. 571.

Joseph Elbridge Bartlett of Puyallup was the widower of Mildred Ross Bartlett, niece of C.W. Stewart, Vice President of the First National Bank of Puyallup. The Ross's were a prominent Puyallup family. Ezra sent Bartlett's letters from Dawson City to Eliza Jane for forwarding.

Mr. Burwell, an acquaintance of Meeker's, worked in the Seattle Hardware Company. Ezra reported seeing him on the steamer *Queen* in 1898 during the voyage to Skagway.

Ella Card; see **Ella (Hilly)**.

George G. Cantwell is listed in the 1900 Puyallup city directory as living with his father, Thomas P. Cantwell, who served on the Puyallup City Council. He was a customer at Meeker's Dawson City store in 1898. He left the Yukon on September 20, 1901, providing a Puyallup forwarding address.

James P. Chilberg, from Sweden, appears in Washington territorial records by 1879. He was the proprietor of the Chilberg & Macready Hardware Store on Tacoma's Pacific Avenue, close to the International Mine Development Company office. Canadian records indicate a "J. Chilberg" building and registering a boat at Lake Bennett in May 1898. In March 1899, Chilberg became one of the investors in Ezra's Yukon mining claim. Andrew Chilberg, James' brother, served as vice consul for Sweden from 1879 to about 1900, and eventually became King County Assessor.

A.H. Clark of Sumner, Washington, owned the mine in Little Skookum gulch above Bonanza Creek, on which Meeker took a 60 percent lay in March 1899.

George L. Cline, in 1897, resided with his family at a livery and feed store on Pioneer and Poplar streets in Puyallup. A former horse and sheep rancher from the Horse Heaven Hills near Yakima, he had moved to Puyallup in 1890, buying Ezra Meeker's livery stable. In partnership with William M. Slythe, he ran the Park Livery Stable and Puyallup Truck Company. In December 1897, Cline left the business to become part of the Klondike venture, joining in a freighting partnership with Meeker. In late May 1898, Cline unexpectedly quit Skagway and returned home, stranding Meeker with tons of vegetables on the Alaska side of Chilkoot Pass. It appears that Ezra, though angry and disappointed at the time of Cline's abandonment, held no grudge. Later, as a contractor, Cline built fully one-half of the roads in the Puyallup valley. He also helped construct the covered wagon that Ezra made so famous when retracing the Oregon Trail from 1906 to 1912. According to different sources, however, Charles Hood is credited as the wagon builder.

Dr. John H. Corliss of Sumner conducted physical examinations of North-West Mounted Police recruits arriving from Victoria. He cleared them for duty in Canada's gold rush districts. In later life, he became a Puyallup fixture as head of the Western Washington Fair Association.

Andrew Crandall, a Puyallup dentist, carried a letter back to Puyallup for Ezra.

Mr. Crawford, about whom Ezra said, "a long time ago used to have a carpenter shop in Puyallup," could have been Judson, Frank, William, or Alanzo Crawford. All were listed in the Puyallup city directory as connected to Crawford & Sons Contractors.

I. Crites and A.C. Dyer started for Dawson City in March 1898 from Spokane, traveling north all summer (1,500 miles overland). After arriving at the Stikine River, they came down on a steamer to Wrangell and thence to Skagway, where Meeker met and hired them to help with his second voyage down the Yukon River. They are listed as passing through a NWMP checkpoint on September 14, 1898, in the same scow as Meeker and Roderick McDonald.

Jennie Decker (widow of James W. Decker) was the daughter of Dan and Martha Igo of Puyallup. She left for the Yukon in January 1898 with a group of Puyallup residents, including a **Miss Bean**. An uncle, who had been in the Klondike a decade before, also joined the party. Jennie returned to Puyallup in the winter of 1899, but went back to the Dawson City area in 1900, where she helped nurse the infant Wilfred McDonald back to health at the MacDonald's home in Grand Forks. In 1903, she was back in Puyallup according to the *Puyallup Valley Tribune*. The purpose of her visits to Dawson City remains unknown.

Arthur C. Dresbach, a longtime Puyallup native, served as the public school principal of Puyallup in 1890. He was the Puyallup City Attorney in 1893–94, and in 1897 a partner in the law firm of Shank, Murray & Dresbach. His home in Puyallup stood at the corner of Pioneer and Lincoln. He announced plans to go to the Yukon in December 1897. Forty years old when arriving in Skagway, he went on to mine in the creeks near Dawson City.

Emma Feero and her four children traveled from Tacoma to Skagway in August 1897. They joined her husband, John Feero, who worked as a packer. In 1898, he died of exposure in a snowstorm while packing to Lake Bennett. Emma stayed on in Skagway with the children, earning a living as best she could. In 1900, she helped Olive McDonald with household duties in Skagway.

R.J. Gandolpho/Gandolfo, of Tacoma, arrived in Dawson City during the 1898 rush with 16,000 pounds of candy, oranges, lemons, bananas, and cucumbers. He opened a five-feet-square fruit stand, renting the space for $120 a month. Selling tomatoes for $5.00 a pound no doubt helped pay the bills.

Mr. Gilbert, a former employee of the Puyallup Hardware Company, and worker at the Meekers' Little Skookum gulch mine.

Mr. Green may have been **George S. Green**, an acquaintance of Meeker's. Green traveled north from Seattle to Skagway on the steamer *City of Seattle* in 1898. The Klondike Gold Rush National Historical Park in Skagway has a copy of Green's reminiscence.

Will A. Hall, a Meeker acquaintance, patronized Ezra's Dawson City store in 1898. At the time, he must have been faring well because Ezra described him as being "fat as a pig." He is listed in several Puyallup city directories as a clerk at Edwin Rodgers and J.A. Raymond's grocery and dry goods store. He resided on Harrison and Union streets in Puyallup.

John Hartman Jr., of Tacoma, was an attorney for the Union Pacific Railroad and a longtime friend and business partner of Ezra Meeker. He arrived in Skagway in August 1897 soon after word of the Klondike strike was announced. Hartman joined with George A. Brackett and two other entrepreneurs in building Brackett's wagon road over White Pass, and soon after associated with the businessmen constructing the White Pass & Yukon Railway. He served as the railroad's legal attorney, a position benefitting Meeker's Klondike interests, as Hartman became a player in Ezra's vegetable business. In February 1898, Hartman was in Washington, D.C., conferring with President McKinley and the Alaska Boundary Commission, which was settling boundary claims with Great Britain over Lynn Canal. In that year, he also prepared legislation that Congress passed establishing Mount Rainier National Park.

Hartman was involved in numerous other accomplishments. In 1888, he was a delegate to the Republican National Convention that nominated Benjamin Harrison. In 1899, along with five others, he helped form the Northwest Steamship Company. He served as a University of Washington regent, 1905–11, and on the Board of Directors of Seattle's 1909 Alaska-Yukon-Pacific Exposition. He also was one of the 14 founders of the Washington Good Roads Association. He received a Honorary Master of Laws degree from the University of Nebraska (1908) and a Honorary Doctor of Laws from the University of Washington (1930). He personally was acquainted with every U.S. President from McKinley to Harding.

Ella (Hilly) Card and her brother **Willy Hilly** originally resided in Puyallup. Melanie J. Mayer chronicles the story of Ella Hilly Card in *Klondike Women* (1958). On journeying to the Klondike in 1898, Ella buried an infant child at Lake Lindeman. She made a good living operating cafes in Dawson City despite her husband's dissolute habits, but then in 1904 lost everything when the hotel she managed burned down. She moved on to Fairbanks following the Alaska gold strike and started over, without her husband.

Benjamin Franklin Jacobs, an attorney, was a longtime Meeker friend and neighbor in Puyallup, and became one of the partners in Meeker's Yukon mine venture. In Puyallup, he resided on the corner of Harrison and Merrill, and was a partner in the firm of Stewart, Jacobs & Co. selling real estate, insurance, and loans.

Mrs. E.C. Le Fevre sailed for Skagway near the end of February 1898. When her tent burned down, Ezra noted: "All there was reported saved was 'two jugs of whiskey' which tells the whole story of her real business." The 1893–94 Puyallup city directory listed her as a seller of notions. Because of the uncommon last name, she likely was related to Henry Bellfield Le Fevre and his wife Ida who were the editors and publishers of the *Puyallup Citizen*.

Milt Logan, who in 1898 gave Ezra a ride in his sled, remains unidentified. However, a Robert Logan is listed in the 1897 Puyallup city directory as a fruit grower living at Hester and Miller. Perhaps Milt was a relative.

J.B. McIntosh is listed in various Puyallup directories as an assayer, miner, and plasterer. He accompanied Fred and Marion Meeker on their 1896 prospecting trip to Cook Inlet, Alaska, and came along with Fred to the Kootenay mines in 1897. Fred reported in a letter: "Mr. McIntosh, the old gentleman that came with me, could not stand the altitude & after sticking it out half sick for the last month, had to give up & is now down at Three Forks some 2500 feet lower, where he is doctoring. He may have to go home." In 1883, a man named J.B. McIntosh had accompanied Lt. Frederick Schwatka's expedition over Chilkoot Pass and down the Yukon River. Although a military expedition, Schwatka listed McIntosh as a private citizen and a miner, who had lived in Alaska. It is not known if this is Fred Meeker's "old gentleman."

Mr. Moore, identified by Meeker as a young man from Kent, Washington, whom he hired to work in the Dawson City store. Nothing more is known about Moore except for Ezra's comment: "I do not think he will develop much."

Paris I. Packard was born in Washington Territory in 1864. His family had a rather unique connection with the Meekers. In 1854, Paris's parents came over the Oregon Trail in a wagon train that included Ezra's parents and siblings. Ezra himself guided the wagon train during the final stretch over the Cascade Range. In 1894, Paris

left his Portland bookkeeping job and went to the Yukon. In 1896, he formed the Yukon Mining, Trading & Transportation Company, which surveyed a 140-mile railroad route from Taku Inlet to Lake Teslin. He came out to Portland in September 1897 with dreams of starting construction the following spring, but the scheme came to nil.

J.R. Pesterfield from Tillamook, Oregon, was Fred Meeker's partner for a time. Whether they were previously acquainted or newly met in Skagway remains unknown. They traveled over Chilkoot Pass together on July 21, 1898, and down the Yukon in boat No. 14309 according to the NWMP register. For a time they shared a cabin on Bonanza Creek.

George Saar, another Puyallup acquaintance, visited Meeker's Dawson City store in 1898. George was 35 years old at the time. He grew up near the White River, just north of Puyallup, where the Saars farmed as early as 1880.

Alva C. Sands of Tacoma was the northwest superintendent of the Sunset Telephone Company. Sands built the telephone system in the Puget Sound area starting with 29 subscribers in 1884. By the summer of 1891, Sands had extended a line between Tacoma and Portland, Oregon, and controlled most telephone service in Washington. He had traveled over the Chilkoot route twice prior to January 12, 1898, when he left Tacoma with a crew of 16 men bound for Alaska on the *City of Seattle*. There he built a telephone line from Skagway to Chilkoot Summit. While in Skagway, Sands introduced Ezra to Mr. Woolsey, who built and piloted Meeker's first Yukon scow.

William M. Slythe was in Skagway in March and April of 1898. He returned to Puyallup without going into Canada. William lived in Puyallup as early as 1889; the early city directories listed him as a farmer. In 1897, he operated the Park Livery Stable and Puyallup Truck Company on Pioneer Avenue in Puyallup in partnership with George L. Cline.

Mr. Troger worked for the Canadian Development Company in 1900 at Whitehorse. He was John Hartman Jr.'s brother-in-law and in a position to occasionally do Meeker a favor.

Frank H. Vining, a Tacoma merchant, opened stores in Skagway and Dawson City, selling stoves and other hardware. Meeker sent mail out with him when Vining traveled from Dawson City to Tacoma. Vining lived at 606 South L in Tacoma and operated a store in nearby Parkland.

Hugh Wallace of Tacoma was the president of the Chilkoot Railroad & Transportation Company. He opened his Chilkoot tramway operation in the spring of 1898, which moved 9 tons of freight an hour, 24 hours a day, from tidewater to the summit. He also owned a Puget Sound steamship company that became heavily involved in freighting to Alaska during the gold rush. In later years he served as U.S. Ambassador to France.

Tom Wallace was Hugh Wallace's brother. A number of Meeker's letters sent home were entrusted to Tom in lieu of the unreliable U.S. Postal Service.

T.G. Wilson, a business acquaintance of Meeker's who made it to the Klondike, had been the superintendent of the Snoqualmie hop yards near North Bend, Washington. At Dawson City in November 1898, Ezra was impressed with how Wilson's hat and face-covering protected from the cold, and wished a similar arrangement for himself.

Warren P. Wood of Sumner eventually made it to Dawson City. When Wood failed to open vegetable sales at Lake Lindeman as promised, Ezra was so displeased that he "felt like letting out the word." In 1890, Wood resided in Sumner and served as the county surveyor. His next-door neighbor was Meeker's half-brother, Aaron. Wood was a civil engineer and blueprint draughtsman and had an office in Tacoma at the National Bank of Commerce Building in 1892. To date, however, no documentation other than the Meeker letters has surfaced putting him in the Yukon in 1898.

Teamsters on the trail through Dyea canyon, 1898.
Hegg #2109A, Special Collections, University of Washington Libraries

off to Dawson as I am really needed here and as I wrote you before think I had best go with it but will see what the next four weeks brings to light.

EM

Dyea
April 15th, 1898

Dear Roderick

I am in receipt of your letter of 31st and also one from mother *[Eliza Jane]* in same enclosure. I had hoped to sell considerable of the vegetables but so far have not succeeded. The falling off of the immigration has put a damper on business all along the line and I do not now

see the way clear to realize and send you more money immediately. Cline had sent you $400 and Catterly *[person unknown]* $100. I mention this not knowing whether you had received the advance; both were drafts on Dexter Horton & Co.

I have written *[John]* Hartman my impressions about the Skaguay trail and I will not go over the ground again; he probably will show you the letter. It certainly was good policy to accept a position as you mention *[probably referring to a personal employment matter for Roderick back home, where he and Olive were experiencing some financial straits]*.

Our teaming business has dropped off and unless the travel begins again there will be but light business. I intend to close up this business and gradually sell the teams, if possible, all of them before I start in and send you some funds. Cline has worked very hard but has spread out too much but with a general decline in business it is difficult to draw into bounds without loss.

One of our drivers had both legs and one arm broken by a falling tree. I am here with him, but will go up to camp again today and push the shipments over the summit. I wish I could only know you have received my letters about my contracting for building a ten ton boat and suggesting you advertise for express & letters, etc., but if you have not received it and acted it would now be too late so I will not go over the ground again in detail. The lack of mail facilities breaks up all calculations for business. I may yet succeed in coming home first before the start, but as to that I can not write definitely at this time; in fact must stop writing now to attend to some matters pressing for attention.

E. Meeker

Dyea
April 15th 1898

Dear Wife

Yesterday I received your letter of 27th and one from Roderick of the 31st all in one enclosure that came on one of the steamers.

I have not received your letter in which you told of your success in eggs. It is very difficult to get letters here though now, I think the mail will do better. That express is no good at all; if you deliver letters at Hugh Wallaces office Tacoma or on board any of that line of steamers in care of Thomas Wallace think I will get them. I am sending my letters by those steamers.

My Dear, you must keep up and be cheerful. I know it is lonesome for you, but I will be with you again in time and then we can and will have a "tarnation good time." I am like Clara in this, that I don't like Alaska.

I am curious to hear how you manipulated the eggs; I had high hopes it would pay. It seems as though every avenue is full.

All kinds of business has fallen off on account of the decrease in the number coming. Enough are coming though, God knows, for their own good. It is a mad rush for many who are illy prepared and otherwise unsuited for such a trip while with others the case is different and they will succeed.

One of our drivers got badly hurt by a tree falling on him during a wind storm. He had both legs broken and one arm but will recover. Neither of the teams were

injured. I came here night before last to arrange for his care and the army doctor took him in charge. He had saved his money and can take care of himself financially.

I am well. Loved as ever

E.M.

Dyea
April 17th 98

Dear Wife

I overlooked these letters when I wrote you from here but now enclose them although I am much inclined to believe that I will come home to see you soon after this reaches you. I may not, however, so we must wait for the present what course will take. I continue well.

E. Meeker

Dyea
April 25th, 1898

Dear Eliza Jane

I love to write and speak your name in full, reviving old time memories of our younger days and would do so oftener were it not for a certain element of ridicule that has sprung up at the use of so long a name.

I am well and came in here to adjust some business which my letters to Roderick will explain and passed the day (Sunday) quietly. The P. Office was closed all day so I had to wait over until this morning to inquire for mail.

Things are looking a little better for us than I wrote Roderick a few days ago but not very bright yet. We collected one account for $100, which I was afraid we were going to lose and there now seems a little better inquiry for vegetables though have a great inquiry for raspberries, strawberries and rhubarb, all of which we can prepare at home.

Our dried potatoes are gradually selling off at 50 cts. a pound but the soup vegetables go slower. We now have a call for dried carrots, but onions, Oh my; but this market is chock a block and running over. We did not however have many and full half of what we did have are sold without loss and perhaps at a little profit.

Henry Baggs was in this evening looking hale & hearty. I did not ask him what he was doing, but Mr. *[Warren]* Wood says he thinks he has a horse & small wagon and does job work around town. You must see his mother and tell her.

[Thirty-two year old Henry Baggs was the son of Clarke and Maria Davis Baggs of Puyallup. Warren Wood appears to have been a neighbor of Ezra's half-brother, Aaron, in Sumner. Wood had served as a county surveyor, and a civil engineer and blueprint draughtsman with an office in Tacoma.]

I enclose a letter of Mr. Woods which you can put into the mail but I am getting sleepy & must go to bed—I will send you a hundred dollars next week.

Loved as ever & ever & ever so much.

Husband

Canion City
April 27th/98

Dear Wife

I wrote to Roderick this morning but was cut short by the early departure of party carrying this letter to Dyea; there is no P.O. here though there are electric lights. I stopped in camp all day, "all my love" and you may rest assured I thought of <u>you</u> when I come to do my washing and sewing on buttons & such like work—natural you know. Well, I thought to take the day and wash up and an all day rest up while waiting on the movement of the freight up to the scales. I had to some extent neglected this but I don't mean to do so again. Thanks to the Great Good God I am vouchsafed good health while I see many succumb. My system seems to remain in good order and while an incident like yesterday as recited in my letter to Roderick this morning is not pleasant, yet I rally at once in "good order."

As heretofore written I am quite on the anxious seat as to the outcome of our venture up here and can not certainly say what I can do. I have not succeeded in selling any of the two last shipments of vegetables; meanwhile have had to take up the freight bills (about $160) and now we are moving in that intended for the trip, that is absorbing money. I certainly believe we will sell some soon though I can not say what a day will bring forth. The almost cessation of travel has thrown many teams out of employment, while the successful operation of the tramway from here has about caused a panic among packers so that the bottom has dropped out of values. I notice, though, that there is a steady trade although much reduced in volume and price. A good many teams have been shipped back to Seattle; others are going over

the divide & more, I think will go each way so that finally it will transpire that what is left will do well. So far, our teams have continued to earn money with fairly good profit and as we can not sell them and could not ship this class of horses to any advantage, I think we will "stand by our guns" until the change comes. Everybody here thinks it can't get worse as hundreds of teams are idle— while I was writing a man came into the tent, 1 Wm. McDonald of Dyea, and paid in $72.00 for a freight bill; He inquired about vegetables and said he thought he would buy a lot to take in with his outfit, to sell. I am to see him at Linderman *[modern spelling is Lake Lindeman]* in a few days—well as I was writing hundreds of teams are lying idle while as yet we have been able to hustle and get some business at a profit. Two or three times it seems we had nothing in sight but some how or another something turned up. I think the tramway work is going to cheapen and expedite the movement of freight so much that the greater part of the trade will come this way and will open a trade for light traffic that will keep many teams employed but everybody here seems to think it will kill all other business—its the same old story we heard in the early days of railroad building—anyway the tramway moves freight in a steady stream over our heads when in operation, take all they can get and are competing sharply with the packers. I think they send out a bucket about every two minutes but those I saw had but 150 pounds. I think though they are now loading them heavier.

So, if it transpires that I can not make ends meet so as to go in the interior as intended, I think I had better stay by the business here for the summer. I do not intend to give up the trip unless I am literally compelled to and in any event will send in some vegetables if I can't go myself, yet if I come to that point that I can't go, I think there is business ahead to warrant my staying here and here-abouts between the lakes and Dyea for the summer.

When the first treasure ship comes out there will doubtless be many to follow back during the summer & they will all or nearly all come this way, meanwhile the great surplus here now will have scattered. It will be a great disappointment to me not to be able to carry out our plans and while I mean to do my best to do so, yet if I can not I think the policy outlined will be the best alternative. I wish I could write you a more cheerful letter or rather one that would be more definitely cheering, but I can not do so now. I know it must be very depressing to Roderick to have this turn as it has but all I can say is that I am striving my best (now against odds) to bring things out.

Lake Bennett, May 1898.
Hegg #266, Special Collections, University of Washington Libraries

28th—had a splendid nights rest, scrambled eggs and hot cakes—good ones too of my own cooking—for breakfast and am now off for Sheep camp.

E Meeker

**Canion City
May 8th 1898**

Dear Wife

I am feeling in a much more cheerful mood this evening. During the last week I have sold about $100 worth of vegetables,—potatoes at 10 cts, onions 50. Soup vegetables at 27 and today closed a sale of $360.00 worth to pay for moving our stock from the Summit to lake Bennet. And what is more got the freight at 3 cts which is low, and sold the potatoes at 15 which equals 12 1/3 at Dyea. So that disposes the freight question in a measure and clears the way for proceeding on the trip when the lakes open. Roderick wrote he had a mind to go in. If he were here I would be willing to remain; the fact is I believe that there will be a revival in trade here and that a profitable summer may yet be put in; anyway two can work to a much better advantage than one. If however, I do go in I believe I will return in July over the Dalton trail. Again I notice a marked increase in the inquiry for vegetables and I hear we will have an opportunity to sell at Bennet and I don't intend to miss an opportunity to sell and try send you folks some money before going in.

Clara is here and we are sending Fred's outfit to the Lake. She is going in to camp with it until Fred is ready to go in. Fred is at work at Skaguay; Clara is not going further than the lakes.

We are still finding something for the teams to do and still making a little gain which in itself these dull times is encouraging. George is in Dyea with two of the teams rustling job work for the dray and freight for the other team and freight for the barge. We will take freight for 55 cts and passengers for $1.50.

I am starting for Lake Bennet to arrange for storing the goods but expect to return in three days with no settled place to be at from this on though George will forward my mail.

Hereafter address letters Box 109 Dyea. I had intended to write you a long letter last evening but was prevented from various reasons and now we are packing up for the start and I must say good bye for the present. I am well and hearty for which I am thankful every day of my life.

E Meeker

Dyea
May 23rd (Monday) 1898

Dear Wife

I was indeed pleased to receive your letter of the 13th, upon my return here today from my second round trip to lake Bennet.

I of course had no opportunity to receive mail while out on the trail and but very indifferent facilities for writing and doubtful chance of getting to a Post office, so I did not write, but reserved myself for this occasion.

I can not well see how the change could now be made for Roderick to come and make the trip though in fact I believe there would be ample time even after you receive this letter for I doubt if the lakes will be free of ice by the 10th of June.

I now despair doing much if any more with the teams and consider them about a total loss.

I feel encouraged however as to progress on the main proposition for I can see that I am making headway though slow—but sure—and will get a good shipment over to the lake. I have most unwelcome news to write and that is I can not get any money to send home, as I see things now. I will describe my weeks work, which I will repeat this week and that will give you an idea why I can not send you money. First but very light sales are possible here now; the business is all, or nearly all gone to the lakes where near 10,000 people are camped. I arranged with Warren Wood during my first try to send 23 cases vegetables to Bennet and to put them on sale at Linderman also and he did neither, so that week for sales was lost. I felt like "letting out the word" when I came to know what had happened and soon got them on sale

at both places but had to return before knowing actually what the results would be though I could see sales would be made and in fact were made before I left to the extent of about $25.00 the day first offered.

[As stampeders descended from the Chilkoot summit in Canada, they encountered a series of lakes connected by a fast moving stream running 14 miles northeast to Lake Bennett. First encountered was Crater Lake, followed by Long Lake, Deep Lake, Lake Lindeman, and finally Lake Bennett, at the head of the Yukon River.

The channel connecting Lake Lindeman and Lake Bennett was less than a mile long, and rocky and dangerous to navigate in a small boat. Despite the obvious hazard, many stampeders chose to build their boats at Lake Lindeman and take their chances in the channel. At both Lindeman and Bennett lakes, tent cities with substantial populations waited out the spring thaw until the ice finally went out. Meeker was selling vegetables in both locations, but his continuing challenge was to get the vegetables there. At this time, he remained based on the other side of the pass.]

I have passed 135 cases through the custom house and it absorbed 15 cases to settle the freight bills. We are selling potatoes on the Lakes at 25 cts; soup vegetables at 40 & onions at 65. The added expense of freight & duty is about 10 cts a lb so Roderick can see from that what we are getting by deducting 10 per cent commissions.

I pay for selling. I have been doubtful if I could move another lot and pay the freight in vegetables but I thought there was nothing like trying and lo and behold have succeeded in making contracts for freighting another 100 cases on the same terms except the freight is 1½ cent per pound higher and also as yet haven't yet succeeded in arranging for the freight up the scales, which is a cent a lb—I think though will succeed in that also.

Then today I arranged for 50 sacks potatoes here or the right to assort out the best of them and pay for them July 1st by leaving some soup stock in store as collateral, so tomorrow, Cline and I will assort and wrap them in paper and put in canvas bags all out of the 50 sacks that we think will do to ship. Cline took two loads 40 cases of the dried vegetables to the canion this afternoon and they will be packed to the scales tomorrow and then we will take the fresh potatoes up as soon as assorted and about 30 cases more of the dried—as we already have about 30 cases at the scales of the last lot—which will make up the 100 or in all 235 cases put over the mountain.

I will then go out to the scales, arrange somehow or another to get them to the summit and pay the duty and finally into the hands of the party contracted to take them *[page missing…]* leave them on the way though after all got them the same evening having gone through four different hands. Clara [in Dyea] is now installed at the telephone at $40.00 a month and food.

Mrs. [E.C.] Le Fevres tent and all her things was burned last week and she narrowly escaped with her life having some of the clothing on her burned. All there was reported saved was "two jugs of whiskey" which tells the whole story of her real business. She is coming home I hear [back to Puyallup].

Well, my dear I have written quite a long letter even if it is rambling but I hope it will interest you. I may not write you again for a week as I expect to start tomorrow for my third round trip to Bennet so for the present goodbye.

E.M.

Office of International Mine Development Company, (Incorporated)
942½ Pacific Avenue.
~~**Tacoma, Washington**~~ **Canion**

May 25th 1898

I have held my letter to put it on the *City of Seattle* but she has not yet arrived and now I think Cline will go on her and carry this letter—anyway, Cline is going home and will take two of the teams with him which will clean out the freighting business for us. Clara is duly installed in the Chilcoot Tramway office and says she likes the work.

[As previously noted, Meeker seemed well acquainted with Hugh Wallace, which perhaps helped Clara get the job with Wallace's tramway company. The firm had warehouses in Dyea, and power plants in Canyon City and Sheep Camp and at the end of the line in Stone Crib. By the end of summer, Clara worked at Sheep Camp.]

Cline is here with me tonight but will go to Dyea in the morning; it will be quite lonesome without him but I will discontinue this camp at once, move the tents to the lake, sell some of them (as we have four) and make my headquarters "on the line" but my P.O. address is Box 109 Dyea as heretofore.

We succeeded in getting a ton & three quarters of potatoes at Dyea and about half of them wrapped in paper and in canvass sacks. We have them all here and will wrap the remainder tomorrow and then—well, then comes the time to get them over the summit. I missed getting the mail in Dyea today as it was not yet in from

the *Queen* and now I may not get it for a week and you may not get another letter written for a week as I will be out between here and the lakes looking after freights etc.

Cline will try rustle some chickens for the return steamer if Roderick has not already shipped some; I do not believe the lakes will be open before the 10th—anyway when they do open we do not want to start for a week and let the ice get out of the way; but its 11 O'clock and I must high me off to bed so good night.

E.M.

Office of International Mine Development Company, (Incorporated)
942½ Pacific Avenue.
Tacoma, Washington

May 26 1898

Morning. George is harnessing to go to Dyea. We are all "torn up" in the preparations for moving. I thought as a rest, to drop you one more line, to say that I could & did eat hearty last evening, slept soundly last night and that my health is good. The weather is warm and I must need be careful of my diet. Dresbach just passed the tent door with a pack on his back going to the lakes; he is shipping his bunk house outfit to Dawson and going with it. But Cline will tell you so much that I need not write these items of news so now again good bye.

E.M.

Scales
June 1st 1898
[The Scales were located at the base of the "golden stairs," the last steep stretch to the Chilkoot Pass summit. Loads were reweighed, as packing rates were higher for this section. Here stood a tent city of five restaurants, two hotels, a saloon, freight offices, and warehouses.]

Dear Wife
I am camped here under the shadow of the summit of the Chilcoot pass but 2,000 feet distant horizontal and about 1500 feet perpendicular.

This is a picturesque country indeed and one that furnishes food for thought and observation of the human character and motives prompting actions of individuals.

View of Chilkoot Pass, March 1898—Meeker bargained with 20 packers to haul his freight from the Scales at $40 a ton.
Hegg #105, Special Collections, University of Washington Libraries

This morning, fully twenty women have passed my camp at the foot of the scales and resolutely started up the incline. Early this morning in 200 feet they would disappear in the cloud or fog that hung on the mountain above us.

The rain fell part of the night and as my tent was not up I tucked my robe closer about my head and fell off into as sound a sleep as if in our cozy east room. My dear, I am well and let us be thankful to the Great God for the blessings bestowed on us and not magnify in our minds our trials of life.

You will have read my letter to R[oderick] about Cline. That action hurt me beyond what you can believe. I thought a great deal of that man and to be betrayed by him gave me great pain. I have however, dismissed the incident from my mind except causally or now while writing.

[George Cline, who moved vegetables northward for five months, had left Meeker. Freight was not yet to the summit and with no obvious way to get it there. This is the only criticism of Cline appearing in Meeker's letters.]

Time flies; its two days since writing the foregoing. Being alone it is needless to say I am busy. I came here sunday to find and bring with me about five tons of dried vegetables, fresh potatoes, outfit, etc. without money except about enough to pay the duty. I had a contract to freight in from the summit to the lakes for vegetables but none to get up the scales to the summit. Monday to my infinite delight and surprise I traded with the scales packers and put up 4700 pounds; the next day 1300 and today about 800. I was fortunate enough this noon to arrange for funds to pay the duty and so this evening revived the packing gait by paying cash for every alternate trip and so now hope to get moved up to the summit tomorrow; these <u>are</u> busy days indeed but really I enjoy it. I have had about twenty packers to keep tab on; then the camp work—for I can't afford to go to the restaurant; then yesterday I traded a can soup vegetables for a box of tea; today a case of potatoes & can of vegetables for 75 pounds of bacon and in this wise build up my outfit. *[In The Busy Life of Eighty-Five Years of Ezra Meeker, he reported a charge of $40 a ton to haul vegetables from the scales to the summit. Meeker also noted: "I started in with fifteen tons of freight, and got through (to Dawson) with nine." It appears he hired 20 packers to haul freight to the summit, rather than using the tramway.]* When I reach the summit I will put myself in communication with Woolsey who is building the boat, make a hurried trip to Dyea for mails and some specialties needed and then back to the lakes for the start down the river. I now see that I will reach the goal and load the boat with vegetables without much else but an outfit of provisions. I will of course have the lemons, pickles, etc. shipped by Roderick. I do hope Fred *[still in Skagway]* will get ready and go with me. Lake Linderman & Bennet are both open but we are not losing time as Le Barge *[Lake Laberge, further north]* is reported closed and besides I do not want to follow the ice down too closely. Thousands of boats I hear are starting already; it will be at least a week before I am ready and that will be soon enough.

Again—time flies, since the foregoing was written I have been to the lakes, seen Woolsey, seen the boat and will begin loading tomorrow or next day at Linderman; I am on my return from Skaguay to Dyea; Fred thinks he can't get ready before the 15th and I will not wait on him; will write you more before mailing, after I get ashore & get more paper.

On Board, At Bennett
June 14th 1898

My Dear Wife

One by one things have been accomplished so that now I think we can surely make a start tomorrow, provided—that fickle old dame, the weather—wind—is favorable. I will not call this a farewell letter as I know there will be abundant opportunities to send you letters. In fact, a steamer line is running from here to Dawson with passengers and freight but make one or two portages.

The scenes around about me are very similar to what we saw and experienced on the plains in 52 only one must substitute the boat for the wagon and water carriage for land *[Ezra is referring to their 1852 Oregon Trail journey].* Many people are poorly outfitted like in 52, while others are perfectly at home; some have already met their mishap even before starting. Our craft is one of the best I have seen and is safe.

15th I was too sleepy to finish my letter last night and too busy to write much this morning. We now have the cargo nearly all on board and so far as I can now see will be ready for the final start in a couple of hours. We have a 12 x 14 tent set up in the middle of the boat with boxes & crates of vegetables piled 3 high upon which we make our bed—and I have a good one—The cook stove is just outside the tent door and stands on boxes of vegetables and I can see ahead, a very comfortable handy little kitchen of about 3 x 4 feet of a space to stand, with the stove on one side; a provision box on another and the mess box on the third so that one can stand still in one place and get breakfast. We of course have no water rent to pay although its very convenient so all and all I think we are going to be comfortable and happy. If the steamer line up the river from Dawson is a success, I will doubtless come up that way instead of by the Dalton trail so now good bye for the present.

E Meeker

Whitehorse
June 21st/98

Dear Wife

We have arrived here all well, safe & sound after 4½ days of baffling wind, except for the first day—however, yesterday for awhile we were favored.

There is a tramway around the rapids but even in the Tramway office they advise my running the rapids loaded as we are and after examination by the Government pilots, we have taken two on board and are now preparing for the trip and the pilots will bring the letter back. They have examined the boat and say its perfectly safe and that they have not yet lost a boat.

This is the last letter I expect opportunity to send back to you until we arrive in Dawson. I am well—4:50 P.M. We have run the rapids with cargo aboard all safe=30 minutes five miles=cost $35.00=will be underway in one hour.

E Meeker

A scow "taking a ducking" in Whitehorse Rapids.
Anton Vogee #269, Yukon Archives

On Board
June 22nd 1898
4 P.M.

Dear Wife

It is difficult to say when you will receive this letter, if ever, but having leisure this afternoon thought to write you as you have been much in my mind. I am well.

We are sailing lazily down lake La Barge with a breeze scarcely perceptible, having run about 25 miles of Lewes river below White Horse rapids and six or eight miles of the lake. We left the "Rapids" at 4 this morning, it was our intention to leave at 2 but I overslept myself two hours.

[Maps dating from 1949 and later indicate the Yukon River beginning at Lake Bennett. Prior to 1949, however, Canada officially identified only that part of the river downstream from the Pelly River as the Yukon; the long stretch upstream from the Pelly to Lake Bennett was known as the

Lewes River. This identification dated from the 1840s when Hudson's Bay Company explorers arrived at the Yukon-Pelly junction. They mistakenly judged the Pelly River as discharging the greater volume of water, leading to the conclusion that the other branch was a tributary of the Yukon and thus needed a name. John Lewes, a HBC chief factor, was honored with his name attached to the upper Yukon.

Over time, however, common usage gave the name "Yukon" to the entire river, but only in 1949 did the Canadian government officially remove the Lewes name from maps. To confuse matters further, the 30-mile section of the Lewes (Yukon) River north from Lake Laberge to the Teslin River was called Thirty-Mile River by stampeders.]

An ill advised promise as the adage runs is better broken than kept; so acting in accordance with that theory I ran the White Horse rapids on our boat and must say that I enjoyed the ride greatly. The confidence shown by the pilots employed, their thorough preparation for the trip, with the evident skill displayed dispeled all feeling of distrust as to the results of the trip so that I felt no more doubt than I would on ship board when the ship was in the hands of the pilot entering port; in fact, there is no danger with a suitable boat and skilled pilots. You will remember the rapid jumping water we saw in the Niagara river a few miles below the falls; well the canion and White Horse rapids is like that though the waves are not quite so large and do not spout up quite so high; in all conscience they are big enough and high enough to make it interesting for all hands on board. Probably a barrel of water in all slopped on board during the trip but I did not get wet from that source. I did though get a ducking from a heavy shower that struck us soon after we started. In the hustle & bustle of the preparation I forgot my coat and when the tent was let down the coat could not be got at and so I had to "take my medicine." It was only a 30 minute run for the 5 miles from the head of the canon to the foot of the rapids. The regular licensed pilots have not lost a boat this year though they have run thousands through the rapids so you see there was small wonder that I should prefer to stay with the boat instead of taking a five mile tramp along the bank of the river or rather paralel trail with the river.

[A different version made its way into Ezra's later writings. In The Busy Life of Eighty-Five Years of Ezra Meeker, *he wrote: "I received a good ducking in my first passage through the White Horse rapids, and vowed that I would not go through them again." There is no mention, however, that the "ducking" came from a rain squall, leaving readers to wrongly assume he was soaked in the rapids themselves.]*

In Taggish lake, after the South wind sprung up that struck the mosquito fleet of small boats, first there finally came in sight eighty boats within a stretch of view of say 5 miles. These small boats could all outsail us and we were soon in the midst of the fleet passing us. In the evening we passed them at the foot of the lake where their camp fires lined the shore while we passed on down Lewes river and ran till 1 O'clock in the morning; just now, about 40 boats are in sight in part of the same fleet and in part new neighbors; according to the Police reports about 10,000 boats have passed down the river so far, a mighty exodus.

June 27th Passing through 30 mile river *[the section of the stream immediately below Lake Laberge]* we saw numerous wrecks of scows & boats—I should say a dozen in all. Some of the scows were broken square in two parts in the middle when they struck the rocks. It was the grossest kind of cruelness or lack of preparation that caused this. I had heard of these disasters before starting down the river and had shipped two more men to work their passage down to Dawson. I don't think we

came within a hundred feet of hitting any of the rocks that had caused the disaster or in fact any. One life was lost. A curious circumstance occurred. One man, whose boat was broken was left on the rock in a very perilous position as it was next to impossible to get a boat to him. He stood on the rock warning other boats until finally one boat either did not hear or become demoralized and pulled the wrong way and so struck the rock and swung off but not until the unfortunate man on the rock had jumped into the boat and went down the river safely.

We have just passed the mouth of the Pelly river and consequently are now on the Yukon. We are now landing at Fort Selkirk and I go ashore to try send you this letter.

E. Meeker

Dawson City
June 30th 1898

Dear Roderick

As there is a chance to send a letter by the *Seattle No. 1* this 2 P.M. I thought but to at least write you of my safe arrival here last night, or rather this morning just after midnight. We anchored 3 miles above town and I came down in the small boat about 10 P.M. and then sent back for the scow. Meantime, I looked around until the scow arrived to pick up the lines.

I am now writing while the men are getting breakfast, and hence have had small opportunity to examine as to condition of the potatoes but think they are in fair condition and will sell readily for about 60 cents per pound. I think there will be something over 3500 lbs.

I opened up negotiations last night to sell the cargo for 50 cents a pound taking potatoes dried & fresh, onions, soup vegetables etc. and if I make that kind of a trade a go, we will have done fairly well as I have over six tons in all of such.

I hear that dried vegetables are dull of sale and about 50 cents a pound but one can't tell much about it as all sorts of prices prevail, in one instance high another way down. Many kinds of provisions are low while some others are excessively high, steak, for instance is 1.50 per pound.

There is no overstock of fresh potatoes, so I will have no difficulty in clearing them up speedily—and in any event will not detain long but expect to be on my way out long before you receive this letter. As to which way I will come home I can't yet determine. The Yucon is very low for this season of the year, but has been excessively high early in the season, hence it is thought travel

Dawson City waterfront, early July 1898, where Meeker sold vegetables from his scow.
UW #26816, Special Collections, University of Washington Libraries

by the river route will be quite uncertain; if I finally find that I can safely come that way without probably being detained, will take an up river steamer to 5 fingers *[Five Finger Rapids, 200 miles south of Dawson City]* and then on out to Pyramid Harbor by the Dalton trail.

The output of gold is going to be disappointing if one can judge anything by the street talk of which there seems to be no difference in opinion. Of course I shall lose no time in getting out and do not expect to see any of the mines as I am still of the opinion that we ought to make the second trip in this fall if I can sell out this venture so as to make it possible for us to do so.

I am well, thanks to the Great Good God. Last Monday or Sunday I started in with one of my periodical "dumps" and applied my medicine of dieting and straightened up again speedily and felt as well as ever—eating too much I think caused it. I went on a spree last night while the men were bringing the scow in and had a $2.50 dinner on moose stake, granulated potatoes & coffee.

E. Meeker

[Throughout most of his adult life, Ezra suffered from a hernia for which he wore a truss or padded belt to help keep the intestine from bulging. He had ruptured himself in Indiana at a log rolling in about 1851. On November 18, 1913, the hernia finally was surgically repaired. He noted in a February 14, 1914, letter: "Charley came to my rescue and saved my life by a surgical operation and what is most marvelous cured my rupture and now I don't have to wear a truss at all and can do all sorts of things without danger."

"Charley"—Dr. Charles Templeton—was one of Meeker's grandsons. Three surgeons performed the operation at Seattle's Providence Hospital. Remarkably, Meeker had been able to perform at a high level of physical activity for 62 years with this condition. When the hernia acted up, he usually referred to the discomfort simply as severe indigestion. His cure was a period of fasting, usually bringing relief. In 1913, the condition became life-threatening and could no longer be ignored. Meeker claimed he was but hours from death and credited his grandson for preserving his life.]

2 P.M.

I find that the soup vegetables are a drag on the market and will probably drag.

I have opened the price of the potatoes at 65 cts & I think they will sell at that but I will need pay a 5 per cent commission out of that. The granulated potatoes I think will sell at 50 cts. It is a great pity I could not have gotten here 2 or 3 weeks sooner as prices were then better and market more active; however, we have only just now gotten into position to begin to do business and must await results before reporting anything definite.

E. Meeker

Dawson City
June 30th 98

My Dear, now that I am at my journeys end and expect soon to be on my way back, my thoughts are with you more and more.

My little brush of which I write to Roderick did not cut me down at all. I think I took some cold, but if I did it all appeared in my breast and side as I had quite a pain but which is now nearly all gone.

As I will be home soon, probably before this letter reaches you, I will not try to write you any farther than to say that I am well, but oh, _so_ busy today that I will hardly be able to tell "where I am at" or to write you more. Our little expedition, to say the least, will not be a failure and I feel that it will be a success but I will feel surer when I get the gold dust in my pocket.

Loved as ever
EM

Tell the "Lady of the house" that it is not for the reason that I have forgotten her but that I am so busy that I can scarcely call a moment my own. We have a regular string of customers and it keeps all hands busy to sell, deliver and collect. A gentleman came on board _[Ezra was selling from his boat]_ a couple of hours ago—a restaurant proprietor— and asked "what's the price of potatoes? "Sixty five" I answered. Send me 300 pounds. Shortly afterwards they were delivered and the gold was laid out to pay for them.

Sunday July 3rd 1898

Dear Wife

After I had written the foregoing to finish my letter to Roderick sent off yesterday, I was interrupted and finally forgot to enclose even what I had written on this sheet.

Dawson business is closed on Sunday—saloons and all—and so I will have more leisure today; so I thought to write you though I am not without hope that I may go on the same boat that carries this letter; if not I certainly think I can on the next about a week later. The steamer runs from here to Rink Rapids—Five fingers—and from there, passengers take the Dalton trail. That is the route I intend to take. I am to have a horse to ride, have meals furnished, shelter to stay in and blankets packed for $200 from here to Pyramid Harbor with a probable time of 15 days; so even if I do not get started until the 10th it is yet possible to reach home by the 1st of August.

Thursday afternoon, Friday and yesterday the sales ran from a little over $1500. The little dab of Squash we had sold for $1.00 a pound and now great numbers are wanting more. I could easily sell a ton of it in short order. When I first opened and asked $1.00 pound for onions, I was told the town was full of onions and had been sold for 50 cts. Nevertheless I stuck to my colors and finally sold some at that which brought others on account of their quality and now ours are all gone and calls for more is repeated time & again; we can always sell freely of these and if it is found practicable I want to prepare some of both for our trip this fall. It now looks as though I will get home with over $3,000—it may be $4,000, but anyway it will not be less than $3,000 I think and I will have special orders enough to ensure the success of another expedition this year. I have had a like experience with our soup vegetables as related about the onions. I was told that the town was full of soup vegetables and so it is, but parties that bought a can Thursday came back yesterday and took a case with 12 cans. The stock of Soup vegetables on hand here in Dawson is not good—in fact one might say is trashy and ours will finally all sell off, but not so rapidly as the balance of the stuff. We will not want to manufacture any more of this this year, but we ought to have some turnips, cabbage and carrots if found practicable to obtain them.

We ought to have some Sauerkraut in small buckets or rather light kegs. Of course the main thing will be to get in here with fresh vegetables in good condition and as they cost least and sell highest; it inclines one to run more in that line and so I think we will bring in at least half of that kind of stuff and maybe more. All our shipments

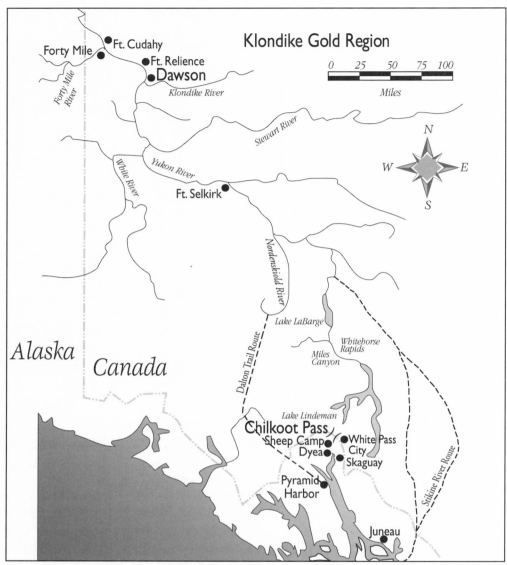

Revised from William Shape, *Faith of Fools* (WSU Press, 1998)

must reach Dyea <u>not later</u> than September 20th so that I can leave Bennet by the 1st or not later than the 5th of October. I called yesterday on Father Judge, the catholic priest here, who has been on the Yucon for twelve years and he says ordinarily we would be safe to count on the whole month of October for an open river this far and surely until the middle of October.

[Father William Judge came to Dawson City in March 1897 and started a hospital—first in a tent, then a log building. He worked long hours caring for the sick and dying, and also established a parish, erecting St. Mary's Catholic Church next door to the hospital. He contracted pneumonia and died in January 1899 at age 49, and is buried beside the alter of the church.]

I know where we can get the lumber on short notice at Bennet for building the scow; we will build one decked in and make it frost proof so that everything will be safe from injury from either frost or water. We will put in an air tight stove so that the temperature can be regulated and keep them stored in the scow until sold. We will double sack the vegetables and wrap the inside sack in a large sheet of heavy paper before putting into the outside sack. This will protect them in transit on the trail should we encounter cold weather and besides may bring some blankets or robes to cover over night. By the way, I sold my robe yesterday for $65.00—that one we bought for $17.00 at the Seattle Trading company. I could easily sell more if I had them but all say the demand will be much greater later on.

I believe there is a chance for us to get hold of some mining property but feel that we had best turn the funds over more, take time to examine and then buy later. There are men here that have good properties that here & there on account of sickness and from other causes become determined to sell out and in that way one finds an opportunity to get a claim; better than to take the time, incur the risk and make the outlay incident to prospecting.

I will not say that I do not dread the trip in again for I do dislike it greatly but I think I ought to make it. I believe I can make it safely but I expect it will be prudence for me to arrange to remain all winter and there's where the rub comes in. If I only could have been here this season with the first boats three weeks ago, I could have easily brought out 200 ounces more gold than I will now be able to do, and then maybe we would have been content for the year. Well, anyway, we will get out on a basis of some profit and which is in results so much better than it might have happened, that we had better be thankful rather than complaining.

Loved as ever
E. Meeker

[The Dalton Trail, Meeker's route toward home, left the Yukon River near Five Finger Rapids, about 200 miles south of Dawson City, and proceeded up the Nordenskiold River drainage toward Chilkat Pass. Travelers on horseback or by foot trekked 250 miles through mountain wilderness to the coast at Pyramid Harbor at the head of Lynn Canal—near present day Haines, Alaska, and not far from Skagway.

By the summer of 1898, steamboat traffic on the Yukon River extended as far south as the rapids, allowing Meeker to complete the first 200 miles of the journey in relative comfort. If Ezra wrote a letter or account about his journey on the rugged Dalton Trail, it has yet to be found. He likely left Dawson City in about mid July and reached the coast very early in August.

A fellow stampeder, William Shape, kept a diary describing his journey over the Dalton Trail about a month after

Most of the Dalton Trail passed through uninhabited wilderness.
H.C Barley #4687, Yukon Archives

Ezra's trip—see Faith of Fools: A Journal of the Klondike Gold Rush *(WSU Press, 1998). Shape portrayed the trek as 18 days of difficult travel with packhorses. He also described the "shelters" that Ezra assured Eliza Jane he would be sleeping in—actually, they were mostly their own tents. Only a handful of shacks were found along the trail. The Shape party arrived in Pyramid Harbor haggard and exhausted.*

With Ezra's arrival at Pyramid Harbor, members of the extended Meeker clan had now followed the four main Klondike routes—the Yukon River between Dawson City and St. Michael on the Bering Sea, the Chilkoot/White Pass route, the Stikine River route, and the Dalton Trail.] ❋

Klondikers on the Yukon River June 1898. Ezra tells of taking a tow like this in his letter of September 14, 1898.
Hegg #709, Special Collections, University of Washington Libraries

SECOND TRIP TO DAWSON CITY, 1898

[Ezra Meeker had left the Klondike around mid-July 1898, and most likely arrived home by early August, but there apparently is no written record of the journey or of his stay in Puyallup. The visit was brief and busy, as indicated by the date of the following letter—he left Tacoma for Skagway on August 13.]

[*Partial letter*]
On Dock at Tacoma
7:30 PM [August] 13th

Dear Roderick
We are not to sail until 9 P.M. Harry Ollard *[a Tacoma boat builder]* has arrived home. I tried to see him but failed but from what Will *[Slythe]* says think he is not inclined to go, so I will look elsewhere for help *[Will Slythe gave up on the Klondike and had returned to Puyallup]*. *[Albert]* Heilig *[Meeker's attorney and IMD Co. business partner]* told me a friend of his who has been through the mill says his experience is that short hair dogs were the best so I thought after all it might be best to….

[The Tacoma News *reported that the steamer* City of Topeka *sailed for Dyea and Skagway on August 13, 1898, with "a large amount of provisions of various kinds and several large consignments of fruit, vegetables, etc." Unfortunately, the report did not include a passenger list, leaving to surmise that Ezra was aboard.]*

[*Partial letter*]

my letter to Roderick, you had better mail it to him if he does not come home soon. I am writing up town at the Fife hotel but must close and go aboard and to bed so good night and pleasant dreams for you.

E Meeker

Roderick McDonald.
Puyallup Public Library

[The later recounting of the Meeker venture in the September 21, 1939, Puyallup Press *reported that the partners went north with 500 chickens, but "the presence of the chickens on the boat necessitated a stop in route to Alaska while they could be made more comfortable." Roderick McDonald's reminiscences in the December 17,*

1936, Penticton Herald *mentioned that the 500 chickens were shipped in improperly built crates, necessitating a long enough stop at Vancouver for repairs.*

It appears Ezra departed for Skagway earlier, leaving Roderick McDonald to come along later in charge of "the dogs & chickens, etc." Following Meeker's August 13 departure, the next two Alaska sailings from Tacoma were on Tuesday, August 16 (the Rosalie*) and Friday, August 19 (the* Alki*). Roderick probably left Tacoma on the* Rosalie, *and after the Vancouver stopover to repair chicken cages, he perhaps finished the journey on the* Alki. *The chickens sold for $5.00 each in Dawson City.]*

Skagway [*Ezra's first use of the modern spelling*]
August 23rd 1898

Dear Wife

Roderick arrived here yesterday afternoon with dogs & chickens, etc. all right except two chicks drooping a little. We did not get off the dock in time to get them out of the coops until just dark and had to handle each one separately to get them out. We got a very comfortable warm place for them though. This morning we constructed a wire fence for them and turned them out but it wasn't half an hour before half of them were out, scratching and rolling in the dust as contented as if they were at home and so we will take down the fence. When I left them more than half were in the house taking an afternoon nap; so Roderick is now not afraid they won't come to the coop to roost.

The dogs—well they were just a terror to handle— wild with delight to get off the steamer. They gave us both a sweat to hold them back going up the long wharf.

We are both well. I finally received both drafts that Dresbach sent out; the first & large one was at the Canion. Saw Clara. She is well—gets $75 a month for cooking. She thinks the Tram will shut down last of October in which case she will lose the job and will then go back.

[Historian Karl Gurcke of the Klondike Gold Rush National Historical Park in Skagway believes Clara Meeker at this time would have been stationed at the tramway's Sheep Camp power plant, as there were no nearby restaurants at that facility, thus a need for a cook. The tramway company's Dyea and Canyon City operations, on the other hand, had access to nearby restaurants.]

Well, the steamer whistle is liable to blow at any time and so I must close. Roderick will have his first

experience in camp life this evening as we have taken a tent near by the chickens & dogs. Will write you from Bennet.

Loved as ever
E Meeker

[The August 26, 1898, Skagway News *announced Ezra's recent return to Alaska: "Ezra Meeker, of Puyallup, is here on his way to Dawson City with seventeen tons of fresh and preserved fruits, vegetables and all kinds of delicacies. He also has several hundred young chickens, and two hundred turkeys." There is no mention in Ezra's letters, however, of 200 turkeys as reported by the* Skagway News. *Meeker would note, on the other hand, that he brought in over 20 tons of goods.]*

Bennet
Sept. 6th 1898

Dear Wife

I arrived here yesterday with the first installment of our goods and now more will follow each day. I am very sorry to be detained but we did our best but could not get through earlier. It transpires that we have over twenty tons though the excess has not detained us more than two days as we sent three tons by the Chilcoot route.

I saw Mr. King last evening and learned from him that our scow is ready. *[On November 19, 1897, the* Skagway News *had run a front-page story identifying King. The newspaper reported that M. King of the lumber and contracting firm, King & Casey, of Victoria, was building a sawmill at Lake Bennett: "In connection with the mill a boat building establishment will be erected, the intention being to supply boats to all who may need them for the trip down the Yukon." King's outfit built the scow that Ezra used on his second voyage down the Yukon in 1898.]* We brought the dogs & chickens in yesterday but Roderick and Mr. Dyer (one of our men) stayed back to look after the freight and payment of duty while Mr. Crites (another of men) came into Bennet. We have lost one way and another about half dozen chickens; everybody says they are the finest lot of chickens they have seen. Roderick will stay out at the "Log Cabin" (eight miles back on the trail, custom house) for several days until all our goods arrive so he can pay the duty on the remainder. He got a little taste of enjoying the "hardships of the trail" of some rough and tumble life,

Roderick passed through Canadian customs at Log Cabin after crossing White Pass.
H.C. Barley #4829, Yukon Archives

but I notice he passes his cup for a second and sometimes third cup of coffee.

[*The December 17, 1936,* Penticton Herald *reported that Roderick went over White Pass to Log Cabin and, "the only hotel there (White Pass City) had no windows or doors, and the guests had to supply their own stove and bedding. When Mr. MacDonald [sic] was asked about the rates at this first class hotel, he said he had forgotten what they paid, but he was quite sure it was enough for the services they received….On one occasion when the pack train had been delayed, Mr. MacDonald and his party found a few potatoes which were their only food for two days."*]

Whether we will get another scow and run it ourselves, or whether we will let out the excess of freight to others to take down, have not yet determined but will soon do so. We have good help but not enough to run two scows but think would have no trouble in getting more. The two men we have *[I. Crites and A.C. Dyer]*, started for Dawson last March, from Spokane, traveled north all summer (1500 miles overland) fetched up on the Stickeen river, came down the river on a steamer to Wrangle, thence to Skaguay where we met them and they are still on their way to Dawson. They were out of reach of mails all summer—did not know there was a war with Spain untill it was all over with—I now think they will get to Dawson in about 2 weeks more.

I am well and hearty. I still hope I may get out on a steamer in October but all the while making preparation to come later if necessary. The dogs are in good condition. Jack don't know much but I think he will be all right to work. He is not at all playful like the other three but is good natured. ~~Jeff~~ "Pat"—the one I bought at Auburn is inclined to be quarrelsome. Almost everybody thinks that "Jeff"—the last one bought at Tacoma is the best of the lot. I think we will have a good team.

Well I must close as breakfast is just now ready and I will have spring chicken—one of the Plymouth Rocks—that had a leg broken yesterday so good bye.

E Meeker

[*North-West Mounted Police records archived at the Dawson City Museum indicate that "E. Meeker" and "R. McDonald" of Puyallup passed through a NWMP checkpoint on September 14, 1898, and proceeded down-stream in boat No. 14636. The records identify the hired hands as "A.C. Dyer" and "I. Crites."*

For his previous entry into Canada in June 1898, Ezra does not appear in the NWMP records, perhaps because he received some kind of waiver from Major Walsh when meeting with him in April. Meeker never identified the two men he hired to help George Woolsey on the June 1898 downriver run.]

Sept. 14th 1898

Dear Wife

We are nearing White Horse and will go through in the morning. We took a tow yesterday from Bennet and have had a pleasant uneventful trip except for two dogs overboard in the night while lying near shore during the night. The pounding of their fore paws in the water in swimming woke me up. I had laid down with my clothes on and was ready on short notice to help them. They both come to me at command and I leaned over the boat and caught hold of their collars and with their own help scrambling to get on board easily got them safely aboard but lost my glasses out of my vest pocket in the melee.

All hands are well. The dogs and chickens have both fattened up and seem to be feeling well. The roosters crowed this morning on board at 5 O'clock and kept it up until we got up.

We may take another tow from White Horse to 30 mile river and if we do we can easily reach Dawson in eight or nine days. Our scow behaved well today in the roughest water of Windy Arm and Taku through just a little water splattered aboard. We finally hoisted sail and perceptibly slackened the steamers long line and increased the speed materially. Our tent is large and roomy and comfortable and our bed is splendid. Roderick says he likes it better than a spring mattress. I made the bed down by first doubling the robes, then two comforters for foundation, then Roderick's eider down without doubling and over that, that single grey blanket. That left the double red blanket, Roderick's heavy brown double blanket and two shawls over us—more than we needed in fact.

I find I can write quite well without my glasses but of course I could not read but as I have neither time nor inclination to read nor reading matter I will not miss them so much—any way its better so, than to lose my

sight altogether. Supper is about ready so I will defer writing more until we arrive at White Horse.

Loved as ever
E Meeker

[In The Busy Life of Eighty-Five Years of Ezra Meeker, *he later noted: "In all of this experience of the two trips by the scows no damage resulted, except once when a hole was jammed into the scow, and we thought we were 'goners' certain, but effected a landing so quickly as to unload our cargo dry."*

This misadventure had to have occurred on the September trip downstream. No mention of such an event appeared in the June letters, which are more comprehensive. The December 17, 1936, Penticton Herald *confirms this by noting Roderick McDonald's presence: "The scow was jammed and started to leak. Things looked very serious for a time, but a quick landing was effected and the cargo was unloaded, which was no small task. In order to find a safe channel Mr. MacDonald [sic] went out in a small boat to investigate. This venture might have been disastrous, for the current was so swift he was almost swept away."*

Meeker made no mention of employing a guide for the September voyage down the Yukon, though he likely hired a government pilot to run the scow through Whitehorse Rapids. He must have felt that he, Roderick, Dyer, and Crites could manage the rest of the Yukon River. Second thoughts may have arisen when they nearly foundered.

Meeker's September letters end just before they reached Whitehorse and do not resume again until late November in Dawson City. The provenience or fate of any letters written during this time period remains unknown.]

Saturday night *[Dawson City, November 19–22, 1898]*

Dear Wife

The days work is over and I am feeling in "good order" and ready for a good nights rest. I thought to gossip a little with you before going to bed so to have a letter ready on short notice as now there are numerous opportunities to send out letters. Our weeks trade has averaged $150.00 a day less than last week which we attribute to the cold weather keeping people indoors. There is yet a cold wave on and may continue for several days. It is reported that three men were frozen to death about thirty miles up the Yukon river from here. It seems they started up the river to go to some new creek to stake claims and

The first store operated by Ezra in 1898–99. It stood on a frequented alleyway off Church Street in the southeast part of Dawson City, just behind the Yukon Hotel, and not far from Front Street along the Yukon shoreline. Wilfred McDonald later identified his father Roderick as standing directly under the "Log Cabin Grocery" sign, while his grandfather Ezra is at far right. This probably is the photograph of the store and dog team mentioned by Ezra on November 19, 1898. Today the structure is gone.
#0200-04, Eagle Historical Society & Museums

had no tent or stove and perished; also that two others were frozen on the "dome" or summit of the mountain going to Dominion creek. In each case it is very evident that the men had not exercised sound discretion and had neglected to take ordinary precautions against disaster.

We had the dog team hitched up this morning to be in front of the cabin when the photograph was taken. After it was taken Osmond & I jumped on the sled and had a spin around Dawson in great shape. We hitched Pat with the team and he trotted off with his head and tail up as though he was proud of his company. I do not know that he had ever been worked before except one day when I hitched him up for a short time. We will send him up in the team this morning to haul wood. I now think I will not sell him but bring him along and sell the Sheppard.

<u>Sunday morning</u> Roderick just now asked me what I would like for breakfast. I told him some "home dried eggs" with a bit of ham and toast and so now while I am writing it is being prepared.

Those eggs you dried are simply delicious as compared with the La Monts. Roderick had opened a box of the La Monts to let a lady have some to put in a cake and had been using out of the box. I simply quit eating eggs for I don't like them.

The weather has moderated just a little and is about 5° warmer than yesterday. As soon as it moderates a little more, numerous parties will start out but the trail will not be at its best for a month or more.

The frost has softened the light on our windows so that we cannot now look out on the street. Some of the panes show most beautiful fre[s]co work. One in particular showed figures like sheaves of grain, fern leaves, etc. the whole field looking like some tropical region of luxuriant growth. Here & there a pane will show a clear margin out of which we can "peek" and see a little of the street. A cold country shows some curious phenomenas. The glass inside our cabin as I have written is covered with frost but some places it is veritable ice an inch thick; the margin of the doors shows ice also inside the cabin though the thermometer right alongside shows 50° above. Every nail head near the windows or doors is a spot of ice. Whenever the door is opened a cloud of steam or fog appears but disappears suddenly when the door is closed. Everybody that comes into the store has ice on them somewhere. The top of the dogs head shows frosty from the effect of their breath.

Noon; I have just returned from a little run on the sled up the Klondike. Osmond finished loading up two sleds & hitched in four dogs, Jack, Pat, Jeff & his own and started up the creek with about 400 pounds of stuff, part of which was for Fred's camp. I went with him half a mile or so to see how the dogs started off, test my clothing for a cold drive, etc.

[Fred Meeker and J.R. Pesterfield of Tillamook, Oregon, came over Chilkoot Pass together on July 21, 1898, and floated down the Yukon in boat No. 14309, according to NWMP records. Ezra would have been on his way out of the country over the Dalton Trail as Fred came downriver toward Dawson City. Fred and Pesterfield set up camp on Bonanza Creek about 15 miles outside of Dawson City. They eventually built or acquired a cabin near Little Skookum gulch. Clara Meeker remained behind working for the tramway company.]

It is astonishing how quickly the dogs take hold to work. Jack & Jeff simply pulled like oxen; going up a little hill I noticed when the sleds pulled harder they simply leaned into their collars heavier and took the load with them. Every now and then a dog would look back over their shoulder and look at you as though they wanted to say "am I doing all right? is this the way you want me to do?" I rode a part of the way, getting on and off the sled while in motion.

I sent you a draft yesterday for $50. I had previously sent you one for $100, I will send you another this week probably for $100, and as I previously mentioned we will continue to send you small drafts from time to time so as to be sure that some of them reaches you. We have had no word from home since we left Skaguay and as to whether we will have any during the winter is problematical. We hope however there will be a mail in, in about two weeks. It does seem a long time to wait. It is a long time before my fresh supplies can be gotten in—nearly six months before the river will open—and by that time I look for a shortage in a number of articles. Sugar and syrup, condensed milk. Honey are now hard to buy; oat meal is getting scarce; butter has been scarce, but just now more is offering. All hands agree that there is a great abundance of fresh beef, bacon, flour, canned meats & fruit, beans etc.—in a word of the substantials. I believe

that granulated potatoes will become scarce as also fresh potatoes although as yet several parties have stacks of the granulated; of the fresh potatoes I think there are but few but it is difficult to ascertain exactly but all of these questions are intensely interesting to us as bearing on the final outcome of our venture in here but I think now I will stop writing and take a sunday afternoon nap, so my Dear, I will write Good Bye.

Monday Morning 21st Nov.

There is no room for me or "Shep" while the mush is cooking, so I am in by the front stove and thought to write you while Shep sits nearby on the floor looking at me. It is yet not daylight, but as cold as "blazes" outside—39 below zero—but comfortable enough in the cabin for me to be writing in my shirt sleeves.

This cold weather makes one feel lonesome and for myself, I feel the "necessity" of exercising great caution. I have not yet found the face covering that fits my case. I can be comfortable everywhere else but my face; if I get that fixed up I will be all right. I saw *[T.G.]* Wilson (formerly of the Snoqualmie hop yard) last night and saw his cap and face covering and will now have one of those cat skins that I brought along fastened on to my Seal skin cap that I think will do the business.

Roderick bought him a new suit of clothes for $25.00 and they are good. I think of getting a suit also. R goes to the Presbyterian Church service quite regular and is going into the choir. I have not been to church yet but thought I will some evening or perhaps day.

[The Presbyterian Church played an important role in Roderick's life. He participated as a church elder for 60 years and a clerk of the session for 53 years. When living in Puyallup, he was instrumental in organizing the Presbyterian Church there. He also served as the superintendent of the Presbyterian hospital in Dawson City for a time.]

Business is suspended here on Sunday though we have some trouble keeping intruders out on Sunday—living in the store as we do—of people who have forgotten something wanted or are going out "up the creek" or have just come in. Sometimes we accommodate them and other times do not. We only have two meals on sunday but I noticed this morning the remains of what looked like an evening lunch, evidently taken after I had gone to bed and to sleep. We have one chicken left—a large one—that we are keeping for some extra occasion and have been debating in our minds whether it shall be on Thanksgiving day, Christmas, Fred's & my birthday or a new years crack. The chicken is hanging up in the back shed, frozen "stiff as a joker" and will keep all winter, hence we can look at him Serenely and enjoy the anticipation for as long as we have a mind to—Breakfast is ready—

22nd. I thought I would write you good morning while the "Pone" was baking and R made the mush. Roderick has been having the tooth ache and that's a good excuse for not getting right up on time, so I had the "Pone" making well under way. I have just read the thermometer and found it 37° below zero. Our cabin is a little open—one might say a good deal—so that near the door jams and window this cold weather creeps in and freezes ice while the general temperature of the room is above 40° above. The floor is not very close but yesterday Roderick covered the kitchen and lower kitchen walls with heavy building paper and over that on the floor a heavy canvass we had on the deck of the scow coming down. So last night was better.

[The Puyallup Press *and* Penticton Herald *articles reported that Ezra rented this abode for $200 a month. Perhaps he paid with notes on his defunct Puyallup First National Bank, as Pierre Berton describes in* The Klondike Fever *(1958): "Miners discounted their gold in order to obtain the less awkward banknotes and before long paper currency from almost every country was circulating in Dawson, including Confederate notes and bills on the Ezra Meeker Bank."]*

[Milt] Logan was in yesterday and reports he killed a moose weighing 800 pounds. He is all right and stands the cold weather well. Dresbach is also well but is in the cabin up the creek.

There are dozens of Puget Sounders in the store off an on. George Cantwell and Will Hall were both here yesterday. Will looks as fat as a pig. Tom Crown & George Saar are both here. Crown has been sick but is better now. *[Warren]* Wood is up and gaining strength and also Winecoop as also Jacobs. Jacobs has not been exactly sick—only "grunting a little" but is out. There are great number of people here without employment and many are getting restless.

[George G. Cantwell was listed at his father's residence in the Puyallup city directory. His father, Thomas P. Cantwell, served on the Puyallup city council. George Cantwell left the Yukon on September 20, 1901, giving Puyallup as his forwarding address.

Will A. Hall worked for years as a clerk at the Puyallup grocers, Rodgers & Raymond.

Thirty-five year old George Saar grew up just north of Puyallup. As early as 1880, his family farmed along the White River.

B. Franklin Jacobs, a Puyallup attorney, was a longtime neighbor and friend of Meeker's.]

Fred has not struck anything yet; in fact he has not tried to get work as he wants to either get a "Lay" (lease) on a claim or get one of his own. He went up the creek last Thursday while his partner *[J.R. Pesterfield]* stayed in and helped us.

There are a lot of Sharks around that has been trying to unload worthless claims on us but without success. Fred thinks there are fractions to freely be uncovered

"The Klondike Team" included in *The Busy Life of Eighty-Five Years of Ezra Meeker* (1916) is the only picture Ezra personally published depicting the time he spent in Dawson City.

right in the richest mining district that he hopes to get on one. *[Many mining claims had been hastily staked and when proper surveys were done, it was often found that small parcels of unclaimed land, called fractions, remained between them. Laura Berton in* I Married the Klondike *(1961) tells the story of Dick Lowe taking a fraction just 87 feet wide that yielded some $600,000 in gold. Fred Meeker, no doubt, hoped for similar luck.]* Well, we think we are "yarning our grub" while "fishing" for a slice of the gold field. I think there is a splendid good field for making money right here in this business buying & selling but Roderick sometimes gets to chafing that it would have been better to have sold out and gone out home. I don't think so and any event its no difference now what we think we could not change.

Everyday brings us customers to sell as well as to buy. Yesterday a man came in and sold 3 sacks of flour and 10 lbs tobacco; in an hour the flour was sold and before tonight the tobacco will be sold. We have to sell on a close margin but its all for cash and we can see just what we are doing and so it goes—breakfast

Wednesday 23 *[November 1898]*

We had a lively time last night with a lady visitor next door but one to us, who cooks and caters for the printing house mess (The Turner) of six persons. She has been in and out frequently and so we have become acquainted but allways in a great hurry. Last evening Roderick and I & Pesterfield had rather settled ourselves down for a quiet evening when she came in (about 8 O'clock) for a sack of rolled oats. Trade over; R. *[Roderick]* I think was reading, P. *[Pesterfield]* mending while I had just began preparation for making a kettle of corn meal mush to fry for breakfast.

Some remark drew her out about her trip up here. She said her friends told her she was a fool for coming up here and she believes now they were right; said she cried all day sunday but all the while interspersed her talk with fun making remarks that set us all in a roar of laughter. We all enjoyed her visit while at the same time pitying the woman. Cannily and gradually the facts came out that she lives in Oakland, that she was sending money to her children there; that she had a husband that did not support her—by inference we drew that he was lazy— "so good naturedly amiable that it was exasperating" as she put it and so on in that vein. Another lady, a doctor's wife, was in the store Monday that gave us a lot of fun for a short time. The talk came up about keeping warm.

She declared that the first ten dollars she got hold of she intended to expend to hire a man 10 hours to build fires in the stove and let her "be free from care for that length of time anyhow." She too was not contented here, but like the first lady was ready to make the best of matters she could and have a little relief in fun. We have quite a number of lady customers that relieves the monotony of selling bacon & beans to miners—but the mush is fried and I must get ready for breakfast.

23rd Evening; "Now I lay me down to sleep" etc.— we have had quite a busy day and miss Pesterfield not a little as he went up the creek this morning to their camp where Fred is and so R & I are here alone tonight. I wrote you once about the beautiful figures on our windows. Two panes in particular have assumed a realistic scene of a forest and mountains in the background. One group is an exact representative of the conical trees on our grounds and one figure has a little leaning at the top, just like I have seen at home all of which as you know is the handywork of old Jack Frost. The weather continues cold but I seem to stand it better. This morning I went to the river for water and was out of doors quite awhile. R has just handed me a cup of hot lemonade, a cup of which he is sipping. I have just learned that the mail to carry this letter will not start tomorrow, so, I will write you more before closing.

24th Evening Notwithstanding this is thanksgiving day, we have had a fairly good days trade, a sort of steady stream all day of small orders in the aggregate, $215.00. The sales yesterday were $294, making for the two days $509.

Roderick at times takes a discouraging look at things and predicts that our trade won't hold up while I think it will increase largely—time only will tell who is right. We have been keeping tab on the profits of each sale made and find the average runs higher than either of us thought and so R. tonight is feeling better over it. Its no wonder one gets the blues a little at times especially when he has the tooth ache and the lamp has to be lighted at three O'clock. We would not light so early were it not the frost and ice on the windows deaden the light. It was a common remark today how mild the weather is—its only 20° below zero—and how glad they were the weather was warmer. In fact it does not now seem very cold at 20° below zero, having experienced 40° or more below.

Fred has been up the creek a week and we do not know whether he has accomplished anything or not but we are on the lookout for the chance of a good mining claim, he up there and we at this end of the line. Milt Logan was in again today hearty and well. He is engaged in sledding up their winter provisions. He spoke about writing home today but did not have the time but asked me to mention him and say the last letter he had from home was dated in May. We all hope now to get some mail in soon. It certainly will be refreshing after so long a silence. We have not had a word since quitting Skaguay.

25th Morning; while R is getting breakfast I thought to write you a little more before closing this letter. It is doubtful if I can write you tomorrow as I am "going up the creek" to look at some mining property nearby where Fred is camped. It is about a 16 mile walk but when I get there I have arrangements for a good bed in a nearby cabin—a sure enough feather bed, the one I occupied when I was up there before. While I am exceedingly anxious to try our hands on a mining claim yet we have felt all the time it was good policy not to be too much of a hurry and it transpires that it was best as now property can be had on better terms and all the while we are becoming better acquainted with the surrounding mines and what properties to avoid.

The weather has moderated and it is a little above zero, being 42° warmer than five days ago. Nobody here thinks it is cold weather when it is only at zero. In fact one does not feel any inconvenience from it. Anyway I am going up with parties that will have their dog team and I expect to put in our "Shep" dog if we succeed in getting a harness and so have some fun on the way up as well. I may possibly stop at Logan's & Dresbachs and get lunch. The road will literally be lined with dog teams and men hauling their own sleds, footmen etc. so that in places it looks like a war on a frequented street.

25th Evening; R *[section of page is torn off and missing...]* up that is out 5 feet from the wall and we have a lantern behind it which makes the sign show as transparency and is catching quite an evening trade. We have had it up that way but a few days; well it's 10 O'clock and I will go to bed; my but I slept Sound last night and fell greatly refreshed this morning. Loved as ever.

Husband

Dawson
Tuesday Noon
Nov. 29th

My Dear
Here I am back again. Roderick detained my letter for the draft, No. 270 Bank of British North America for $50 payable—NY. I have a duplicate of this draft and will send it also so that if one miscarries you can use the duplicate.

I made the trip up the creek all right—up one day and down the next. Fred came down the day I went up and we missed each other on the trail. I however looked at the property we are talking of buying and Fred has gone up today and will make a more critical examination; Fred now has a comfortable cabin and has undertaken to represent a claim on "Little Skookum" for a half interest in the claim. This will not interfere with his working on this property we are negotiating to buy as it is near by.

Evening—we have not had a heavy days sales though a fair trade $132, though the profits run low. We are keeping a tally sheet of sales and set out the profit on each article sold. Yesterday the profits ran to an aggregate of $24.50 on goods bought here and today, though the sales were larger the profit were but $15.00. In addition to this is the sales of goods that we brought in with us which is much larger though the sales do not aggregate so much.

There is undeniably a superiority of those eggs you dried, over those of La Monts or in fact any other brand on this market. We are selling the La Mont eggs for $2.50 a pound; that is the price all over this city and I doubt much if they sell for a lower price. I think we ought to construct a small drier to dry eggs and berries, rhubarb, etc. for this market. If we had had two tons of the dried sweet corn we could have easily sold it for 50 cts a pound and now I think more. We are selling blackberries we packed up here at 75 cts a pound and *[page missing...]* practice. Mr. *[Warren]* Wood is stopping with us tonight. The weather continues warm—only 8° below zero you see. This morning I went down to the river for 2 buckets of water. At the waterhole I met a dutchman. "Its warm this morning," he said (it was then 8 below zero) "Yes," I said, "Its very pleasant," and so it was. We have had a good fair days trade and tonight until 10 O'clock before it fell off entirely.

Wednesday Morning Nov. 30th

We did not meet with an opportunity last evening to start this long epistle on its long homeward journey so this morning while Roderick and Mr. Wood are getting breakfast I thought to add just a little more of the latest date.

Men are coming down the river now daily on the ice from Stewart river and farther up and report good traveling. Mr. Chilberg came up from Eagle City about a hundred miles below and reports the traveling fine. We hear that a heavy mail is approaching and will be here soon so our hopes are revived as to hearing something soon from the "outside" and from home.

[James P. Chilberg, a Swedish immigrant, is listed in Washington Territory records as early as 1879. He operated the Chilberg & Macready Hardware Store on Pacific Avenue in Tacoma, near Meeker's IMD Co. office. The NWMP recorded "J. Chilberg" constructing and registering a boat at Lake Bennett in May 1898. In March 1899, a person identified as Chilberg became one of the investors in Ezra's mining claim, almost certainly the same man.]

Roderick is to go to the banquet to night on "St. Andrews" night and so meet the "Scottish Clan." The tickets cost $6.00 but was fortunate enough to have one presented to him. *[St. Andrew's Ball was a major occasion in the wintertime social life of Dawson City. Laura Berton in* I Married the Klondike *describes an event so formal it would have done London proud. There was an opening grand march following strict protocol, an orchestra and printed dance programs, and a midnight break for a large meal. Many of the men wore "swallow-tail" suits and women were adorned in their finest Parisian gowns with long white gloves. Dancing included two steps, schottisches, and even the French minuet, and continued until the early morning hours.]* I bought me a suit of underwear last evening but Mr. Wood and Roderick both say that I have made a mistake and so this morning I will take it back and get another. I need this to complete the change when wearing two suits at a time. The suit cost $7.00; it would cost about $3.50 at home. The weather continues moderate and pleasant though now the days are so short that one seldom sees the sun unless in a most favorable position. I do not remember having seen the sun for a month until last Monday while coming down the creek I caught a glimpse of light so saw just about half of the sun above the crest of a distant high hill. I have however quite often seen the sunshine on the mountain on the opposite side of the river that we can see from the front door of our cabin. The more I think about it, the more I am inclined not to try make an early trip out. The longer the trail on the ice is traveled the better the trail gets; then besides, if I wait, the days will get longer and weather more moderate; but over & beyond that is the fact that I am needed here and that even if I did not get home before the middle of March I would have time to make a return trip in when the ice breaks up in June but as to all that more anon—for the present I must attend to the breakfast call. ✳

Dawson
Feb. 27/99

Dear Ezra *[to Ezra Blaine Meeker, 14-year-old son of Marion Meeker]*:—

I received your nice letter all right—Jack is one of the best dogs in the Yukon Country; he is big and strong and grandpa wouldn't take $100 for him—He works on the sled fine—we work him behind & call him the wheel horse—

Grandpa & I drove him & Gige & shep up Bonanza to the forks the other day. They took us there in 2 hours and a half. It is 14 miles we went a spinning sometimes—its lots of fun too but you have to jump off & run behind once in a while to get your feet warm unless you have a heavy fur robe. There are a good many little boys & girls here & they may start a school here in the spring so they can go to school. The big Yukon river is froze over solid now so you can walk right over it. They cut holes through the ice to get water. If you don't do that you have to melt snow to make water. This letter will start here by the Northwest Mounted Police tomorrow afternoon at 4 O'clock so you see how long it takes to come to you—with love.

From your Uncle Fred

Dawson
March 3rd 1899

Dear Wife

At last, the papers are signed, witnessed and delivered and we enter into possession Monday morning of one mining claim 250 x 250 feet square and the half interest of another 250 x 175, adjoining.

Fred spent about a week prospecting the claims and in one shaft found this $5.00 nugget and in 6 pans found the remainder—70 cts to the pan.

We have taken a sixty per cent lay, that is we get sixty per cent of the gold taken out, out of which we have to pay half the royalty—5 per cent so that we get net 55 per cent.

I think we have a good property that will take nearly if not quite a year to work out. The claim is well prospected as shown in this diagram *[illustration follows]*; you can scarcely imagine what a relief it was to me to get the papers signed for a property that I had so much confidence in and on such favorable terms. The property belongs to A.H. Clark, whose wife now lives at Sumner *[NWMP records note "A. Clark" leaving the Yukon on August 16, 1899, on the steamship* Nora]. I feel that we have made no mistake and am very hopeful that we will make a good showing. We can work it winter and summer so that now we need not have our thawer lie idle a day for at least a year. Back of this is property that can not be worked during the summer at all by ordinary methods and at any time speedily with the windless as the shafts are so very deep. We can reach them with our tunnel in time and so may find a two years run without moving.

Long before you will get this letter we will be already actively at work and I hope to soon be able to report a daily output of pay dirt.

Fred and his partner *[J.R. Pesterfield]* will both go to work and can have steady work from this on if all goes well. They intend to take an interest in the thawer.

As soon as we can get to it we will establish a boarding house and get a woman cook. We have three applicants; in each case the husband wants to work in the mine. We intend to give good wholesome food for a good generous diet so as to preserve the good health of the men. It is a pretty place in summer I am told with an abundance of pasture for a large herd of cattle—what a pity it is we could not have cows, and "sure enough" milk.

I will send my bedding so that I can stop at the mine when I want to and will spend my time between there and the business here. The possibilities are good for getting a large return out of this venture, nevertheless in mining one can't most always tell, so we must need wait for developments.

My Dear, how nice it would be if you could but make that trip in here and look in on us some morning with steam up and a busy crew of men at work.

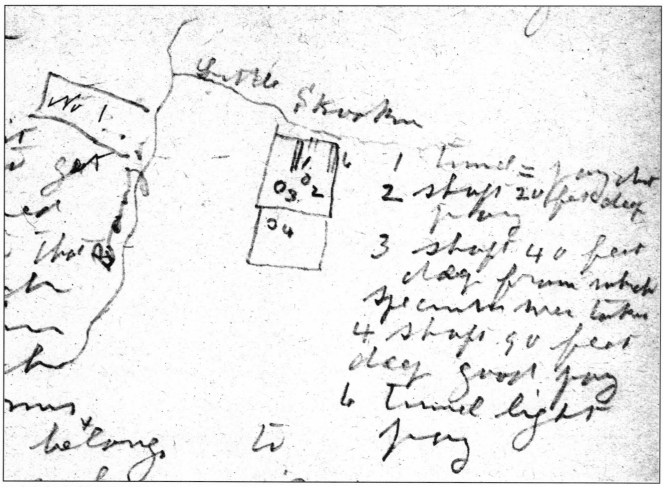

Meeker's sketch of the mining claim on Little Skookum gulch, drawn on the edge of his March 3, 1899, letter—"1 tunnel = pay dirt / 2 shaft 20 feet deep pay / 3 shaft 40 feet deep from which specimens were taken / 4 shaft 90 feet deep good pay / 6 tunnel light pay." Bonanza Creek is at left.

We are still having quite cold weather (34° below zero this morning) but the days are beautiful. The days are now quite long, Yesterday morning I called Roderick as usual at 7 O'clock. A few minutes later he said "see the sun shining on the hill" and sure enough, there it was.

[Partial letter]

2 PM

Roderick will now go and mail the letters and just before closing I write to say that we have just bought Mr. Wrights interest in the thawer for $1000. This gives us with the 1000 already paid a half interest after we set out $500 of the Wright purchase for Fred. This will give Fred and his partner nearly a one sixth interest. We buy Wrights interest for $500 cash and $500 on bed rock.

Fred and his partner has enough money to pay $250 now and will pay $250, on bed rock. Roderick said yesterday he would much prefer to go up to the mine instead of staying in Dawson but I think if he did go up there to stay that he would soon find he would rather be here where he has a wide acquaintance in church circles and which he enjoys greatly.

Roderick is ready so Goodby

Dawson
March 5th/99

Dear Wife

As this is sunday I thought to write you a chapter of our life here though there is nothing startling or for that matter anything of very great importance to chronicle.

Grand Forks grew up at the junction of Bonanza and Eldorado creeks. The Meeker mining claim was located nearby.
Anton Vogee #121, Yukon Archives

Fred is going up today to move over to the mine and our machinery will be moved up Tuesday. I will send up a part of our bedding and probably will go myself some day of the week but only to stop in for a day or two. By the way, tell Mr. and Mrs. *[Clarke and Maria]* Baggs that their son *[Henry]* will move our things; he has a horse and sled and is freighting and also in the wood business.

We are now all astir to get things in shape to turn the steam on the face of the tunnel. *[B.F.]* Jacobs is looking after "unlumbering" the machinery and moving it, Fred and his partner look up the wood supply question and get that under way; *[James P.]* Chilberg takes in hand the building of a track into the tunnel and cars and other things. A workshop tent is to be put up, a boarding house established; I am looking after this end of the line getting things together for the move; Roderick has charge of the books and cash and so on and so on. We will at first only employ about eight men but we think in about four weeks that number will be doubled and soon after be quite largely increased. I think eventually we will employ

25 or 30 men—provided the panning out shows up to justify it. As the tunnels are driven in, samples of earth will be taken and panned out so we will know what earth to save for the sluice boxes and what to put into the waste pile and also to know how the mine is paying. We expect to start two rockers at work; if we encounter as rich earth as that Fred found, three men can rocker out several hundred dollars a day but the bulk of the dirt will be run out on the "dump" where it can be shoveled into the sluice boxes when the spring opens and we can get a sluice head of water. After the water comes we will run the dirt direct from the tunnel to the sluice boxes as long as the water lasts which we think will be until the frost locks it up again in October or possibly in september.

There has been "luck in leisure" with us; we now all think as we have gotten a better property we think and on much better terms than we had before been thinking of taking.

When we once get steam up unless some accident to machinery or something unforeseen occurs, we do not expect to let the fires go out night and day.

Last week has been a revelation to us on the vegetable question. I wrote you about one man carting five tons of potatoes over the bank of the river—rotten. This week one of the big companies sent out men to canvass to sell of their potatoes at 25 cents a pound. Two different men offered them to us and finally submitted samples.

The samples were soft and unquestionably will soon be rotten and realy is not now fit for use; however, the restaurants and hotels are buying them freely and what are not now sold and used will also soon go "over the bank" of the river. We have lost but very few—culls—and what we have are in fine keeping. Our sales go steadily along at 60 cents to our regular customers who would not use the other potatoes even at a gift. We have in fact the best quality in town and everybody that gets them are pleased and come back for more. We are getting low on them and before April is gone there will be none left.

We will want to bring in a large shipment this fall again and maybe one of us will come out to select pack & ship them, after all,—certainly will if the mine turns out well and the work is well organized.

Now again about Riverside *[Meeker is referring to property in Puyallup]*; you may have taken action however before you receive this. Of course if the last crop gives a large return and makes a large payment on the mortgage, the equity would be much larger and of course the place could be saved; the same applies to the upper place but it would be a long story to explain to you how to proceed and as there is no danger of losing it I will not go into that now but wait until I see whether I can come out in July or not.

The weather is simply perfect—bright sunshine, dry under foot and bracing cold. I can not for the life of me see why this is not a healthy climate; I believe it is if people will take care of themselves. Roderick complains of cold feet and his stomach don't serve him like mine does me but all the same I can write, "we are all well and hope you are enjoying the same blessing." God be with you my sweetheart until we can be remembered in my prayer.

Husband

March 6th/99

Now it transpires that a weekly mail is to be dispatched hereafter instead of twice a month as heretofore and so the mail will close tomorrow.

I write to say that we are busy—had a splendid days trade. We have actually made the start to move the thawer up to the mine and I hope to be able to report steam up within a week—ten days at most.

Today I received your letter of Jan. 15th. Now my dear, it would be as impracticable for me to buy into a mining proposition and then go home and let it run itself, or by others as it would have been to let the hop yards run themselves or let someone else attend to the London trade. I think we have gotten hold of a good proposition but it must be looked after closely. However, I may be able to get away for a short season and come home and make a shipment of vegetables, etc. for next winters trade.

Loved as usual
Husband

[Partial letter]

…and getting bare and is soft and sloppy during the day—afternoon—hence the early start. This is the fourth night and we intend to keep it up until all our supplies are up which we think will be in about a week. We have already sent up about 5000 lbs. and expect to send 3000 lbs. more.

The store begins to look quite bare of goods and we will soon be ready to close it. Trade is good and we could have been doing a big business had we continued. I do not however regret the move we are making and believe it for the best.

We have bought two cabins at the mine and rented two more. One cabin near the work we use to store our goods in and as a sort of an office. Fred & I sleep there and also Mr. Gilbert who used to work for the *[Puyallup]* hardware company. Mr. Gilbert has charge of the pipe work and takes one watch at the boiler.

Our cook house is about 300 feet away and lower down near the little creek bottom. Mrs. Anderson does the cooking and everybody votes her a first class cook. We have put up a 12 x 14 tent in front of the little cabin—which is used as a kitchen—that is used as a dining room. A 12 foot table is near the centre of the tent and on each side a hewed sapling answers for seats. My little Yukon stove that Charly *[Charles Hood of the Puyallup Hardware Company]* made for me is set up in one corner and regularly every morning a fire is built in it as the mornings are cold though the days are warm.

Fred and I generally go down to the first table together though sometimes he goes into the tunnel first between watches.

There is a lot of detail to look after in running a mine; the "face" of the tunnel must be watched and pans of dirt taken and washed to see if there is pay dirt. Timbers are to put in here and there; steam pipes will sometimes leak and must be looked upon; a hose may blow off and must be "fixed;" a "nossel" may get to blubbering and blow back some steam into the tunnel; the question as to when the thawing is finished is to be decided; then where to insert the nossels and hundred of like details to look after so you see we are not asleep but have plenty to keep us awake. My light gum boots come in nicely as the tunnel is wet in places so I have at last found use for them but I must stop "prattling" and get down to business.

You will no doubt have received a letter by the hands of Robert Heningson who has agreed to buy and bring in some goods for us. You will know whether he is carrying out the agreement, for if he is, he will have called on you with reference to potatoes etc.

I enclose a draft on him for $150, which he authorized us to draw on him if we need to do which you can present. You can find where he is by applying at the Anderson Wooden ware company at Tacoma.

Of course if he has purchased the goods and shipped the potatoes and started back to Dawson then it would not be advisable to press for payment, but if he is in Tacoma then I would say to collect it. He does his banking at the London and San Francisco bank. I think though he will pay it at sight.

I had intended to send you another draft from here through the bank but we need the money here to carry through this enterprise and I knew of course that the good Lord would take care of the Widows?

So my dear wife I must again say good by

Loved as Ever
E Meeker

[In an eight-page letter preserved at the Yukon Archives in Whitehorse, a William Mollett mentions working for Ezra Meeker in 1899: "I did some awful dirty work for him." Mollett broke a hip and left the Klondike in the spring of 1900. Aside from the "Mr. Gilbert" and "Mrs. Anderson" mentioned in Ezra's letter, William Mollett is the only other

Grand Forks in summer.
H.C. Barley #4754, Yukon Archives

As Ezra noted in his letter of March 3, 1899, the mine in Little Skookum gulch belonged to A.H. Clark of Sumner, Washington, not to Meeker. Ezra took what was called a lay or lease on the property. Ownership remained with Clark. Meeker would keep 60 percent of the gold taken out, but had to pay one-half of the royalty on the gold, netting 55 percent for him; plus he had to pay the actual mining costs. Taking lays was a common practice for those who arrived too late to stake their own claim.

The property was a bench claim, meaning it was located on a hillside above a creek. In the early days, miners scoffed at bench claims until they realized rivers once flowed on the benches. Some of the bench claims proved very profitable but required tunneling, which was difficult and dangerous work, made even harder due to permafrost.

Ezra's lay was about 15 miles south of Dawson and included 2 tunnels and 3 shafts. Since Ezra shortly returned to Dawson City and continued to sell vegetables, he seems to have turned the day-to-day operation over to Fred and J.R. Pesterfield.

Why did Meeker choose Little Skookum gulch as the place to try his luck? The November 14, 1897, *Tacoma Ledger* may provide part of the answer. In the early days of the gold rush, a front-page story had reported a "Remarkable Find on Skookum Gulch… the rich strike reported to have been made on the barren hillside of Skookum gulch, 15 miles from Dawson. News of this strike caused great excitement at Dawson City and a stampede immediately took place notwithstanding a violent snowstorm. Within twenty-four hours nearly 400 bench claims were located on the side hill and men armed with guns were standing guard over their new found treasure. Boulders were turned over and often disclosed nuggets lying in the gravel. The moss which is about a foot thick was torn up and there lay golden nuggets, right on top of the ground so thick that two men picked up $800 in a single day."

Being a regular reader of the *Ledger*, Meeker in Puyallup no doubt was impressed by the story. Less than 1½ years later, he put his money down at Little Skookum gulch.

In the September 21, 1939, article about Ezra's life, the *Puyallup Press* noted that, in 1899, a deep freeze came a month earlier than usual. Miners could not keep the ground thawed nor obtain enough water for sluicing.

By late 1899, Meeker lost his investment. Ezra wrote his own version of the story in *The Busy Life of Eighty-Five Years of Ezra Meeker*: "Fate or something else was against me, for the mining experience swept all the accumulation away 'slick as a mitten,' as the old saying goes." His letters made no mention of the mine after 1899.

The *Puyallup Press* account in 1939 stated that Meeker lost $19,000. This figure is repeated by Frank Green (1969) of the Washington State Historical Society who catalogued, indexed, and archived the Meeker papers. The origin of this figure is unknown, as Ezra never mentioned the dollar amount in his letters. However, it seems unlikely that the total loss was as high as $19,000.

Meeker estimated he returned home with $3,000 to $4,000 in his pocket from vegetable sales during his first trip to Dawson City—much of this probably was reinvested in the shipment for the second trip, when he took about twice as much freight to Dawson City. Perhaps, this involved a total of around $10,000 for the two 1898 trips to the Yukon. Any profit accrued and available to invest in a mine would have been considerably less, since in addition to regular business expenses, he now had to pay rent on his cabin store and he sent income home to Eliza Jane. Even if all the mining partners chipped in a share of the purchase price and operating costs, $19,000 still seems too high. These miners did not have that kind of money.

The *Puyallup Press* story of 1939 further noted: "A Puyallup man who was in the Klondike at the same time Ezra was said recently that the Meeker claim eventually proved to be of great value." Roderick's son, Wilfred McDonald, in a September 17, 1971, letter (now archived at the Dawson City Museum) seconds this opinion. Wilfred wrote: "Grandfather Meeker and my father acquired a claim which turned out to be very rich, reportedly several hundred thousand dollars of gold in the first clean up, but they were maneuvered out of it and got none of the gold. My father then went to work for the NATT Co. [North American Transportation & Trading Company] and was manager of their store in Bonanza, Grand Forks from 1900–1904." Unfortunately, Wilfred never explained how the Meekers lost their claim.

After more than a century of continuous mining and dredging, today's landscape in the Bonanza Creek drainage is altered beyond recognition, with willows growing amid the Little Skookum gulch tailings. Active mining continues.

The White Pass railway was built to Lake Bennett in 1899, aiding Meeker's shipments.
H.C. Barley #4648, Yukon Archives

hired hand working at the Meeker mine who has been iden-
tified. MSS 273 (2000/7R) Textual Records.]

July 5th evening

Well, my dear wife, I will be with you soon. I sold all our fresh potatoes today and was so busy delivering them that I forgot to mail my letter until after the steamer had gone so now I will enclose you $100 to help out on pressing needs. We have met with a loss of about $1000 on the fresh potatoes but have nearly made that up on our dried potatoes sold but there will be about one third of that part of the shipment unsold until I come back here in September, so I will have but a limited sum of money at command with which to buy with.

I will go up to the Forks tomorrow to visit for a day or two and then come back and get ready to start back

home and may surprise you and follow this letter in about ten days or two weeks at farthest.

I will leave about $3000 worth of goods here until I return; which will help us out on freight bills in september when the new shipment arrives; will write a little in the morning when I mail letter and enclose draft *[page missing...]*

[In April 1899, a major fire had destroyed much of the Dawson City business district. Meeker's July 5, 1899, letter, however, indicates that his Log Cabin Grocery probably survived, or at least the stock and merchandize did, since he still retained "$3000 worth of goods."

A two-month hiatus follows in the letters; the Meeker Papers provide no information as to when and how Ezra returned to Puyallup in the summer of 1899. However, steamboats now plied the entire length of the Yukon River from Lake Bennett down to St. Michael. It can be assumed Ezra went upriver by steamboat to Lake Bennett, then transferred to the newly completed White Pass railroad to Skagway. Track laying to Lake Bennett was completed on July 6, 1899, just ahead of Ezra's departure from the Yukon. His stay in Puyallup would have been six weeks at most before starting north again.]

Sept. 3rd 99
Arrived at Vancouver at 6 P.M. Sail in half an hour

Dear Wife

We did not leave Seattle until about 6 O'clock but I slept soundly until one of my room mates came in and said "old man you had better get up or else lose your breakfast." As it was I got a ticket for the second sitting at the table, so, now I can have my morning nap.

We did not go to Victoria but will arrive in Vancouver about 5 O'clock this afternoon.

The steamer is worse crowded than you saw and every available place is occupied where there is room to make down a bed on the floor. This is a good and fast boat so I am very content even if my state room is dingy (its the engineers room) and especially as I have nice room mates that are willing to have all the ventilation we can get.

I did have a feeling of depression when I separated from you last night, but its all gone and now I am living in the sunshine of hopefulness and do hope your spirits may rise to equal my own in buoyancy. I believe I am going to succeed and that gives me courage to try.

At Port Townsend I had time to get a line of magazines that will give me reading matter (8 in number all for september) among which I have the *Farm, Century, Leslies* Mags etc. You see these will also find another reader in Dawson.

Well, I thought this much of a note would be welcome by you even though there was not much in it. But it shall bear witness that I love you as ever

E Meeker

P.S.
Skagway
Sept. 7th/99

We landed here this morning and I am now this 2 P. M. writing in a little restaurant while the lady is preparing a light dinner of poached eggs on toast.

I have meanwhile since landing "picked up the line" and find there is quite a jam of freight here, but perish-

able goods are moved first, so, I am promised to have our shipment moved to Bennet tomorrow or next day.

I learn that the transportation companies are unable to move the freight from Bennet to White Horse as fast as it arrives so I have about closed a contract to have our freight go down from Bennet in two scows along with some sheep—expect to go to Bennet tomorrow but will write you again from here. I was <u>very</u> much pleased to see our freight come out of the hold of the steamer in first class shape, not a single crate that I saw landed was in bad order, so you see our fears were not well founded. I now have no doubt but they will go through to Dawson in like good order.

I now have no uneasiness about getting the shipment off from Bennet promptly in safe hands so that I can go to Dawson by steamer and which is a great relief to me as I did not want to make the trip down the river by scow.

I met Dr. Gandy *[person unknown]* here today; he will go by the *Alki* tomorrow or next day and I will try send a letter by him so now good bye.

Loved as ever
Husband

Sept. 15th

We will be at Selkirk in about an hour—that <u>is</u> provided we don't stick on a bar—and I hope to be able to mail a letter to you there. We have had a delightful trip though not without some enlivening incidents. Everybody was up this morning early to see the steamer shoot "Five Fingers" and there was quite a ripple of excitement as we glided through the narrow gateway missing the rock on one side by about eight feet and not much wider margin on the other side. It is a marvel how well this steamer is handled though I sometimes almost hold my breath fearing least she will not swing in time on short turns but seemingly does as like a "thing of life" that knew and did its duty. At Rink Rapids a line was put out and payed out letting the steamer down stern foremost; at this point apparently a reef extends clear across the river and we touched bottom lightly; then below this about twenty miles we "bumped " again but passed on over without detention.

The passage through Thirty Mile river was an almost unbroken succession of bell calls to the engineer to "back" "go ahead" "slow" "slow" etc. but we made every turn in the crooked rapid river seemingly "to the mark"

One of the White Pass & Yukon route steamers passing up through Five Finger Rapids on the Yukon River. Ezra's September 15, 1899, letter describes his passage down Five Finger Rapids.
Claude and Mary Tidd #8415, Yukon Archives

without a miss or mistake. I only wish our freight now on two scows were safely landed in Dawson and sometimes wish (almost) that I was with them but as I could not be with both of them become content as it is especially as I am having such a nice time of it. I have taken a two hour nap today, reading myself to sleep like I often do at home. One thing I am always ready for my meals three times a day and feel decidedly rested and well but now a little "work brittle" or restless or whatever you might call it.

We are booked to be in Dawson tomorrow (Saturday) and I think fully a week or more before any of our freight arrives—have just scraped bottom—which will give me a good opportunity to get ready to take care of it.

If we could and have the same kind of market I met on my first trip, a week would suffice to sell out but we will not find a like opportunity, however, I do not see or hear of anything that leads me to fear that the venture will not turn out profitable provided always that the freight arrives in good order—whistle stop for Selkirk so good bye.

E Meeker

[Partial letter]

Fred is with me and is working steadily and is getting himself good clothing. He is quite cheerful and companionable. Olie *[daughter, Olive McDonald]* can begin to manufacture eggs and sliced potatoes but I expect to telegraph that out.

I must close as the steamer will sail shortly and besides its getting late and I must go to bed so I must say good night my sweetheart, good night.

Husband

[Meeker's third trip to Dawson City was brief. He had departed Seattle on the steamer Alki *at 9 A.M. on September 2, 1899, and arrived back in Puyallup by October 8, 1899, where he would remain through the winter. The original plan probably had him staying in the Yukon much longer, but something changed his mind. The* Tacoma Ledger *reported on September 10, 1899: "Mrs. Ezra Meeker, Mrs. Roderick McDonald and little son have gone to Seattle to spend the winter with Mrs. E.S. Osborne." On October 8, 1899, however, the* Ledger *added: "Mr. and Mrs. Ezra Meeker went to Seattle to spend two weeks with their daughters, Mrs. E.S. Osborne and Mrs. Roderick McDonald." Ezra was now back home.*

It seems unlikely that Eliza Jane would have made plans to spend the winter in Seattle with her two daughters if she knew her husband intended to return so soon. Ezra apparently left the freight with Roderick and almost immediately returned. There is no mention of his Little Skookum gulch mine at this point, in either the letters or the newspapers. His stay in Dawson City, perhaps, would have been too brief to allow him to pay it much attention.

He spent the winter and the holidays with Eliza Jane. The Ledger *reported that Marion Meeker hosted a pleasant Thanksgiving dinner attended by 22 guests. "The toast was given by Hon. Ezra Meeker." No mention was made of a Christmas celebration.]* ❄

A FAMILY AFFAIR, 1900

Olive McDonald.
Ezra Meeker Historical Society, Puyallup

[A break in the Klondike letters continues from October 1899 to late April 1900 when, of course, Ezra was in Puyallup. In this seven-month span, there is but one brief letter, sent by Roderick McDonald from Dawson City on April 2. However, the Puyallup society section in the Tacoma Ledger *provides a glimpse of Meeker family activities during this time.]*

Roderick, of course, had departed for the Klondike at the end of August 1898, leaving his pregnant wife behind in Puyallup. Olive would not see her husband again until late June 1900. Their son, Wilfred McDonald, entered the world on March 12, 1899, in Puyallup. Olive and Wilfred stayed with Eliza Jane until September 1899, at which time they went to Seattle to stay with Olive's sister, Carrie Osborne. It appears Olive was ill during much of this period. According to the Ledger, a somewhat recovered Olive returned with her mother to Puyallup in late November.

On January 21, 1900, the Ledger noted that Mrs. Charles Hood had recently hosted a party for the "Mesdames" of Puyallup. Olive and Eliza Jane were in attendance. Also on the guest list was Jennie Decker, who six months later in the Yukon played a significant role in helping save Wilfred's life. But all that was in the future. It would still be more than three months before Olive took her baby north, accompanied by Ezra, to join Roderick and experience first hand the challenges of living in the Yukon.

In the winter of 1899–1900, Ezra remained in Puyallup preparing a shipment of over 30 tons of vegetables to take north in the spring. The Ledger noted he spent a week in Portland in mid-March, but no reason was given for the trip. Perhaps it was to see Milton Misamore or to purchase supplies for the next Klondike trip. The following letter sent by Roderick from Dawson City informs how the shipment was largely paid for by Ezra. Meanwhile, Roderick had closed the Log Cabin Grocery in March/April 1900.]

Box 71 Dawson
April 2nd, 1900

Dear Mr. Meeker

I have yours of March 13th and agreeable to your request give you list of remittances.

Oct 2 *[1899]*		500 *
Nov 7	No 732	500
Nov 27	754	500 *
Dec 7	7	500
Dec 23	31	450
Jan 2 *[1900]*	41	500
Jan 16	62	200
Feb 3	90	2000
Feb 13	106	500
Mar 6	147	225
Mar 19	184	<u>200</u>
		$6075

I enclose duplicate for all except those that are marked with a star.

[The letter is unsigned, but the handwriting is Roderick's. The sums likely represent earnings made from selling the vegetables that Ezra left behind in the Yukon in September 1899. According to Yukon Archives records and Wilfred McDonald's later reminiscences, at some point in early 1900 Roderick became manager of the North American Transportation & Trading Company store (NATT) at Grand Forks, a position he held for the next four years. The Skagway Daily Alaskan, however, identified Roderick as the Dawson City wharf manager for the NATT. Perhaps Roderick was selling Ezra's vegetables in both Grand Forks and Dawson City; $6,075 was sent to Puyallup that winter and Ezra applied this sum to funding the 1900 shipment.

Meeker's letters for 1900 begin as Ezra, Olive, and 13-month-old Wilfred travel north aboard the steamer Dirigo, *proceeding toward Skagway.]*

On Board Stm *Dirigo*
April (Saturday 1 P.M.) 28th, 1900

Dear Wife

We are now well on our third day out and consequently on the last half of the voyage to Skagway.

I will relate the most important incident first though it did not occur until yesterday. We were crossing Queen Charlotte Sound where the Pacific Ocean came into full view and sent in some gentle waves that caused the ship to roll a little. Olie *[Olive's nickname used by all the family except her husband Roderick]* was out on the deck with the baby both dressed up in their best bib-and-tucker while I was in the room lying down a "spitten" imagining I was going to get sea sick. All at once the door opened and there stood or rather came Olie with baby in her arms, both <u>such</u> a sight as you ever saw. Baby had imagined that he was sea sick and emptied his stomach on his own and his mothers dress until they were both befouled almost from head to foot. Olie, instead of running for the rail or holding him at arms length when the explosion came, simply started for the room with the result stated. Such a forlorn look as was on Olies face I never saw before. I could not help laughing to save my life. The more I laughed the madder Olie got (at herself, me, everybody and everything). I said "poor baby" she said, "I dont care about the baby but <u>just look at my dress.</u>" "I cant see what there is to laugh about," and neither could I but nevertheless I could not restrain the mirth.

I took Wilfred in hand and had to strip off three garments before getting deep enough to get clear of the mess; meanwhile the poor little fellow would gag and sputter and throw up some on to a cloth that I snatched. He was literally as white as a sheet (all you know from "imagination") but he kept me too busy to get much sick though I "sputtered" some too. Meanwhile Olie disrobed and cleaned her dress which after all did not show bad but baby's dress did. Wilfred seemed to cling to me as the only friend on earth and continued sick off and on until we left the sound and entered a narrow passage and smoother water. In less than two hours after the "explo-

Ezra, Olive, and Wilfred sailed from Seattle to Skagway on the steamer *Dirigo*, late April 1900.
H.C. Barley #5151, Yukon Archives

sion" we were all comfortably seated at the table at supper as though nothing had happened with a good deal of merriment at Wilfred's expense.

We have experienced a remarkable smooth passage—just the same as if we were on a river except for a short time on the Gulf of Georgia and on the sound as described and now we are steaming along through a passage not a mile wide with the snow line down nearly to the waters edge. The weather is delightful—simply perfect, clear cool but not cold, no wind or any thing else to mar the pleasure of the trip.

Baby has a high chair and goes regularly to the table with us. Olie sits next to the captain, baby next, and me 3rd; he "hollers," crows or scolds the same as if he was at home and furnishes the small talk for the table the same as the home talk as he is the only baby on the ship and everybody notices him; so you see Olie ("and I") you see are happy.

He has taken his food as regular as at home and so far as I can see is doing just as well as at home; has never waked up in the night; takes his noon nap, eats hearty, etc., etc., etc.

Now Mamma you must not be uneasy about us for we are going to get on all right; just before I wrote this last paragraph Wilfred had taken his afternoon bottle and showed signs that another nap would do him good although he did not go to sleep with the bottle. so I laid down on the bed with him gave him a glass, a toothpick and an unsharpened pencil to play with and sure enough after about a half hours play dropped off to sleep and is now lying face down enjoying an afternoon nap.

There are four other ladies on the steamer, so you see Olie has plenty of company and there are four other children—two little boys and two little girls, so Wilfred is not without company though he dont go much on the little folks for company. Well two more days will get us off the steamer but just what is before us, how long we will have to wait; just what kind of fare we will encounter in Skagway is all in the future, but we will not borrow trouble over it but meet the emergencies as they come and be thankful they are no worse.

Loved as ever
E Meeker

April 30th Monday

We have just left Juneau this 1 P M while at lunch. The captain says it's a 9 hour run to Skagway as he stops at Haynes Mission then lands us at Skagway at 10 o'clock at night but of course we will not leave the steamer until morning. If we could have had the making of the weather to order it could not have been bettered; it has simply been perfect for the whole trip. Wilfred is the same good little happy boy that he was at home and now as I write is tumbling about on the floor with perfect abandon as though he owned the ship. Except for the little bout of sea sickness which I have written about there has not been anything to create the least ripple of excitement though of course that was enough for one voyage.

Olie had time to go up and visit Mrs. Davies [person unknown] while the ship lay at Juneau and baby slept. Jack says the word is just down from Bennet that the ice is very rotten on the lakes and that a break up is impending at an early date. Our shipment is in perfect order, the vegetables and eggs being stored in a cool place and not a package broke.

Don't fail to have the orchard sown to clover; I forgot it in the hurry of getting ready to come away. I want Marion to get five cords of green heavy bark and have it ranked up in the basement but not broken up fine and five cords of free splitting 14 inch stove wood and have this split up fine but not ranked. I think the stove wood will all store in by the heater while the bark can be ranked in east of the boiler, that is, in the North East corner of the basement. I will provide the funds to pay for this by July 1st and pos-

sibly sooner and I think Mr. Cummings will undertake it if Marion can not wait that long for the pay. It is very important to arrange for the bark while it will slip and in that way get it green and give it time to dry.

If any more letters come from Williams about the little steamer he wrote about, send them to Hartman who has that matter in hand. If any comes from Bird, letters or cables, turn them over to Robert [Wilson] who will answer them. [Robert Wilson, age 51, was a Puyallup insurance and real estate agent who long handled the Meekers' bookkeeping, taxes, and legal matters.]

If Ella [Templeton, Ezra's oldest daughter] hasn't written I think you had better write again. I suppose it goes without saying that you are to send all letters to Skagway until further notice; I will have them forwarded from there, if we go on at an early date.

I am perhaps a little over confident as to the result of my trip but nevertheless I do feel quite sanguine and as I have not missed much in my calculations on either of the three former trips I think I have good reasons for at least half way trusting my calculations.

There is scarcely any freight moving in the direction of Dawson and that is a good sign for a market; then it will make it all the more certain for me to get in on the first boat.

Well little boy is now standing by my knee and reaching up for my paper, so making it difficult to write meanwhile Olie is packing up the odds and ends to be ready to leave the boat so I must bid you good by and God bless you my own dear sweetheart,

E.M.

Skagway
May 1st, 1900

We stayed on the steamer all night and are all up waiting for the hotel coach which will be here in half an hour. Wilfred has waked up in great good humor, has had his "din" and is already for the trip up town.

The weather is fine, clear and cool, but not cold. I went up town last night at midnight and engaged rooms; we get a room with fire, electric lights; bell call etc. for $1.50 a day with one bed and a bed lounge—do not know whether we will stay there or not but can tell better after a day or two trial—think we will like it as there is hot water, baths, closets etc. all on the same floor.

All well.

At Home
Skagway
May 2nd, 1900

Dear Wife

Here we are "at home" keeping house. It seems that our good star is not yet set but is ministering to our wants as occasion requires. Mr. Harridon of Ross Agens & Co. kindly let us take possession of his house for a month while his family is at Astoria.

We have a kitchen and dining room combined, a sitting room and two bed rooms and a good sized wood house. The house is fully furnished and partly provisioned so that we had supper at home last evening and a splendid breakfast this morning. I boiled baby an egg while Olie was dressing which he ate with great relish; then about 9 O'clock the milk came and he had his "bot" while flat on his back on the floor and using his heels for drum sticks keeping time to the music of his grunts of satisfaction. He is just as well as he can be and I <u>know</u> is the best boy in Alaska.

Mrs. Feero milks her own cow and we get milk of her and it is good rich milk. She is here today washing up the clothes and will help Olive from day to day as she needs help. *[In August 1897, Emma Feero of Tacoma arrived in Skagway with her four children, joining her husband John Feero, a packer. John later perished in a snowstorm while packing to Lake Bennett in 1898. Emma remained in Skagway with her children, providing for them as best she could.]* Baby found lots of blocks and playthings that were left here by the two little boys that have gone to Astoria with the mother, and has been very busy since we moved in; he slept all night and did not wake up till 7 O'clock and is now at noon taking his daily nap.

We can not tell when we will "move on" as no one knows when navigation will open. The RR Co are ready to move our freight over to Bennet as soon as I say the word which I think I will do yet this week. The fresh potatoes will keep in better condition at Bennet than here as it is cooler but I feel yet a little doubtful that it might get too cold over there. I am looking after some tarpaulins to cover with in case there was a cold snap.

There has been some sad accidents on the ice, which is now very rotten which you will see is inevitable from the weather conditions as reported in the paper I send you with marked weather reports.

I subscribed for this paper yesterday for two weeks so sure enough, I had my daily to read at breakfast this morning.

Olie is delighted to get out here and away from the hotel. Here, baby can crawl about in his blue dress and have all the freedom he wants and make all the noise he wants and she herself does not feel it so necessary to be "dressed up" so we are all happy.

My dear wife I think of you every day and almost I might say every hour. I would have enjoyed your being with us here but I enjoy the thought that you are comfortable at home and enjoy the anticipation of the return home.

Loved as ever
Husband

Seattle May 3rd, 1900

Dear Mother

Have just a few moments to write you. We had word from Insurance Co. that Father *[Ezra]* succeeded in getting insurance on all his goods *[shipped north]*. Father was not sure he would get it when he left, so wanted you to know. He gets $3000 insurance.

Have not been well this week. Hope you and Miss G. *[Katherine Graham, staying in the Puyallup mansion with Eliza Jane]* are getting along all right. The weather has been so fine I hope the folks had a pleasant trip. My new girl came Saturday and so far proves very willing *[the Osbornes employed maids as late as 1910]*. Sumner *[Caddie's son]* wanted to know if I thought she would be faithful.

Write me a little letter if you have not time to write at length and tell me how it fares with you. Love from all to Grandma

Your loving daughter
Caddie *[Osborne]*

Skagway
May 4th, 1900

Dear Wife

I have been quite busy today getting the shipment off to Bennet and felt a little "lazy" this evening but some how I felt I ought not go to bed without at least a short scribble to my "best girl." We have 932 crates and packages in our shipment a little over 61,000 lbs all told. It is all in fine order and I got our freight bill all arranged through to Dawson and took out $3000 insurance so when I get the storage matter at Bennet fixed to suit me I will probably have several weeks to play with baby or otherwise amuse myself. We dont think of going to the restaurant no more than we would at home. We had a nice stew for dinner today; fresh potatoes, prunes, raw onions, bread & butter etc. etc. enough to satisfy anyone. Baby—well he is hearty as he can be. I build the fire in the morning and soon have boiling water and put an egg on for him which he eats the first thing; then at half past eight the milk comes and he has his "bot" and today went off to sleep early. It was a great find for us getting this furnished house as it gives Wilfred so much more freedom—and he takes it—with lots of exercise accompanied with plenty of his old time grunts. He eats hearty, sleeps well and I cant see but he is doing just as well as at home. He spoke pa=pa today very plainly and measuredly making a long pause between the two syllables but he dont make much headway either in walking or talking.

From what I hear from the interior I think our prospects are very good for making a profitable trip. We seem to be ahead of everybody in our line and the market is bare of these goods, so, I feel encouraged to hope for the best results of any of our trips in—we shall see though, better, after the trip is completed. But I must say good night and go to bed.

Husband

☙❧

Skagway, Alaska
May 13th, 1900

Dear Wife

It is forty nine years today since we were married. To look back to the time of that event seems but a short period; as I write I can see the assembled group in the little house then occupied by your father's family on the gentle slope of the hill near Springdale, Indiana; see the grotesque appearance of my humble self in clothes unsuited to my age and youthful appearance.

I doubt if either of us realized the importance of the step then about to be taken, though if you will remember, that we had previously agreed that "we would be farmers," and which agreement we so long kept that the incident would seemed to show that we did look upon the serious side of life, young as we were.

Now writing forty nine years after that event with the nineteenth grandchild by my side (Wilfred). I can no

more now feel that I am an old man than I could upon our wedding day feel that I was but just a youth but a very little way "out of my teens."

But dropping the contrast between the first event to the present time, the life between, if contemplated step by step seems a long long time. The trip to Iowa in our own wagon; the stop at Eddyville for the winter; the advent of our first born near the banks of the Des Moines; the preparation for the trip across the plains; the crossing of the Missouri river the 18th of May "52"; the long trip across the plains; the incident on the barge on the Columbia river; the landing at Portland and the subsequent removal to St. Helens; then to Kalama and finally to Puget Sound all seem to come uppermost in my mind as like a veritable romance though, as we know, was incidents of real life.

[In The Busy Life of Eighty-Five Years of Ezra Meeker, *Ezra tells the story of floating down the Columbia River from The Dalles to Portland in 1852. Among those on the scow was a young couple; the husband was clearly dying. In an attempt to cheer the couple, the ladies began singing "Home Sweet Home." Then the men joined in. Soon, sobs and outcries of grief followed as the song echoed across the river. After the outpouring, smiles replaced tears.*

In another account by a person with this party, it seems Eliza Jane fell off the scow and was floating downriver with her dress billowing up around her, yelling at Ezra to save her. Ezra noted she was about to drift up on a sandbar and thus no heroics were needed on his part. The scow rowed over to the sandbar and picked up a very angry Eliza Jane.]

To think of these incidents referred to occupied only a little over a year and a half of our married life will serve to remind us of the multiplicity of incidents of a half century now nearing the end; of the family born to us, reared and married; of the numerous grandchildren grown to manhood and womanhood with the nineteenth here making the start in life. One would think such reminiscences would make one feel old but candidly, though I often playfully resent being called old, over and behind that, the fact remains that I can not and do not think of myself as an old man or upon you as an old lady—banish the thought.

I look forward to a long experience of life and who knows but we may not only celebrate our golden wedding yet also our diamond anniversary as well. Whether we do or not, is of course beyond our knowledge but for myself I can truly say it is not beyond my desire nor beyond my hope. Be that as it may, we have both grown to look forward to the end with more complaisance than in our earlier years with more willingness to lay down our lives at the call of "Father Time." And yet I have an intense desire to live; we have had joys piled up mountain high round about us during our married life and have yet such manifold blessings that our daily theme should be one of daily thanks—and is, if we turn to our innermost hearts. I have always felt that it was good that we came together in married life. While I know and realize the great disparity of our dispositions yet we must acknowledge that the union resulted in the improvement of both; that each tempered the other, so to speak, and brought us happiness and contentment in the cabin or out of it, in prosperity or adversity so long as we had each other.

Now my dear wife, all these things you knew but the thrice told story of the lover never loses its zest and so shall it be between us until the end.

Little Boy has just "waked up" but would not take his "bot." He has taken a notion to sup from a cup or eat bread and milk fed him from a spoon. We did not have breakfast until nearly ten O'clock but Wilfred had had his boiled egg and some milk before that; he is however somewhat national in his eating and we can not always tell what will satisfy his fastidious taste. Any way he sometimes gets milk straight, sometimes milk & mellow food, the eggs or crust to knaw at or bread and milk and so it goes but all the while doing well and as "lively as a cricket."

I wrote you the other day of my dream about the selling our shipment for $9000 net. Of course that is what I hope to get out of it if all goes well. But I must get it down the river to Dawson safely and early and maybe will "slip a cog" somewhere and fall short of that calculation. I think though the chances are favorable for realizing that much.

Loved as ever
Husband

Skagway, Alaska
May 22nd, 1900

Dear Wife

There has not been any mails in for several days nor any outgoing mails either way; so that we have been "by our lone" sure enough. Baby boy is just as well as he can be. He has not had the least bit of cold since we left home. He refused to take the bottle part of last week and fretted a little but his new teeth are now near nearly through and he is as lively as a cricket and has gone back to the bottle like any other old taper.

We are all well and will soon begin to pack up again to "move on" though I doubt if we get away from here for another week—in fact I dont expect to though lake Bennet is nearly clear of ice but Caribou crossing at the foot of the lake is too low for steamers to cross and besides the ice is not out of the lower lakes yet, but we will start as the water is raising a little every day now.

We were out this afternoon for about four hours with Wilfred and called on the Treens and afterwards went out to a restaurant for dinner. We had a box, but Wilfred made himself heard all over the room by his playful outcries and made all the more noise when he found there was an echo. On the street just before we entered the restaurant a lady smiled on him and he gushed right out like you have seen him with me after being away from home and reached out to get to her. I half believe he thought he knew her. It was a pleasant incident, though we did not stop but Wilfred twisted his head around to get a farther look at the lady while holding up his hands to go to her.

I have been reading "Lorna Doon." It is a real nice sprightly romance. I wish you could read it. Olie says she thinks their copy is in the library.

I learned yesterday that our fare from here to Dawson is $80.00 each, rooms and meals included; I expect to see a jam on the first boat.

Husband

Skagway
May 25th, 1900

Dear Wife

From some cause there has been a break in the arrival of mail steamers hence we are without mail from you.

We are all well. Olie says she feels better than she ever has since baby was born. As for Wilfred, he is still that happy little boy and as I often say "the best boy in Alaska." Olie is having but little trouble with him now as he now knows why he is set in the little low box with the chamber under it. He has not had the least indication of a cold since we left home though some days the wind blew hard when I had him out.

I think we will be here for at least ten days longer. I was over to Bennet yesterday and find that the water is yet too low to go to White Horse and besides one of the lakes (Lake Marsh) is still closed by ice. Lake Bennet is open but quite full of floating ice but this gives the opportunity of resuming track laying on the Railroad from the foot of Lake Bennet to White Horse which is estimated will be completed in ten days and then we can go on to White Horse anyway; by that time there doubtless be more water and let steamers run from White Horse to Dawson. Little Boy is down on the floor by my side having the "goodest" time you ever saw, talking to himself and not asking anyone to entertain him. The door is wide open and the sun is pouring into the room as likewise a gentle breeze; he has had his morning nap outside the house near the door in his baby carriage and consequently two hours of fresh air. We will go out with him about four O'clock, get our dinner at the restaurant and probably make some calls and have a "drive" around the city.

I met a Mr. Sloan the other day that came from Uncle Usual's neighborhood *[in Indiana]*. He lived in Uncle Usual's house at the time we were there. He has been away from there several years and could not give me any news though seemed to enjoy talking over the old time incidents.

I enclose a sheet of the *Oregonian* containing Harry's picture. I confess it makes me sad to think of as bright and good a boy as Harry is to bury himself in that way teaching old time errors; maybe he will come out on the liberal side, yet I cant help but feel that it is the mistake of his life.

[The May 13, 1900, Oregonian *printed a sketch of the Reverend Harry S. Templeton, one of Ezra's grandsons. The caption announced that Harry was the "New Pastor of Westminster Presbyterian Church." Ezra, on the other hand, was a Unitarian. Over the years, Ezra and Harry debated politics and religion in their correspondence. An interesting exchange occurred in 1919 as they debated whether the United States should join the League of Nations. Templeton was in favor of joining; Ezra was not. Harry had this to say: "I hope you are well and not too worried over your liberal and progressive grandson. You may be somewhat responsible for my liberality in theology, so you will have to take the consequences if it carries over into politics." Harry Templeton later presided at both Eliza Jane's and Ezra's funerals.]*

I received a letter from Marion in which he told of Mr. Ross' death and by the *P.I. [Seattle Post-Intelligencer]* learn that Jonathan McCarty is also dead; there are but few of us "old Timers" of the original stock left. Well it seems that we are to be among the last—perhaps the very last—who knows—but as time moves on I feel an increased cheerfulness looking forward to the end, without in any way releasing my desire to live and enjoyment of life.

My <u>Dear</u> wife, I want to see you ever so much and think of you often and often and some day—about two months from hence—I will drop in on you to gather some of those roses, help eat one of those spring chickens and have one of those good old time talks and have a "tarnation good time" generally.

Husband

**Skagway
June 3, 1900**

Dear Wife
We have spent a quiet sunday and have just returned from dinner at the restaurant kept by two ladies where we got a real good dinner for 25 cts each. Wilfred is just finishing up his second bottle of milk and is in his wagon and will soon be off to sleep.

The railroad will be finished from Caribou to White Horse Thursday (June 7th) and I expect our shipment will be shipped to White Horse yet this week. We will not however go over there until we know definitely certain when steamers can leave White Horse with freight as we can not get accommodations there and we do not want to go ahead of the freight. Another crowd arrived here this morning from Dawson by a second steamer that got up nearly to White Horse so you see the time is approaching when we can "move on."

We are all well and hearty as can be; none of us has had colds since we come up here so we have no kick coming on climate.

Loved as ever
Husband

June 5th, 1900

We expect to go away from here Friday, and go as far as White Horse without detention. As yet there is not enough water below White Horse for steamers to run and carry freight, but may be by the time we get there.

Our freight has been loaded in cars in Bennet and by this time probably transferred to Caribou to go over to White Horse by the first train Friday or possibly not until Saturday so you see our coming early is bearing fruit. *[The railroad was not completed to Whitehorse until July 29, and a section of the route at Caribou still needed to be negotiated by water, requiring off-loading and on-loading of Ezra's 61,000 pounds of freight.]*

We will now get off on the first boat that leaves White Horse that carries freight. The *Alki* is in but as yet the mail is not distributed but I hope for letters meanwhile I will not close this until I get down to the P. O.

Well the Post Office remained closed nearly all day but at six O'clock I finally received your letter without date but post marked May 25th.

I bought our tickets to Dawson this afternoon for $80.00 each over the White Pass railroad and the Canadian Development boats *[plying the Yukon River between Whitehorse and Dawson City]* and as I before wrote expect to start for White Horse Friday Morning. We will reach White Horse Friday evening if all goes well; I think we will get quarters on one of the C.D. Company's boats lying near White Horse but if not will cross the river and go up to the Canyon and stop with Mr. Troger *[employed by the Canadian Development Company]*, Mr. Hartman's brother-in-law, but not as their guests but by invitation of Mr. Burns who is the superintendent and part owner of the tramway. From this point we can watch the movement of the steamers, ascertain which one our freight is going on and then get on the same boat and go with it.

Our expenses have been comparatively light here. Our rent and fuel has cost us $21.75; our meals when we go out 25 cts each and provisions we buy only a little higher than at Puyallup, so, all and all we have made a bit by coming up early as our freight is at the front and will go in ahead of the very large accumulation that has arrived since we came here.

Little Wilfred becomes more interesting every day. He now understands a good deal more that is spoken to him or said in his presence but he wont try much to talk or walk. He knows now very well what he is put on his little low chair and does not usually delay long. He plays very hard and is now well pleased when night comes and he is put to bed and usually sleeps all night without waking up. This morning he woke up and got hold of an earthen dish on the table cloth to pull so that he broke the dish and woke his mother up by the crash. When I am down town for a few hours and return he is very demonstrative in his joy in seeing me and has quite a fashion of loving me by patting my shoulder and talking some baby talk that I do not fully understand, but he evidently wants to tell me something. We have several times given him some condensed cream diluted with water (the St. Charles brand) and it seems to agree with him the same as milk. He is yet very fond of his soft boiled egg and usually have

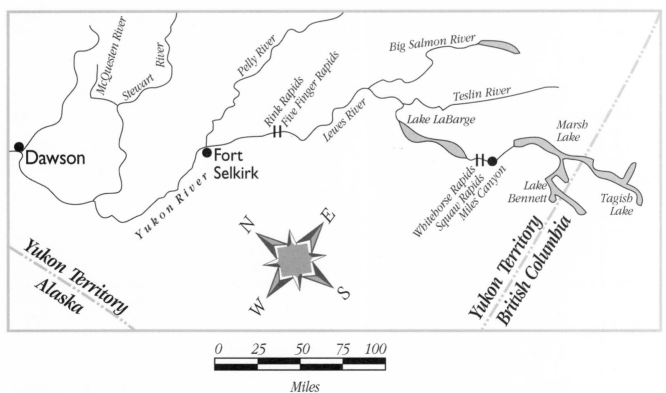

William Shape, *Faith of Fools* (WSU Press, 1998)

one bottle of milk and a soft boiled egg for breakfast with a hard crust to knaw between times and on this he will make his little teeth fairly rattle like a little pig cracking corn. Well we enjoy him as you see and only wish you could have been here for this short month. Will finish up tomorrow.

June 6th. We are repacking our trunks, satchels, bags etc. preparatory to checking and having them examined by the custom house officer tomorrow so that we will not be bothered with them Friday morning when we take the train. Wilfred is the busiest body of the three, first one place, then another and is in a very great hurry. Just now he is taking the bottles of mellow food out of the box and scattering them on the floor without any reference to the order of their going.

The *City of Seattle* is in but we can not get at the mail yet and this will probably be the last mail, if any, that we will get here but any letters arriving after we leave will be forwarded to Dawson.

We are all well. Wilfred is particularly hearty and regular in his food, sleep and stools. He has an egg every morning for breakfast besides his bottle of milk and then nearly two bottles of milk for his dinner and then a two hours nap at noon; my—but he is a restless boy—never quiet a moment when awake. Well, I wont say good bye for I will write you again from here.

Loved as ever
Husband

On Board Stm *Columbian*
White Horse
June 19th, 1900

Dear Wife

As I have from day to day for a week hoped to write you something definite, I have refrained; trying to comfort myself that "ignorance is bliss" and that if you did know anything of our bother before it was over there would be no worry over it. We arrived here on the morning of the 10th (Sunday) at 2 O'clock in the morning and went immediately on board the Steamer *Canadian* where we were cared for in bed and board not dreaming but in a day or two we would be on our way rejoicing.

The next day the *Canadian* was ordered to take passengers only for Dawson so we transferred to the Steamer *Victorian* that was booked to leave two days later with pas-

sengers and freight; but behold when the time of departure arrived our freight (and but little of any) was [not] put on board, so I concluded not to go, but transferred to this steamer and here I am yet. The trouble is low water; but as Olie had secured one of the large staterooms on board the *Victorian* we both thought it was best for her to go on and accordingly she did. The boat she was on stuck on the bar at the head of lake La Barge thirty miles below here, for five days but finally yesterday managed to get through and proceed on the way to Dawson and if not farther detained will be in Dawson tomorrow.

[According to Roderick's reminiscences in the Penticton Herald *of December 17, 1936: "The journey took some time as the boat was so heavily loaded, it went on a bar, where it remained for ten days. Mr. McDonald knew his wife was on the way and from the time the boat was due he walked 13 miles each way several times a week, expecting to meet her." Dawson City newspapers printed passenger lists of those departing Whitehorse, which allowed Roderick to know that his wife and child were on the final leg of the journey. Ezra's letter noted that the steamer remained stuck on the bar only 5 days, rather than the 10 days mentioned in the* Penticton Herald.]

Meantime the water is rising very slow and I may and probably will be delayed here another week before the steamers can take freight. This detention throws everything out of gear, so much so that I now think it is more than doubtful about my going out by Nome but I now rather expect that I will return direct up the river.

[Meeker's intention for going to Nome was never fully spelled out. Perhaps he planned to drop off a portion of his freight with Roderick in the Klondike and then continue down the Yukon to Nome and sell the remainder. According to Pierre Berton (1958), over half the population of Dawson City had departed for the Nome gold rush by the end of 1899. Thus Nome was a fertile new market.

The Skagway Daily Alaskan *reported on May 2, 1900: "IS BOUND FOR NOME" "Ezra Meeker Among the Stampeders to Descend the Yukon." " Ezra Meeker, the former 'hop king' of the coast, who is here on the way to Dawson, is not only again to visit the Klondike, but with his characteristic irrepressible spirit will push on from there down the Yukon to Nome. He is accompanied by Mrs. O.G. Campbell, his daughter, who is going to Dawson to join her husband. She has a thirteen months old son who has never seen its father. Mr. Meeker, although with white hairs and many years upon his head, does not hesitate to make the long journey down the Yukon and on to the Arctic camp. He is one of the oldest Argonauts in the great rush to Nome. He was also in the rush to Klondike." Despite misidentifying*

Olive and Roderick's last name as "Campbell," the story makes it clear that Ezra originally intended to visit Nome.]

The market for fresh potatoes has become demoralized by the heavy arrivals by scows which have been going down the river now for three weeks. I made a great mistake that I did not take a scow as soon as navigation opened but I did not dream of this detention and so now its too late to take advantage of the early market. Meantime our shipment is in good condition and will keep for six or eight weeks yet so I hope the glut will pass by towards the end of the season. The market is in good condition for our dried potatoes.

I am well and living here comfortable on the companies boat and at the company's expense; have enough reading matter to keep me busy and have refused to be worried. I have been very careful about my diet, so that my system is in good condition.

I miss Wilfred very much; he had become so closely drawn to me that I was sorry to give him up, poor little boy; I wish you could have the care of him—you know why.

[In this Ezra does not elaborate on why he thought Eliza Jane should "have the care" of Wilfred. However, Ezra and Wilfred obviously formed a special bond. In subsequent letters, Ezra stated his concern for the rigors on a toddler living in the north.

As Wilfred was growing up, he and Ezra corresponded over the years, even when Meeker was off retracing the Oregon Trail. Wilfred's letters, when writing from the north as a young boy, were especially delightful. He told Ezra of his adventures with his dog "Bummer," and gave Ezra a recipe for curing the croup. Ezra in turn, as in this 1911 letter, provided Wilfred with advice: "Now Wilfred, let me preach to you a short sermon. Be content with your lot, but not so satisfied as not to strive for better things; be hopeful and look on the bright side of life, but do not overlook the darker side and try to better it where possible."

In later years, whenever in western Washington, Wilfred made efforts to visit Ezra. In the next passage, Ezra provides Eliza Jane with much the same advice as given Wilfred 11 years later.]

Well, there are many sad things in this world but let us be thankful that we have each other and try look upon the bright side of life for there are many many joys in life to be thankful for.

My dear wife I hope you are well and that I will be with you again in due time as appointed.

Loved as ever
Husband

Yukon Hotel
J.E. Booge, Manager
—AMERICAN AND EUROPEAN PLAN—

Dawson, Y.T.
June 26th, 1900

Dear Wife

I arrived here yesterday at 11 O'clock AM, two months to an hour from home. I have been oh so busy and realy have not had time to read all your letters (six I believe) that Roderick brought down to me this morning.

I find fresh potatoes market overstocked and prices so low—a little below cost—and so difficult to find a buyer that I have stored them in the brick warehouse— a cool dark place—and will await developments. Our dried stuff is high and scarce but in limited demand on account of the cheapness of fresh potatoes. I had to borrow funds of the bank to pay our freight bills which must be repaid out of our first sales so that it is problematical as to just when I can remit. The fact is I have not had time to set a price or make an offer to sell but tomorrow will begin to feel of the market. The detention in getting here and dulling of the market I think precludes my carrying out the plan of going out via Nome but as to that I can not yet say definitely certain.

Fred met me at the steamer—poor boy— not in good condition though seemed to cling to me for a visit until 11 O'clock last night after which he started back up the creek. I think he has not saved anything of his wages.

Clara has gone out *[to the creeks]* but I missed her. I will go up to the Forks Saturday *[June 30]* to spend sunday and maybe Monday and will write you and in fact before then and often as steamers go up the river now nearly everyday meanwhile just bear in mind that I love you as ever before. Thin the apples on the trees so they will grow to a large size and I will bring them in here September.

Husband
Show this to Marion

[For the previous year, NWMP records indicate that Clara, "Mrs. F. Meeker," had proceeded from Lake Bennett on the steamer Nora, *July 12, 1899. Thus, Clara would have reached Dawson City by the beginning of August 1899 and seems to have joined her husband Fred out on the*

Grand Forks, where the McDonalds made their first Yukon home.
H.C. Barley 82/409, #2, Yukon Archives

"creeks," in the heart of the Klondike mining district. The city of Grand Forks was established at the junction of Eldorado and Bonanza creeks, about 15 miles southeast of Dawson City. By 1900, the "Forks" with approximately 10,000 people was the second largest community in the Klondike, with electric lights, dozens of stores, and telephone service to Dawson City.

Clara found employment two miles south of town, cooking for workers in an Eldorado Creek mine owned by a Mr. Campbell. After the loss of Ezra's mine in the fall of 1899, Fred seems to have spent some time working for wages. He continued to prospect, and worked a claim south of town in which he and Roderick had invested. Ezra's comment that Fred was "not in good condition" suggests he had not fared well during his father's absence. Roderick, on the other hand, became manager of the North American Transportation & Trading Company store in Grand Forks.

The town, standing on prime gold bearing terrain, eventually succumbed to dredging. All that remains today are a few decaying shacks and an interpretive sign.]

**North American Transportation and Trading Company,
Merchants and Carriers**

OFFICERS:
Ely E. Ware, President
John J. Healy, V.-President
William W. Ware, Second V-President
Charles A. Weare, Treasurer
C. H. Hamilton, Secretary and Traffic Manager
John C. Barr, Manager River Transportation
Chicago Office: Old Colony Building Room 290

Dawson, NWT

July 2, 1900

Dear Grandma *[Eliza Jane]*

Olive and baby are now in their new home here at the Forks and I am very glad to have them here. Baby has had a cold during the past two days but I think he will soon get over it. Olive is well and busy getting things in shape. We expect a visit from grandpa any day now. I do not think he will go to Nome but rather go out and prepare for another shipment in here. Fresh potatoes are very cheap just now and there is little or no demand for them.

The weather is very hot here now, much more so than it was this time last year.

Well I suppose you will want to know what I thought of baby Wilfred. I think he is the dearest little boy I ever saw. He is certainly a good and pretty child.

Olive will write you more fully but I wanted to get this off to you by this mail.

Yours Sincerely
Roderick McDonald
[Twenty-two months had passed since Roderick last saw his wife Olive and he was meeting his young son Wilfred for the first time.]

July 5th

I have been busy this morning—sold up to 11:30 at this writing $192.00 of stuff—if all the potatoes would sell like those this morning our loss would be light and as none are now coming in maybe the market will stiffen up.

Loved as ever
EM

Grand Forks
July 8th, 1900

Wilfred is sick with a cold which has run into a fever, disturbance of the bowels and partial congestion of one lung.

I <u>do</u> wish he was at home, but that can not be now and so we must do the best we can. His temperature is lower this morning by a degree and a half (102 today)

Wilfred McDonald.
Ezra Meeker Historical Society, Puyallup

but he seemed to have more pain after eating; however, that has passed off and he is sleeping again. In fact he slept nearly all the time the first five days. I came up here *[Grand Forks]* yesterday to find him a very sick boy and was much concerned about him but feel entirely more hopeful now after being with him now for nearly two days. He did not notice me when I first came or in fact scarcely anyone at all but this morning he would look me square in the eyes and make signs of recognition and at times want his mother to be near him while yesterday he did not seem to care whether anyone was near him—I have just given him about a table spoon full of new milk diluted ¼ boiled water and he does not exhibit much pain. This morning Roderick let him have about a third of a bottle which seemed to pass through him with great pain, so much that he rolled and threw himself all over the bed. Dr. Grant is here and has called twice and he said to give the food in very small quantities and often.

While I was writing I gave him another small portion and just now followed it with a tea spoon full of peperin. We keep the room at an even temperature of 72 degrees on the wall at the head of his bed. The heat comes from the cook stove in the adjoining room so we have the air from two rooms and if the temperature runs up a little I open the kitchen window and let in fresh air from the outside.

Roderick and I went up the Eldorado creek yesterday two miles to see Fred and found him well and cheerful. He is hopeful and was at work on the property they bought an interest in and think they will do well. Roderick has put $500 into the venture. As we came back, I told Roderick that I thought Wilfred ought not to stay in here this winter and he said he had been thinking about the same thing and—

Dawson July 11th. I was interrupted and came down here Monday to settle up some business; and will return to night. Wilfred is about the same and Mrs. *[Jennie]* Decker has gone up to nurse him. I will stay there too until a change comes.

I am hopeful and that is the most encouraging word I can write.

Husband

[According to the Tacoma Ledger, *Mrs. James W. (Jennie) Decker of Puyallup first started for the Yukon in January 1898. NWMP records indicate she passed through the Lake Bennett checkpoint in the mad rush of June 1898. The* Ledger *also reported she came out in the winter of 1899–1900, first to Victoria, B.C., and then to Puyallup. She attended Mrs. Charles Hood's party along with Eliza Jane and Olive as reported in the January 21, 1900,* Ledger. *She returned to the Yukon in 1900, arriving in time to help care for Wilfred McDonald. Jennie was a widow.]*

July 13th, 1900

Dear Wife

Wilfred is better. I write this first to relieve your anxiety but he is yet a very sick boy. His temperature this morning is but 100 & 2/5ths as against 105 two days ago and his pulse is correspondingly lower but I haven't the exact figures.

It is surprising how well he looks for one that is so sick. I can not write that I believe he is entirely out of danger yet we are all together more hopeful and believe he will recover. Both lungs seem to be congested and Mrs. Decker who is now here with him says she fears he has had typhoid; anyway this is the 13th day but he does not look reduced. A few hours ago he laughed at his mother and I think that was the first time since he has been sick.

Mrs. Decker is a good nurse and is with him all night and Olie and Roderick during the day. I came up here night before last in response to a telephone message from Roderick that he was worse. Dr. Grant said a change <u>must</u> come in 48 hours if he recovered and it has come as I have written.

[Dr. Grant was the Reverend Andrew S. Grant, who trained as a surgeon before joining the ministry. He came north as a missionary in 1898, served as minister of St. Andrew's Presbyterian Church, and also became involved in the construction and operation of the Good Samaritan Hospital in Dawson City. Grant and the Meekers crossed paths often, as Roderick became active in the church almost from the moment of his arrival in Dawson City. In an October 6, 1900, letter, Ezra indicated he and Roderick were going to church "to hear Dr. Grant." Grant also presided at Fred Meeker's funeral in 1901.]

I will stay up here now for a few days & until Wilfred is still better but I am anxious to get started back home.

We are all well though Roderick showed a care worn look yesterday but is up and about in the store today.

The water is bad here and so this forenoon I have been getting material to make a filter and we will have it in operation by night and that will be a great gain as to their future health.

My dear wife, we should never forget to be thankful every day, morning, noon and night for the great blessings of health that has been vouchsafed to us and particularly to myself. I feel strongly and vigorous and enjoy the trip of life as much as ever and so may we hope and pray that it may be to the end.

Loved as ever
Husband

Grand Forks
July 15th, 1900

Dear Wife

Rejoice with me for Wilfred is better, so much so that the doctors are willing to say that he is out of danger. He has been a very sick little boy and we were none of us satisfied with the doctor here and Roderick has been for two days striving to get a doctor of large experience and high repute to come up and consult with the doctor here. Finally this noon one came and has given him a close examination and tells me the child will get well with good care which they are giving him.

Mrs. Decker is here with him of nights and Roderick and Olie day times. I am surprised to see that he looks so well as he does knowing how sick he is and how little nourishment he has taken. This is the fifteenth day since he was first taken.

I expect now to start home in a few days and can tell you altogether about him but now it is entirely impractical to bring him home but I <u>do</u> think he ought to go before winter sets in.

Loved as ever
Husband

Dawson July 16th, 1900

Dear Marion

I wrote to mother yesterday about Wilfred's sickness. After writing there was such a marked change for the better that I felt justified in coming away and at 5 O'clock this evening telephoned to Roderick and he told me that he was sleeping nicely and continued to improve.

I can not yet write definitely when I can start home as my absence at the Forks while Wilfred was so sick has delayed business here but I hope to be able to start soon. The market has been a bad one all round for me except with the sliced potatoes which I had to sell at a lower figure than I intended to protect the freight and duty bills, but all and all hope to get out without loss. I can not realize on the granulated potatoes and dried vegetables except by making large concessions and now think will store them until my return in September so you see I will go home without being flush of money. I intend however to try it again and buy as large a quantity of potatoes, onions, etc. as possible and ship here in September.

As I expect to be home so soon after this letter reaches you I will not write more particulars farther than to say that Fred thinks you could get work in here this winter at good wages but it is hard to say what winter will bring forward. I will make a strong effort to manufacture 20 tons of sliced and granulated next winter but I think we ought to have a larger house.

E. Meeker

Dawson
July 19th, 1900

Dear Wife

I am yet unsettled as to when I can start home. I want to remain long enough to sell sufficient to have money enough to buy the shipment for September and as sales goes slow I cant say exactly when I can start home. Anyway I must start within two weeks but I might get ready in two days so I thought best to drop you a line to say that I am well and that Wilfred is <u>very</u> much better and is now realy out of danger.

Ezra stayed at the Yukon Hotel when arriving in Dawson City in late June 1900 and for a time contemplated purchasing the business. Constructed in October 1898, the building remains largely intact today.
Canadian Museum of Civilization Collection #778, Yukon Archives

I am feeling first rate and now that I have found my own bedding and have my own cabin (next to the Yukon Hotel) and good company in the adjoining room. I do not feel so lonesome as when I was stopping at the hotel. However, I go out for my meals as I did not think it best to fit up to board myself. I have toast and coffee for breakfast about nine O'clock and then a good hearty dinner about 5 O'clock and that is all I want and my system is in good shape.

But I will be with you soon for a short season, so I will not write you a long letter but this much to let you know that you are Loved as ever.

Husband

[It appears that Ezra had checked into the Yukon Hotel when first reaching Dawson City in June 1900, since the June 26 letter he wrote home was on Yukon Hotel stationery. He spent a good deal of the first two weeks out at Grand Forks with the McDonalds, helping care for Wilfred.

He next found temporary lodging in a cabin next to the hotel, sharing it with a Mr. L.L. Votaw and his partner Mr. Houck.]

Dawson
Saturday July 21st, 1900

Dear Wife

Wilfred is <u>very</u> much better. Mrs. Decker has just come down from the Forks, where she has been nursing him and tells me he takes and retains his food well; sits up some, plays a little and begins to talk; also is able to scold if things don't go to suit him.

She says he is gaining strength rapidly but gives it as her opinion that he would not be strong enough to travel for a month or six weeks even if they concluded to send him out.

You will doubtless be disappointed in receiving this letter instead of greeting me at the door. I am disappointed myself as I had expected to be on my way out before this. The fact is the market here is dull at best yet there is lots and lots of business passing but the remainder of our shipment unsold is really winter supply and people are adverse to stocking up so long ahead. For instance granulated eggs sells when it does sell at $1.50 a pound, but just now everybody is using fresh eggs. I was offered yesterday $1.00 a pound for 200 lbs. in gold dust which really is but 94 cts per lb. Now this will sell

for $1.50 a lb. when winter comes, but I must sell something more to have money enough to go out an to get another shipment for if I stop now I wouldn't have over $900 in cash and leave $2500 worth unsold. So you see I am in a dilemma and do not yet know just what I can do or when I can start for home. I will however have to go quite soon if I make another trip in this fall.

I am well and feeling first rate though I dont get up very early. It is so light all night that everybody stays up late and I with them, seldom going to bed before 11 O'clock; then I remain in bed usually till about half past 8. Then I get a breakfast of toast & coffee at half past nine which costs me 50 cts. Then I get my hearty dinner at 5 O'clock and have found a place where I can get it for 50 cts so you see my living is not now expensive.

Night before last I got hungry and ate a lunch before going to bed and I did not feel good over it during the night—it was just that much too much, so last night I omitted it and this morning (and last night) felt ever so much the better for it.

I enclose two letters from Bartlett that he left with me to take out but as I do not know when I will go thought best to send them; better take them over to Alice Stewart and she will have them delivered. *[Alice Stewart in Puyallup was the wife of C.W. Stewart, Vice President of the First National Bank of Puyallup. "Bartlett" appears to be Joseph Elbridge Bartlett, a widower, whose wife Millie had been C.W. Stewart's niece.]*

Loved as ever
Husband

Dawson
July 23rd, 1900

Dear Wife

I write again as I am yet unsettled about the trip out. Roderick will be down here tomorrow and then maybe we will come to some definite conclusion as what best to do. I haven't money enough in hand to warrant going out for a shipment and the remainder on hand is not selling and will not sell to any advantage it seems until winter. There is nearly $3000 worth of this that is unsold.

Roderick just now telephoned me that Wilfred was improving fast. He is now out of danger. It may be that we will send out for Marion to buy a smaller shipment. It would cost me $250 for the trip out and back and that expense would not be warranted unless I could make a

Meeker's Third Avenue cabin, which opened as the second Log Cabin Grocery, in early October 1900. It stood nearer the center of the Dawson City plat, three blocks west of his former store. The structure is abandoned in this ca. 1970 photo. Today it is gone.
#1998.22.383, Dawson City Museum

larger shipment than is possible with the funds in sight now. However, I am yet trying to arrange so that I can go out and make the shipment myself. Roderick is inclined to come to Dawson and open up the Log Cabin Grocery again. He sees now the mistake made in closing that business. I believe there is just as good an opportunity now as there was when we closed and in fact better as there are a great many more families here now and you know (we) are or were popular with the women folks.

All jesting aside, we did draw trade from the families from all over Dawson and it was that trade that paid us so well. *[Roderick had continued to operate the grocery during Ezra's absences through March 1900 but apparently shut the store down when moving to Grand Forks that spring. In October 1900, Ezra reopened the Log Cabin Grocery at a new location several blocks west, on Third Avenue.]*

You will be interested in knowing how I am living; well, my bed consists of my big robe doubled, two comforts also doubled and that heavy double brown blanket all under me; then I have the two shawls and double blanket besides, so you see I am fixed well with my bedding. I am yet going out to my meals but Mr. *[L.L.]* Votaw and his partner who stop in the east room of the cabin cook for themselves and say I can use their stoves and fixtures any time I want to and so I think I will at least here after get my coffee toast for breakfast in the cabin instead of going out to the hotel and pay 50 cts for it.

As I wrote you last letter I am feeling first rate, and in every way in good health. My hoarseness has disappeared

entirely and so let us be thankful for the blessings of good health vouchsafed to we and think less of the miscarriage of my hopes for a profitable trip; I realy do not think we will lose but the detention in sales upsets the plans made.

Well I must close this letter, go get some dinner, take this letter to the steamer and then read some before going to bed.

Loved as ever
Husband

**Dawson
July 25th, 1900**

Dear Wife

First and foremost, Wilfred is so near well that we have quit calling him the "poor little sick boy." For so long a time he seemed so listless and made no noise that Roderick said they had become real uneasy about him that he might have lost his voice. One day last week Olie set him up in the bed and he began to try to talk every word he had ever tried to say before and to ask questions Eh? Eh? and quickly dispelled all thought of uneasiness on that score. Roderick came in yesterday and was in good spirits. He now talks as though they did not intend to send Wilfred out as I had suggested.

I am as much at sea as ever as to my movements. The remainder of our shipment is selling very slow—so slow that I am afraid I can not accumulate enough money to warrant my going out after a shipment with what funds we have. Meanwhile I am waiting for the arrival of a Mr. Sawyer now on his way down the river from Bennet. His partner is here and wants to join in on a shipment. We closed yesterday for the lease of a large cabin (20 x 40 feet) which is a first class place to store fresh vegetables and will undoubtedly arrange some way to fill it with about 50 to 60 tons but do not yet know just how.

[The cabin was erected in 1900 on Third Avenue, east of King Street, by J.W. Little and C.F. Nelson before they received clear title to the land. Little and Nelson then rented the structure to various scow merchants, one of whom was Ezra Meeker. The lot was still owned by Joseph Ladue (who platted Dawson City) and James M. Wilson. The sale to Little and Nelson was finally completed on June 28, 1901, two months after Ezra left the Yukon for the last time.

After moving in during 1900, Ezra built a warehouse in the back to store vegetables. In June 1902, Marion Meeker (who first went north in March 1901) and Roderick

McDonald purchased the property for $3,000. Over a year later, they sold it for $2,000, taking a significant loss.]

Meanwhile yesterday the old time talk about the Yukon store and hotel was revived and we have been looking over their stock of goods with a view of purchasing them. Mr. Booge is very hard of hearing and is realy unfit for business and Mrs. Booge is very anxious to have him go out of business and go out of the country with her. She has been sick and is going out soon. The son-in-law, Mr. Bents, a contractor of Chicago, is here and brought in a fine line of goods but he wont stay so all and all there seems to be a prospect of our buying into the business and with it a good stock of goods. There may not anything come of this talk but if we do go in to it there is a good chance to step into an established paying business.

I remain in good health and Roderick and Olie is well, in fact I do not see why we should not be well as we all have good food and perfect weather. I think this is as fine a summer climate as one can find anywhere.

There is a steamer leaving for White Horse and the outside nearly every day and generally three or four tied up at the docks unloading or getting ready to start out up or down the river. This makes Dawson a lively place during the summer as all the supplies must be gotten in during a short season. Hundreds more families have come in and are preparing for winter quarters and now white shirts are the rule among businessmen and at church instead of the old time regulation of ye olden times.

Loved as ever
Husband

⬿⬾⬿

The Forks
July 29th, 1900
Sunday

Dear Wife

I came up here Friday evening just to have a visit with Wilfred and was not disappointed this time. He is however much changed but being hungry nearly all the time and taking his bottle well and can see that he is rapidly improving and will soon be his old time self again. His dimples are all gone and movements entirely different; also is slower in his talk but he plays quite a good deal though not so irrepressible—in fact is yet quite weak and inclined to be in his box more or less; a week ago he could not hold up his head but now he helps himself

every way even to robbing my pocket of my glasses cases. He has three double teeth coming which is hurting him now.

My dear I cant yet say definitely as to my movements. I want very much to go out to get the shipment but as yet have not enough funds accumulated to warrant making the trip. I want to ship in fifty tons of potatoes and onions to fill the cabin we have leased but have not yet but $200 over and above the rebate of $650.00 due from the railroad. It will cost me $250 or thereabouts for my expenses out and back and that sum would buy ten tons of potatoes; so upon the whole I am yet unsettled as to what to do except in this that in any event I want to get as big a shipment in as possible. I am hoping and in fact expecting every day to consummate a deal that will change all this but as the time is near at hand that I must decide. I am naturally a little restless but am thankful to be able to write that I am well and that we are all well. Fred is well. I went up to his place yesterday and found him just ready to start down here so we walked down together and he stopped over to lunch. I think the property will turn out well; in fact it is getting more then wages now. There has been unprecedented rainfall here for the past week and given plenty of water, so now mining is very active all over the camp and large quantities of gold is being washed out. This is a wonderful country for gold indeed whether we get any of it or not. I do not think we will lose on the last shipment in the long run though I could not sell the remainder out promptly without making a very much lower price than can sell for in the fall and winter. I have about $3000 worth on hand. Take as an instance, the most that I could get offered for the granulated eggs was $1.00 a pound. Roderick says they will readily sell for $2.00 a pound when winter comes and fresh eggs are out of the market and the same conditions as to our granulated potatoes and dried vegetables

I have no letters from you for some time. I presume you have ceased writing expecting me home. Better give me the benefit of the doubt and write me when you receive this so that I may hear from you in case I send out for the shipment instead of going out after it myself.

I will add something to this at Dawson.

Loved as Always
Husband

July 30th I came down to Dawson today and left Wilfred in his box playing nicely. I had a pleasant trip down and enjoyed my 5 O'clock dinner and am now writing you this to go out on the boat tonight at 8 O'clock.

Olie is much stronger than when we left home and Roderick is looking stout and hearty.

I can not add much of interest beyond what I wrote you yesterday but do hope soon to write you something definite. I am getting reports every now & then from people who have bought our granulated potatoes. They all say these are the best ever brought to this market; some sell nearly every day but only in small quantities but entirely all will sell and at a profit. *[page missing…]*

Yukon Stoves a Specialty
606 South L *[Tacoma address]*
F.H. Vining
Dealer in
TIN, GRANITE AND HARDWARE
Manufacturer of COPPER AND SHEET IRON WARE.
5TH AVENUE, NEAR BROADWAY
SKAGWAY, ALASKA

Aug. 6, 1900

I hung my vest in the room and this afternoon reached for my watch and somehow knocked my arm against the door and broke the watch.

Frank Vining *[a Tacoma merchant operating stores in Skagway and Dawson City, selling stoves and other hardware]* is going out tonight but earlier than I expected so have but a moment to write you. I send my watch out by him for repair and he will return in about 10 days. I wish you would call at his residence and give him my extra spectacles and a small bottle of corn medicine and pay for repairing the watch *[Ezra repeated this information in another letter on August 8; see Chapter 6]*—will write you more tonights mail.

Husband

Dawson
August 6th, 1900

Dear Wife

I have written several letters today and have reserved this for the last for today.

I am well; so is Wilfred and in fact so are we all. I am sorry to feel constrained to make the change and not go out. It was a keen disappointment to me and I know it will be to you but I thought the matter over carefully and when I found that I could only get a limited amount of funds together to buy a shipment I saw that it was my duty to stay and conserve the values we had and not let them slip away. I believe however I can make it a profitable season even if the shipment is small. I hope however that between Hartman and Marion they will get off a pretty good shipment.

I thought to write you about some small things to send in but will defer that until my next letter and after I hear from Roderick and Olie about what they will want, if anything.

I wrote to Caddie today a pretty long letter and told her to either take it up to you or send it, so you ought to hear from her shortly. I will not go over the grounds covered by that letter as you will see it soon after receiving this.

I am well and living well. Those granulated eggs are wonderful nice. I am boarding myself now in the cabin with Mr. Votaw and his partner Hawke *[Ezra spells the name here as Hawke, but hereafter as Houck or Houk. Dawson City Museum records suggest Houck is the proper spelling and, since Ezra also uses that spelling most frequently, from here on he will be referred to as "Houck."]* I have my own provisions but we make coffee and tea together and trade dishes some so that all and all it is pleasant. Yesterday I cooked some cabbage (I tell you it was fine) and they had some fruit, bacon and corn so between us we fared sumptuously.

This morning we had some fried sliced potatoes and today fresh cucumbers and so it goes between us we have a good variety of good wholesome food and plenty of it. I have my bread and butter and doughnuts etc. separate and have my own toast in the morning while they have mush.

I was so busy that I did not get to the post office to get a money order for $100.00 but will do so tomorrow and drop it in the mail but I have a chance to send this out by the steamer that sails tonight. I expected a letter from Roderick today but did not come to hand. I wrote him to send me a list of what he wanted and also list of articles he thought desirable to ship in and when I receive it I will write you.

And now my dear wife you must not fret and grieve because of my absence. I am perfectly safe so far as health goes and I <u>will</u> be cheerful until we can get together again. My, but wouldn't I like to have you come in and be with me this winter. You would be surprised to know how many many ladies have come here this summer; the town is full of them. There is good water here now, better drainage and what's more electric lights.

There are more improvements being made than ever before since I first arrived here.

Well all this gossip which perhaps may not interest you but in any event it shows you how others see it. I don't know what we are to do about our golden wedding—anyway I must try get some nuggets of our own that will be a substantial reminder that we are not as young as we used to be.

Husband ❉

Winter view of the NATT company warehouses, Dawson City.
Vancouver Public Library #2118, Yukon Archives

WINTERING OVER, 1900

Dawson
August 8th, 1900

Dear Wife

I wrote you last evening <u>very</u> hurriedly on board the steamer at the dock and sent the letter out by Frank Vining. I had intended writing more fully but the steamer sailed two hours earlier than I thought she would.

My help sheathing the cabin was going off for a couple of days on another job and as he could not work to advantage alone I stuck by my job all day passing up some dust, so when night (6 O'clock) came I felt like taking a rest while Mr. Houck got supper and so I took off my shoes, washed my feet and laid down and read the paper until supper was ready and felt like a new man but lo and behold before I finished eating the first whistle blew and so then I did not have time to write you much.

Yesterday I took off my coat and vest and hung them on a nail in the cabin we were working on and at 4:25 I went in to see what time it was. In taking my watch out of my pocket my arm struck against the door so that in some way the watch dropped out of my hand and fell to the floor and broke the balance wheel.

Frank Vining was ready to go to Tacoma last night and will be there a week or ten days and will then return here so I sent the watch out by him to give it to Vath for repairing. Vining lives in Tacoma, 606 South L street Tacoma.

I wish you would go down to Tacoma and see him and pay for repairing the watch and let him bring it back to me as I am entirely lost without it and besides I must have a time keeper of some kind.

I wish you would send in by Frank Vining, my extra spectacles and one of those small bottles of corn medicine and the watch.

For a few days after I decided that it was best for me to stay and not go out after the shipment and so wrote you, I felt pretty lonesome I tell you—bordering on the blues— but that's all gone, now that I am busy preparing to take care of the shipment when it comes and at intervals selling

---

LOG CABIN GROCERY
E. MEEKER

Fresh Vegetables
ALL WINTER.

OUTFITTING.

THIRD AVENUE
Near New P. O.

I. M. D. CO.

MANUFACTURER OF
GRANULATED AND SLICED POTATOES, GRANULATED EGGS, DRIED CAB-
BAGE, PARSNIPS, SQUASH, TURNIPS, ETC.

Dawson, Y. T.

Note the International Mine Development Company logo on Meeker's grocery store stationery.
Meeker Papers Box 4, Washington State Historical Society

some that we have here. I now think that I will eventually get $2.00 a pound for most of our granulated eggs and what's more sell them to a large number of consumers that will want more of them. I have been met with the question "well, will they keep?" La Mont had advertised extensively that none but his manufacture would keep; beside this our brand being new people are slow to buy at first but when once tested then there is no farther trouble as they are better than any other brand on this market. I am now introducing them into restaurants, families and "mess" houses and invariably give satisfaction. Each of these when they give them a trial become partisans in our favor and help to advertise them *[Meeker advertised them as "Chechako Eggs" in the* Klondike Nugget*]*. Our sliced potatoes seem to be about perfect; if I had twenty tons of them here they would all sell off at a good profit before the winter is over. Our granulated potatoes are also giving satisfaction and in fact all our own manufactured stuff is good and will all sell at a profit during the winter and is selling now in a small way and at a profit.

Now that business men come to know that I am preparing for warm storage for the winter I have had a number of applications for space and I think there would be no trouble of getting goods enough to store to fill two such houses as we will have at $10.00 per ton a month, so, should our shipment fall short in quantity from what I have written for, then I will fill up with goods from others.

It is amazing to see the dense ignorance manufactured about this warm storage problem. No wonder their potatoes dont keep—a gentleman has just come into the cabin from the Forks and handed me Olie's watch, so now I am fixed until mine comes in—but to resume, I find the storage people keep their warehouses from 20 to 30 degrees too hot but as I am not here as a teacher I make it a rule to be a good listener but say little—their stupidity is our opportunity. I do hope Marion & Hartman will devise some way to get off a good large shipment to me.

Dawson of today is a very different place to that of 98. Seventeen steamers ply between here and White Horse. An average of ten steamers a week arrive from up river and as many depart. Great numbers of families have come here this summer. I saw last week thirteen ladies land from one steamer most of them accompanied with children. I will have electric light in my room this winter. A good supply of pure water is now distributed through the town in pipes. A large number of covered drains have been cut. I visited both hospitals this week and found but 10 patients in one of them and 13 in the other.

When I visited them in 98 both were full to over-flowing. All the fresh fruits—or nearly all—are here in abundance and a full supply of fresh vegetables as well. Freight has been delivered in ten days from date of shipment from Seattle. Passengers have made the trip in eight days. There are at least three times the buildings being erected than I ever saw before. I only wish you could *[page missing…]*

August 10th 7 P.M.

I will put this letter on the steamer at 8 O'clock; am well. I have been canvassing for the sale of our eggs and dried cabbage today in bakeries, small hotels and families. The eggs are liked very much and I have no doubt but all will be sold long before we can get more in; and what's more, at $2.00 per pound. The dealers would hardly talk business to me at all and when they did it was at a dollar a pound or under; with the cabbage the same way. Now I am getting 65 cts a pound for that. Of course it is out of season for either but I thought it would be well to get acquainted and I am satisfied with the result; next week, will be at work on the cabin again. Had succotash, canned salmon, tea, fruit bread & butter and rice pudding for supper.

Loved as ever
EM

Dawson
August 11th, 1900

My Dear Wife

I wrote you a long letter that started on its long journey last evening on steamer *Yukoner*.

I have just noticed the bulletin board that another steamer the *Canadian* sails tonight at 8 P.M. so I thought you write you a little gossip that might interest you. I dont seem to be doing much today but just now as I was passing one of our customers store (Mr. Jones) he said, "I just got those two cases away in time as a fellow up the creek ordered three cases of Meeker potatoes and that was all I had left. This man has bought of us several times and said he wanted some more now in a few days—when the addition to their store was finished. I had just gotten around the corner when I met a restaurant man that does a large business with whom I had left samples of eggs

Log Cabin Grocery Store and Warehouse advertisement.
Ezra Meeker Historical Society, Puyallup

and dried cabbage. He said, "I wish you would come in Monday as I want to give you an order" and spoke highly of the goods.

I have just bought me a box of gravenstein apples of Crawford, who a long time ago used to have a carpenter shop in Puyallup, for five dollars. I put a part of them in front at our old stand to sell and I think enough will sell by night to pay for the whole box, give the boys their commission and leave me a third of the apples for apple dumplings and sauce.

Ella Hilly (it used to be, Mrs. Card now) is here running a restaurant. Their receipts are over $400.00 a day. *[Ella Card came to Dawson City via Chilkoot Pass in 1898, burying an infant child at Lake Lindeman. She prospered as proprietor of the Bank Cafe despite having an irresolute husband. On April 9, 1901, the* Klondike Nugget *reported she had taken charge of the Hotel McDonald Cafe. Meeker apparently knew her parents.]*

I have been all by my lone in the cabin today; Mr. Houck is at work for Frank Vinings folks and they invited him to dinner; Mr. Votaw is up the creek for a day or two so when dinner was ready there was no one else to eat but me. I had not done much though getting dinner—warmed up the succotash in the oven, heated the coffee and ate the canned salmon cold—but there will doubtless be a full house this evening.

I am well but have not heard from the folks at the Forks since day before yesterday.

I had plenty of hot water left over at dinner so I had a bath or scrub or whatever you may call it instead of waiting until morning and feel good all over after it.

Loved as ever
Husband

Sunday August 12th, 1900

Dear Wife

This is a beautiful day. There has been a good deal of rain fall for about a month but as showers and not as continuous rain. This morning the sun shines glorious and makes one feel cheerful. We did not have breakfast this morning until 9:30; then after breakfast I put on my new suit that I wrote you yesterday that I was going to buy *[Ezra may have intended to write about the suit in his previous letter, but failed to do so]*. Well, I bought it last evening. It is quite light bluish gray stripes about this wide === then a black stripe tinged with an orange colored through every fifth stripe this wide ——. The other four stripes between the wide stripes has a bluish cast thread; in fact the gray wide stripes has much the same. The suit is light weight but I got it large enough to admit wearing another suit of underwear for warmth. Because of its light color and light weight the suit was considered to be going out of season and had been marked down from $25.00 to $15.00 but I did not buy it because it was cheap but because it suited my fancy the best of anything I could find. I will not of course wear it much about my work but will slip it on for appearance sake when I am going out on the street. I think the remainder of the stock I have left on hand will sell for $1500 to $2000 more by my staying with it than if I had forced it to sale and so I mean to be content while making the effort to better our affairs even if we fail to get a shipment in this fall.

Of course if the money the White Pass railroad for overcharging on last shipment is not sent you in time to buy with then you may not be able to send me much (if any) in which case I would take in storage in our warehouse from others while selling out our stock in the front end of the warehouse. This stands near the new post office site and is a good place for business as well as storage; some day I will send you a diagram of my rooms as they will be, after we get through "fixing" them up.

Tell Marion that I say that when I come to compare our dried product with other that is on the market, we are "strictly in it" for quality. I could not get dealers to look at or talk about our dried cabbage, but when I come to compare it with what they have had, no wonder they did not want any more. Now that customers are testing ours the case is all together different and I look for a ready sale for all we have and call for more long before the winter is over; I only now wish I had a ton of it.

I have just now ascertained that the steamer *Bailey* goes up the river at 11 P.M. tonight, so you see this is the third day in succession I have been able to get a letter off to my sweetheart of ye olden times. I am well and hearty. Loved as ever.

Husband

Dawson
Sunday August 19th, 1900

Dear Wife
    The steamers seem to have been detained and are arriving and departing in groups so that our daily outgoing mail is interrupted.

I am well and have not been very busy this week, as Mr. Houck has been working elsewhere, but we will resume work on the cabin in the morning and probably finish it before quitting again

While Mr. H. has been working so early and late I have been practicing in cooking with the result that I begin to believe I would make a good cook—Eh—Well anyway I had plenty of time and during the week made a stew with dumplings, fried doughnuts that were realy fine, baked cornbread etc. etc. etc. and what pleased me most was that I succeeded in poaching our granulated eggs to perfection—so now there's brag enough for you for one time.

Our living is not very expensive but like in the winter of /98 is good wholesome food and so, with keeping my person cleanly and clothing in order I can see no reason why my health will not remain good.

Somehow a fastidious streak has struck me (and I hope will "strike in") and so I change my clothes before going out on the street and don my working clothes when I have work to do. My white shirts are good for two weeks that way. I use two suits of underwear alternate days, but use my night shirt without change for a week. My bed is very comfortable and about as high from the floor as the top of the dining table. At the head of my bed is a box on which the light stands when I want to read. A nail near by serves to hang Olie's watch on and numerous nails on the wall serves to hang my clothes on. I have a certain nail for my hat; three certain nails for my new suit so you see I am trying to be a good boy—seriously though I thought it would interest you to know how I am living.

Mr. Houck is now making two fresh apple pies while I am writing—I believe I wrote you of my side speculation of buying a box of Gravenstein apples for $5.00 and selling 2/3 of them for $5.00 so that we have a third of a box for use free gratis for nothing.

What did you have for breakfast the morning you received this letter; how do you like the new chicken house in its new place; do the chickens get through the fence and bother you; how is the bark and wood for winter; what time do you get up in the morning; did Marion's garden do well on the grounds; how are the rose bushes; the ivy on the wall where I cut it off; did the holly trees transplanted all grow well; will you have plenty of holly berries this year; there are lots and lots of things that I would like to know about you and your surroundings.

Better get Robert *[Wilson]* to make inquiry about the assessment on the home. Just as soon as possible I will send out funds to pay the taxes and if that tax suit appealed also goes against us we will have to meet that also but I think it can be done.

Well we will not borrow any trouble about this but it is well to be prepared to help ourselves in the case of an emergency for if we do not, who would. I am <u>so</u> thankful for my good health and hopeful for the future. I would have so liked to have had you come here for this winter but I could not see how you could leave the house and besides was not perfectly certain what effect the cold weather would have on your health. Our cabin will be very comfortable and I expect to be indoors most of the time. I will put in a good ventilator and the floor will be tight so that our feet will be warm. I realize the necessity of taking good care of myself and you need not have any uneasiness on that score.

I now feel perfectly sure that we will need more of the granulated eggs before the winter is over; that I will sell all we have here at $2.00 a pound and have call for more. Since the completion of the railroad to White Horse it will be practical to ship in some high priced goods over the ice. There will be a stage line established carrying passengers out and freight teams running that will carry freight at about 25 cts per pound from White Horse to Dawson so you see it will be practical to ship some granulated eggs that way.

The poached granulated eggs are really delicious and will accelerate the sale of our eggs among families particularly. A keeper of one of the largest restaurants yesterday told me to come in Monday as he wanted to give me an order for his entire supply of cabbage and parsnips (dried) so I expect to make quite a sale Monday—hopeful you see.

Loved as ever
Husband

Sunday August 26th, 1900

Dear Wife

We have just had our breakfast and the church bell has just rung for the second time, but I thought I would rather remain in the cabin and write to you than to listen to an "orthodox" sermon threshing over the old straw of the "fall of man" and "vicarious atonement."

I would this morning <u>very</u> much like to be in Seattle and hear a sermon by Mr. Simmon of the Unitarian church but as that can not be I probably will enjoy myself as much by writing you as I would if I could have my wish to hear Mr. Simmons.

I am well and did a good solid days work yesterday though find an excuse to leave at 5 o'clock. Mrs. Morrison lives near by and in the afternoon came over to our cabin and invited me to dinner at 6 o'clock which invitation I of course accepted, so at 5 o'clock I left the work washed myself, put off my overall and woolen shirt and donned myself in my best suit white shirt etc. and attended to the dinner.

She had other company, a german gentleman and his wife whose name I can not remember, Mrs. M had an excellent dinner though by no means elaborate—mutton roast, brown gravy, potatoes, peas, (canned) lettuce, plum pudding, lemon pie & tea.

I was there in all about an hour and a half before and after and during dinner after which I strolled towards the river front and dropped in on *[R.J.]* Gandolpho *[an Italian-born merchant, from Tacoma, who arrived in 1898 to run a store at the corner of Front and Harper streets, selling fruits, candies, cigars, etc.].* While there, Mrs. Card (Ella Hilly) came in from her restaurant the Bank Cafe near by and selected a large bouquet that was for sale as she said

Gandolfo's Point on the northeast corner of Front (today, First Avenue) and Harper streets, near the Yukon River shoreline.
Canadian Museum of Civilization Collection #675, Yukon Archives

"for a friend." Just as she got near the door she beckoned to me and I went over to her when she said "I want you to come and have dinner with us tomorrow" and so now today at three o'clock I am again going out to dinner and I will warrant you it will be a good one. Ella Hilly (as we think of her) has developed wonderfully, is highly respected and has made her business a success. Her husband has gone to Nome but I hear he both drinks and gambles though when I saw him a couple of months ago he was working hard and seemed real pleasant.

But now for another dinner episode; as I was coming home last evening I met Mrs. Mason near the store and chatted with her, finally went into the store and among other things related my good fortune about the two dinners. She had previously said she wanted me some day to have dinner with them; she said now that they were building and would get into their new quarters by and by that she would speak in time and wanted me to have a Christmas dinner with them. She is a Londoner, (born and raised in London) but one would hardly detect from her talk that she was not an American. Mason is the Agent here of Agan of Seattle in wholesale of butter & eggs.

I have not heard from the folks at the Forks for several days but when I did, Roderick told me over the telephone that Wilfred had been out that day playing on the gravel pile.

Evening
I have returned from dinner with Mrs. Card.

She is so "strung up" looking after things about the restaurant that it is hard for her to get down to visiting as her mind is on business so much. We had a good dinner though and many old time things to talk about. Her mother is living at Walla Walla. Oldham *[Hilly]* has a position there as assistant warden *[of the Washington State Penitentiary, Walla Walla].*

She did not speak of it but her brother—Willy Hilly told me a few evenings ago their receipts run to between $400 & $500 a day. Their expenses are heavy but she is making a good deal of money.

Mr. Houck is going to work in a warehouse and is required to board with the parties so we settled up our little mess account that has run for 13 days and find that it has cost us only about 75 cents a day each for our board, rent, fuel & water—not so bad, as we have had everything we wanted. So now, I will this week live "by my lone," though Mr. Houck will be here every night as he will sleep here and besides its only eight feet across the alley way to the Yukon hotel with our old cabin join-

ing on the front and another one occupied 20 feet in the rear so you see I can't get much out of the way lonesome *[the "old cabin" Meeker refers to is the one he and Roderick shared during the winter of 1898–99].* But my dear wife I would rather have your company; but as that can not now be for the immediate present I will not work myself unhappy by having the "blues" and go moping around because I can't see my sweetheart every day or every hour of the day so let us be happy meanwhile live for each other and pledge to each other.

Loved as ever
Husband

Dawson
August 29th, 1900

I am without any letters from any of you since date of August 5th from Marion, although my neighbors all around about me have mail up to the 18th; for two days ago and now today freight is here shipped from Seattle on the 18th. I am afraid my letters have miscarried but in any event had expected mail from you by this time.

I write to say that I am well and that the folks up at the Forks are well. I have been at work on the cabin today only for three hours and the remainder of the time looking up for the contracts on potatoes, collecting, cooking etc. I had some poached granulated eggs for dinner—cup custard it really is; rice pudding (left over from yesterday) boiled potatoes, bread & butter, etc.

August 30th
Company came in last evening and interrupted my writing and so I add something today.

I am only waiting today = waiting for the mail; waiting for the time to arrive when I expect to get possession of our cabin; waiting for the shipment to come in—almost might say "killing time." However, I do find something to do though now selling but very little.

I think though when the shipment comes in and I get into our new quarters that I will get our share of business; meantime I take good care of myself and feel well but of course not content to lay around and wait.

I have a little more work to do on the cabin and after I do get the mail expect to make a trip up the creeks and canvass with road houses, mine owners, small stores etc. to lay the foundation for future business.

Loved as ever
Husband

[Partial letter/August or September 1900]

If you can send me a rug or a piece of carpet to cover a room 8 x 12, I would put on some "airs" over it.

It would have to be invoiced but the valuation need not be high. I think it could be packed in a potato case. You had better send in what apples you have to spare from the orchard that are ripe enough to ship and are good size and perfect. I have written Hartman the shipment can be delayed safely until the 15th of September.

If you send me anything in the shipment, then send
3 towells
2 white silk Handkerchiefs
3 large rolls of toilet paper
1 suit of good warm underwear soft & pliable, large
1 Dozen turn down narrow linen collars no 16
2 white shirts neck 15½ = sleeve 32
1 pair of suspenders
even now I can get along comfortably without any of these things being sent in for I can buy them here as needed but I thought you might be sending a box in which case these mentioned would come in all right.

I will dress different this winter than when here before as the business will throw me in contact with many well dressed people = merchants, customers, acquaintances, etc.

Dawson (Sunday)
September 2nd, 1900

Dear Wife

I have not received any letter from you for a long time. I had one from Marion yesterday written on the 22nd (a week ago last Wednesday) which as you see came through on lightening speed.

It seems that my letters out had been a long time on the road but Marion's letter cleared up the doubt about whether the shipment was coming.

I finished up on the cabin work last evening and am ready to say "well, I do not know how to do it better"; and will have a very safe place to keep the shipment and a very comfortable place to live. I will now order me an air tight stove with a flat top and a drum bake oven for heating and cooking. We can keep the room an even temperature night and day no matter how cold it is outside. I think I will put on a storm door; will have double windows and expect to put in two jets of electric lights.

I am well. Now that I have heard definitely from the shipment, I am ready to make my trip up the creek, visit a little with the folks, have a good visit with the folks at the Forks and get acquainted again with Wilfred.

Caddie sent me a short letter that Mrs. Egbert wrote to you. I hope you had a nice visit with her. *[Mrs. Egbert came west over the Oregon Trail in 1852, the same year as Ezra and Eliza Jane. She was an old family friend living in California in 1900.]* I am glad to hear from Caddy that she has been up to Puyallup again to see you and that Miss Graham will stay with you all winter. *[Katherine Graham eventually became the full time caretaker of the Puyallup mansion and remained in that role through 1907 when an ailing Eliza Jane moved to Seattle to be under her daughter's care.]*

I hope now almost any mail to begin receiving letters from you again. Friday evening I saw a gentleman just in from Seattle that left there the 24th—just one week from Seattle to Dawson;—the latest letter from any of you was from Marion August 5th 12 days previous.

I have our winter quarters cabin now nearly finished—about all I can do until we can move in to it and relay the floor which I can not do until the present occupant moves out. It is going to be a very warm cabin.

I have time and again almost wished I had written you more urgent to come in for the winter but maybe its for the best I did not; I know it would have been pleasant for both of us—who knows but you have concluded to come,—I hope you have.

September 5th, 1900

Dear Wife

I am about starting up the creek for a few days visit and also partly business putting up our posters and will be gone until Sunday.

When I get back I will move into our new cabin *[Log Cabin Grocery, Third Ave.]* or rather get possession of a part of it so that after this I will not have an opportunity to get very far from the business.

I have just received Marion's letter of the 27th acknowledging the receipt of my telegram but there is no answer required and I am in a hurry ready to start, will see Wilfred tonight.

Loved as ever
Husband
<u>Well</u>

Formally dressed customers and clerks at the North American Transportation & Trading Company store in Dawson City, 1901. Roderick McDonald worked here from 1904 to May 1908.
University of Washington #1235, Yukon Archives

Evening: I have just received your letter of July 14th. This letter arrived here July 26th but because you had addressed it in care of Roderick, it was sent up to the Forks and carelessly let it lay around there until today they sent it down here by Mr. Votaw. Now <u>dont address my letters in care of any body</u>, but simply address E. Meeker Dawson Y.T. Box 71.

I am very glad indeed to receive the letter even at so late a date but feel provoked that the P.O. folks should send it up there contrary to my orders and that Roderick should hold it so long.

E.M.

**Dawson
Sept. 9th, 1900**

Dear Wife

We took our first load to the new cabin on 3rd Avenue yesterday. We do not get full possession right away as there is a wholesale stock of dry goods there but we will get some room and hereafter will be there at the store all day.

Clara came in and was here when I came back Friday evening from my trip up the creek. She came in yesterday to see me and had quite a visit. Poor Fred, he has gone off on another drinking spell. Clara will not go up to him and I don't blame her.

I did not have much of a visit with little Wilfred though is just as "lively as a cricket" and jabbers away as though he was making a speech (in his own language)—like *[William Jennings]* Bryan, talks a good deal but dont say anything, Roderick says. He wont let go and walk but will go around his trundle bed. *[page missing...]*

Sept. 21, 1900

Dear Wife

You must not think I am neglecting you but the fact is I am now too busy to write you long letters.

Fred is with me and is his old time self again and I think will keep his pledge. This I know will be a great relief to you; I know it is to me.

Only the first car load of potatoes have arrived and about 1½ tons out of the second but I look for the remainder soon. We are assorting and selling a few and will get into our new quarters next week so that afterwards we will feel more like at home.

This will give an all winter job for the work but I do not think can get started before December. I am also sure we will want to manufacture more eggs, but not until eggs get cheap in the spring. We are going to have a good trade here this winter I think and plenty to do.

I am well. Loved as ever.
Husband

Dawson
Sept. 28th, 1900

Dear Wife

We are gradually getting moved into our new quarters and by next Monday will have moved out of the cabin where I have been stopping. Fred is with me and is well and hearty and stout and working very industriously. He is taking quite an interest to see things move briskly. This I know will be good news to you; I know it will be a great comfort to me if he only will continue and I believe he will.

29th I was interrupted last evening so will finish this morning. We are admonished this morning that winter is near at hand as the temperature is down to the freezing point but nothing to injure us. In fact we are now in position to hustle everything that has arrived into winter quarters very quickly if need be. If the temperature

should drop 5 degrees more, then we would work tomorrow (sunday) and get everything in the house.

We are all well and now working a pretty strong force—two extra men assorting the potatoes and have Mrs. Lamon get our dinner & supper for us.

I often and often think of you and somehow or another more tenderly and only regret that I could not be with you this winter, or you with me. Dont understand by this that I am fretting or discontented or homesick but simply have that robust healthy longing to be with my sweetheart and am happy in the thought that I have one that I know is thinking of me and possibly at this moment writing to me. I have now been away for over three months and now it is possible that in a little over three months I may be with you again.

My dear, I must cut this letter short as my time is now very full—at my old time occupation of "bossing" and talking to prospective customers; I let the men do the assorting and lifting and like that and tell them its a mighty poor concern that cant afford one gentleman with "store clothes" and so of course, you know I am happy.

Husband

Sunday Oct. 3rd 1900

Dear Wife

We are passing a quiet sunday in the cabin but did not get up very early. I have had an enjoyable week with Fred. He is working with Mr. Houck overhauling the potatoes and will go into the store to work as soon as we get possession and I think will stop with me all winter. He has been last week his old time self again. He is buying new clothing and promises me to dress well from this on and has kept his pledge not to drink.

I believe I wrote you I would soon send you some money; I think I can by next mail. I wish I knew just how your finances stand. Just now I am close run to pay the duty on shipment, first months rent, for a sign, printing, shelving, etc. incidental to getting started. The outlook is that we are going to do well for which I feel greatly rejoiced. Mr. Houck is good help and Fred you know is good (—if he stays sober—and I think he will—) in the store and has good judgment in buying. I think we will get possession of part of our new quarters tomorrow and even if we do not now have all we can do. There are <u>very</u> heavy shipments of potatoes here and on the way that

NATT store, Dawson City, as it appeared in 2007.
P. Ziobron

keeps the price low but there are <u>very</u> few as good as ours and the price of ours has started in at 20 cts per lb which pays well while the general stock on the market is selling for 13 so you that is quite a difference.

The old maxim that "too many cooks spoils the broth" does not hold good in our case as we all have a hand at it but get along well, each bragging on the other by way of encouragement. I am however dropping out of that part of the work as my "store clothes" are too high toned for that. As a matter of fact I now have plenty in hand distributing our cards, picking up the lines of the market, making some sales *[page missing…]*

Dawson
October 4th, 1900

Dear Wife

I have not written for several days as we have been moving and now are snugly in our new quarters. I like it very much; nice and warm. Our heating stove as yet however is not a success for cooking but we have a little coal oil stove that works all right for boiling meat, making coffee, mush etc. I now have good light for reading by, and a good bed three feet wide.

Fred is working steadily but we have not yet gotten down to do much business other than getting things in place. We are all well though.

There is small pox on the creeks and some at the Forks. Roderick telephoned down yesterday to get a permit to come down here but the health office would not grant it, so he must stay up there until the scare is over. This makes business very dull for the time being, but I think it will be better latter on.

There are a great many potatoes here but there are a great many being used and Roderick thinks it will come out all right in the end.

We have <u>such</u> a nice place to keep our stock and <u>such</u> nice comfortable quarters for ourselves that I only wish you could look in on us some day when we were at dinner "joying" ourselves. Well, I would like to be at home with you but as it seems best that I should be here.

I can stay cheerfully and enjoy life and will not go moping around "bewailing my fate" for in fact we have so much to be thankful for.

I caught a little cold in the move, or rather before it, but it is not bad and will doubtless soon be over it.

We have had a little taste of winter but not very cold and the weather is now again bright and mild—freezing just a little—I will finish up tomorrow before the steamship sails.

[Meeker's Third Avenue "Log Cabin Grocery" building was still standing as late as 1984. An interpretive sign above the front doors read: "Ezra Meeker's Place. Ezra Meeker played an important role in the early history of the State of Washington and is acknowledged as one of the state's pioneers. At the turn of the century when he was in his 70s Meeker made two trips over the Chilkoot Trail to Dawson City with loads of potatoes to sell to miners." The cabin has since been razed.]

**Dawson
October 5th**

Dear Wife

As the open season is near the close I thought to write you as often as there seemed to be a probability of getting a letter out. Mrs. Card (Ella Hilly) goes out tonight and will carry out this letter. I will also send out $20.00 by her which she will deliver to you in person with the letter. I had intended to send you more and think I will be able to do so before navigation has closed. After the river has closed there will be two or three weeks that mail will not reach you but you will know that I often will be thinking of you.

Now you must not be uneasy about me, for I am comfortably situated and have not hard work to do; at least I am not trying to do hard work, lifting and the latter as I have two men with me—in fact three, Fred, Mr. Houck and a Mr. Sloan that used to live on the Wabash and knew Uncle Usual's folks. His work is canvassing to sell potatoes, assorting etc. He is quite an agreeable intelligent man and succeeds well in selling. I have the satisfaction of having a good working force and as we get arranged think I can see a fairly good business ahead that will pay.

Roderick came down tonight from the Forks but I have only seen him for a few moments. He says they are not in

danger from small pox and in fact it is not in the Forks but is in some of the cabins on the creeks near there.

Ella Hilly (Mrs. Card I mean) has been doing a large business and I think has made considerable money. I hope she will have time to make you a nice visit; she was well liked here and highly respected and has real good business qualifications. Her husband I hear is no good though they are not separated as he went to Nome after I came in here.

Fred and Mr. Houck has gone to bed, the first whistle of the steamer has blown and it is now half past nine O'clock so I must close and go to the steamer to deliver this letter and then back to "high" me off to bed and pleasant dreams of home and of my distant faithful sweetheart.

Husband

Oct. 5th The steamer goes up the river this morning so I must close and mail this letter. I have just heard that Osmond had just arrived with two letters for me but I have not seen him yet.

I just put some small potatoes into the new oven this morning when I first built the fire and by the time Fred got the breakfast ready they were nicely done and as white and light *[two words unreadable]* as you ever saw. This settles the question about the new oven being a success. I know now it will bake biscuits and "corn bread."

Business opened last night with the sale of an outfit of $160 that ran yesterdays sales up to $250; the day before it was over $200; so you see we are doing a little business but I must now close by saying

Loved as ever
Husband

**Dawson
Oct. 6th, 1900**

Dear Wife

It is now after ten O'clock; Mr. Sloan has gone home and Fred and Mr. Houck have gone to bed. Roderick has gone up to stop with Dr. Grant so I am up "all by my lone" and felt that I wanted to talk to you a little while before going to bed. The fire is nearly all out in the stove but the room is nice and warm and in fact it is not cold outside—just freezing a little.

Roderick and I selected me a nice new suit today and I have it on now. I like it better than any suit I have worn for many years. I also bought a new hat, so now I feel free to go into company, and will go to church with Roderick in the morning to hear Dr. Grant.

We had a good business today and I think the outlook is good for our doing well. I do not make any pretense of laying hold of the hard work or in fact of any work except it is to look after the buying and attending to "odds and ends" of things to be done to keep things moving. We are selling a good many potatoes that we get here at a lower price than we are willing to sell of our shipment; I think we sold at least $250.00 of such today besides other things out of our little stock of groceries.

I received your letter post marked September 24th today and am very glad to hear that you are well. It will soon now that the mails will be interrupted for awhile so that I will not hear from you or you from me but you will know that I will often think of you and also that I know you will often think tenderly of me. Well it is a great consolation for each of us to know that we are loved and have much to live for and be thankful for.

Roderick seems in good spirits and will go home tomorrow after church. Fred seems to be very much interested in making the business successful and is doing his best. Clara has a situation on Eldorado where she was last year. Wilfred, Roderick says, walks from morning til night but does not talk much yet. Olie is well though of course I have not seen her since last week when she made her trip down here and left Wilfred with Mrs. Brown.

I have a real good strong light to write and read by—a glass table lamp with a good large burner. As we gradually get settled in our new quarters and get things placed I like them better and better—I just now stopped writing to wash up my handkerchiefs. We have a broad bottomed tea kettle that sits on the stove all the time so that we always have plenty of hot water at any time we need it and so now I have just taken advantage of it and have three clean handkerchiefs.

Now my dear wife I will go to bed and sleep soundly and bid you a happy good night.

Husband

Oct. 8th

I have not had an opportunity of mailing so I thought to write you a little more this evening by way of reminder that I was thinking of you. I have had a pleasant day in and out of the store, buying sometimes other times selling while yet at other times collecting. The most bothersome thing of the day is that I am short in my cash this evening $3.25 which I think has come by the weighing of gold dust. The business has been lighter today yet made a fair showing for new beginners, of about $200.00.

The steamer that was expected to take out the mail early this week is delayed on the way down at "Hell Gate" a shallow place in the river about 200 miles above Dawson.

Oct. 9th

One of the small steamers will go up the river afternoon and so I thought to send my letter out by some passenger as this steamer does not carry the government mail.

We are all well and have plenty to do though business is not rushing but enough to pay "grub" with prospect for better later on.

The weather is fine—just freezing a little, so now there is no wind and yet it is pleasant to be out of doors—have just had dinner and now do not have time to write more.

Dawson
Oct. 11th, 1900

Dear Wife

The steamer *Canadian* starts for White Horse tonight and probably carries the last government mail out for the season until the ice forms. However there will be some more steamers out so that I expect to get other letters out to you before the close of navigation.

We have had a good trade today—a little over $400.00 which we consider pretty good for the stock we carry and in fact pretty good for quite a stock. Our trade has not been as good as it was in the start in 1898, neither the prices of our shipment is as good as then nevertheless I think we are going to have a prosperous season. We are so far selling but very little of our own shipment and our sales are principally made up from what we buy and sell here, so, when our own shipment does begin to move we will I hope have a pretty lively trade.

Our shipment is not all in yet but we heard from the last fifteen tons today and look for its arrival now any day.

We are all well. Fred was so busy that I took hold of the cooking and done most of it today. I have had me a blue denim apron made and some oversleeves to slip on to protect my shirt sleeves and so come out from the work without getting my clothes soiled.

View west on Third Avenue, apparently some years after Meeker's time in Dawson City.
Louis Irvine #1891, Yukon Archives

Mr. Houck made Fred a cot yesterday, so now he also has a comfortable bed. I am over my cold that I wrote about; in fact it was not bad at any time.

We are having splendid weather—just cold enough to make it dry under foot, yet pleasant bracing atmosphere overhead. Our storage room is working all right and our stock is in splendid keeping order so withal, you see I am feeling pretty cheerful.

I had intended sending you some more money today but the cash was short and will be until our own shipment begins to move; nevertheless I will send you a small remittance by the next steamer. Now my dear wife I want you not worry about me for I am comfortable and happy in the thought that I can be of some service to provide for our wants, to get some money out to you so that Marion *[page missing…]*

I think it is a good idea to rent some of the rooms if you can get good nice people otherwise not.

And now I come to your last letter dated September 12th.

I am sorry indeed to hear that you are not well but you did not write me just in what way you are unwell. I think it is a good idea to see Dr. Misner.

I am <u>so</u> glad to hear that Miss Graham will stay with you all winter. She is such nice company and besides will take the care of the house off your mind. Of course you want her to stay by all means.

The potatoes have not been here long enough yet to sell many of the choice ones like ours. There are a great many potatoes here crowding on the market that won't keep long and when they are gone either by being used or rotting then ours will sell more rapidly. I have sold a few at 20 cts a pound which pays us well.

You say that you are going to come here to me next spring and that it looks a long way off. Now my dear wife I hope to see you long before that if my plans do *[page missing…]*

I doubt whether there will be more than three more boats attempt to go up to White Horse this season and probably the last one will start from here in about ten days. After that, there will be no mail for three or four weeks and then there will be regular mail service over the ice all winter and nearly as quick time as in the summer.

I am ever and ever <u>so</u> sleepy and must go to bed. Both Mr Houck and Fred are in bed so good night.

Husband

Dawson
Oct. 13th, 1900

Dear Wife

This is the coldest morning of the season so far—8 above zero but is calm and not a breath of air stirring.

I get up every morning at ten minutes to six O'clock. I have my kindling all prepared and it but a few minutes till the room is warm and comfortable. What a blessing good dry wood is and plenty of it:—I hope you are enjoying your basement full of bark and wood. Well, when I get up and start the fire, my broad base tea kettle is soon boiling or rather the water in it; my coffee is ground the night before and potatoes prepared and go into the oven as soon as the fire is started so now, as I write the coffee is made, the potatoes are done, the table set and all hands are now up and Fred is frying some bacon while Mr. Houck makes some mush and so now I must stop and eat breakfast at ten minutes before seven.

Sunday evening 5 P.M. I have spent a quiet day "at home" but did not get up until breakfast was ready—about 9 o'clock and so we have had but two meals today.

Frank Vining was at dinner with us and related his experience on the scow on the way in. One scow was swamped on Labarge or rather driven ashore and all the goods wet and some lost but he only had a small portion of his seasons shipment on this scow.

Fred is working as steady as clock work and seems to enjoy the business like he used to enjoy the hop business. There is a great field here for buying and selling—"from hand to mouth"—yesterday he was figuring on a six hundred outfit that two men want most of the goods we would have to buy and he was looking up the question of where we could buy the cheapest and what price to put on them. There is a lot of such work to do and I hope we will build up quite a trade like we did in 1898—but, we will have to work for it more this year than then.

We are not selling but few potatoes as the market is filled yet with the cheaper sorts but ours are in fine order and will keep well all winter. Potatoes are selling now at 13 cts by the sack and large quantities are used daily but I think there are a great many in an insecure place so that the first real cold snap will frost more or less of them and cause them to go off the market entirely.

Our storage room is working fine; the temperature varies but little and the potatoes look as though they would keep forever.

I still hope that I can get out by the stage over the ice before the winter breaks but if I do I will simply go as a passenger and wrap up in my robe all the way. I am this year taking solid comfort in my robe. It seems almost as light a cover as an eider down quilt, yet is just as "warm as wool" and is all the covering I need as yet and I think is all I will need all winter.

The weather has moderated and this evening is barely down to the freezing point and as Aunt Mary Jane would say, is "fixing up to snow." We hope there will be snow as the ground is frozen solid and snow would now make easy work delivering goods on the sled and would make business livelier as miners would then come and buy more freely.

Our new stove is already in place and works fine.

Wilfred is now walking so Roderick telephoned me; they are all well up there.

I intend to send you some money before the river is closed but as yet have not sold only enough to cover current imperative outlay here, but now it will be different and as soon as I am sure of enough to pay the duty on the shipment you will come next.

You can tell Marion that I have a strong probability of making a contract for twenty five tons of sliced potatoes which if it goes through all right can be delivered from time to time at any time prior to the first of March.

Vath did a poor job on the watch and it was not keeping good time and would not run at all when held in one certain position. I had to after all take it to a watch maker here to have it put in order. Vath ought to be ashamed of himself to send out such work.

Dawson
Oct. 16, 1900

Dear Wife

When I opened the box this morning containing the things you sent in my heart went out to you in thankfulness that I had my dear wife to think of me though far away. I lost no time in putting down a piece of the carpet in front of my bed where I dress and undress. The carpet looked so natural that I could almost think myself at home; and then those nice large apples—well, my heart is full of thankfulness this morning. Our shipment is now all in Dawson safely we are well and I am hopeful for a prosperous season that will enable me to bring out some nuggets with *[page missing...]*

I think you could not possibly have a more congenial companion and as you say she prepares the food nicely, it would be difficult to find another person as suitable. I hope you will enjoy yourselves this winter.

Now my dear, the remainder of the shipment has arrived and the men are putting it in the warehouse today, so you see we have a busy day and so you see I have not much leisure time to write you and so you see you must be content with this short letter but remember I love you as ever

Husband
Box 262

LOG CABIN GROCERY
E. MEEKER
Manufacturer of
Granulated and Sliced Potatoes, Granulated Eggs,
Dried Cabbage, Parsnips, Squash, Turnips, Etc.
Dawson, Y.T.

Dec. 4th, 1900

Dear Wife:

I am well. The mail will be deposited in the morning so I thought to write you this much. The weather is very cold now—50° below zero—the coldest I ever experienced—but we are all right inside and just as comfortable as when its warmer. In fact though, I have been out collecting and have not suffered with the cold the least bit, though have not been out for long at a time.

Trade yesterday was the heaviest we have had since we started here—over $500.00. We can plainly see that our business is increasing but of course the profits are not large. Our stock of potatoes are keeping just splendid.

I was interrupted and must close to catch the mail.

Husband

LOG CABIN GROCERY
E. MEEKER
Manufacturer of
Granulated and Sliced Potatoes, Granulated Eggs,
Dried Cab-bage, Parsnips, Squash, Turnips, Etc.
Dawson, Y.T.

Dec. 8th, 1900

Dear Wife:

I am well. What are you doing this afternoon as I write at 2:45 P.M. sunday. I have just finished eating dinner and I got no farther than biscuit and butter with my oyster soup although Mrs. Brown had other things besides.

I said at the beginning that I was well. That is true from the top of my head to the soles of my feet though it does not extend to the end of my toe as I have just a little of that corn left. But I will not "show" you my sore toe but write of something more pleasant. For instance I slept so soundly and sweetly last night; I enjoyed my breakfast and dinner so much; I am enjoying this writing to you as much as if I was eating oyster soup or mince pie; and by the way, Mrs. Brown makes us splendid mince pies but I got too full for utterance before I got that far in the dinner course.

I have not been out of the house today except through the front door to look at the thermometer. The temperature has been about 50° below zero all day. Yesterday it was as low as 58° below—the coldest weather I ever experienced. I was in and out all day yesterday without experiencing any unusual discomfort but of course was not out very long at a time.—as I write a house fly has alighted on the table and is moving about lively. Our living room has never been too cold for flies to live in yet we do not let it get very warm except once and awhile, while baking bread gets a little too warm for comfort; but this does not last long as we have two large ventilators overhead easily opened or closed by a rope attached.

We finally got to the apples and find there was not much loss. I think we will get about $15.00 a box out of them which I think is pretty good. It seems to me they are much larger than usual. That pruning Marion gave them doubtless did the work. Trees ought to be pruned every year and I wish you would get Marion to prune them again this winter and then by thinning the fruit we can have them suitable to ship here.

There are a great many potatoes here that are not keeping well and some of the owners are urgent to sell and have forced down the price to 10 cts. Such however are not very good eating, so, we get some customers for ours at from 18 to 25 cts, but not as many such as we would like. I think there will be a great many potatoes lost here—some by overheating and some by being touch with the frost. Our shipment is in fine shape. It seems that this house that I fixed up last fall is just about right. We do not keep any fire at all in the warehouse part except such weather as this keep a small coal oil stove burning to cause a circulation of air near the floor. I get up about 10 O'clock every night and examine the thermometer but seldom make any change. Our whole stock is solid and fresh while most of the others I have seen are flimsy and wilted. Just how long such will last before they rot I cannot say, but some I know not long but ours I know would keep until the river opens again.

I received two letters from you by the last mail and now that communication is open again hope to hear from you often. The mail leaves here every Wednesday morning and is expected to arrive once a week but not exactly on time. You may be sure that I will send you a letter by every mail that leaves here.

My dear wife, I feel <u>so</u> thankful that you are able to write so cheerful a letter. Miss Graham <u>is</u> a nice companion and a nice lady and I am glad to know will stay with you. I will be home after awhile and then we can visit until we again get acquainted with each other and next time you will come here with me wont you?

Loved as ever
Husband

Dawson
Tuesday Dec. 17th, 1900

Dear Wife

A large mail arrived Sunday—said to be forty five thousand letters—but none from you. I know however that you have written and probably the letter is in the next mail expected to arrive tomorrow.

Two copies of the weekly *Oregonian* came by letter mail direct from the *Oregonian* office and will be mailed regularly all winter as I subscribed for it and sent them postage. I also received a business letter from Hartman and yesterday a telegram from him with reference to freight matters and so I assume all is well at home else he would have made some mention if anything had gone wrong with you.

Oh, my, but I wish you were here. My health seems to be perfect and I believe the change would be good for you but I will not fret about it but rather bend my mind and energies on the business to make that a success.

There is the foundation for a good business here although it does not now promise as good results as I had expected earlier in the season.

I have a little garden in one of our windows—a box of celery to bleach that one of the gardeners brought us. He had failed to get it bleached. I took it in hand, applied some bottom heat, watered it with tepid water and I think will get it ready for Christmas. Already the top leaves are brightening up and the lower part begins to bleach.

We have turnips, rutabagas, cabbage, and carrots besides our potatoes and onions and celery and think I will have some beets soon. We are advertising these in the paper and people are coming to us from all over the city and from up the creeks as well.

It makes me happy to feel that I can be of some use and be busy and I think you would be happy too; I <u>know</u> you would.

Fred is busy and is a great help to me. Clara is on Eldorado cooking and gets $75.00 per month. Roderick is over his cold, and at work again. Olie is all right. Wilfred said "Helloe" to me over the telephone yesterday. They have a telephone in the store and we have one in ours and we can talk as often as we please without extra cost. I have a fine extra good electric light in our dining room and it burns all day when we need it as the curtain shuts off the light partially from our living room. Mrs. Brown is still cooking for us and our diet is good.

Now my dear wife I must close with the oft repeated though true and sincere expression of Loved as ever.

Husband

Sunday Dec 23rd, 1900

Dear Wife

All hands have gone to bed, but I had an afternoon nap so I thought to write my sweetheart a letter before going off to dreamland.

I received your letter of Nov. 29th by last mail and also one from Caddie of same date and one from Mrs. Egbert in which she said she had your "permission" to write me. I have just been talking with Wilfred twelve miles away, over the telephone and could hear him distinctly say "heloe" "Grand Pa" and a stagger at something else I couldn't understand. The intention was for them to come down for my birthday dinner and Christmas but Olie told me this evening that Wilfred had taken cold and his throat was somewhat swollen so I am not sure whether they will come or not.

Well, we are getting business again something like in /98 though not as yet so profitable but it is gratifying to know that it is steadily increasing and is paying. Yesterday was a <u>very</u> busy day and I tell you I enjoyed it for right in the midst of it I thought of you and how I could make you happy by writing you about it. Potatoes are yet low, and that bothers me, but my oh my, if you could but see how nice ours are keeping in comparison with others you would feel confident about the future.

I had my hair and beard trimmed yesterday and bought a light cap to wear indoors which with the "outing" shirt with a white collar makes me look quite "gay." And well I ought, for we are having a good many ladies coming to the store for cabbage, celery, eggs, potatoes, etc. etc. Is this "Meekers"; is this the "Log Cabin grocery" is asked quite often now as new customers put in an appearance. But as I said, profits are small yet in the long run it would seem that the winter work would pay one quite well notwithstanding potatoes are low.

Mrs. Brown is with us yet but will go tomorrow to Eldorado creek to spend Christmas with Clara and so I will have to do more cooking. But that's not much where we buy our bread and boil the potatoes with the "jackets on."

My dear wife how much I would like to have you with me on this birthday occasion. I will be seventy years old. I dont feel it. The fact is I believe my health is just as good as it ever has been though my finger joints do "creak" a little—a little stiffened—and I can notice that I am a little more "lubberly" than—well say "fifty years ago."

I took a walk today up the trail towards home; I didn't like to stop; I declare I could walk out easy enough but of course when I do go it will be by the stage. The low price of potatoes and the uncertainty as to when we can sell unsettles me as to when I can go. Only to think of it here we are already in midwinter and now from this on the days will be getting longer and soon there will be that heart bracing spring weather here—home I <u>do</u> wish you were here to enjoy it with me. But we will take things as they come and be happy in the thought that we can soon be together again and thankful that we can enjoy many many blessings even if we dont have exactly all we want and so by now my dear wife I will write you that I love you lots and <u>lots</u> and <u>lots</u> and will now go to bed.

Husband

Christmas

I ate my dinner all "by my lone" though you were present in my thoughts and I enjoyed thinking of you and how we had in the past and probably in the future would have our Christmas dinner together.

Mrs. Brown went up to have dinner with Clara. Fred & Houck went out to a restaurant but I preferred to stay "at home" and as I said ate all alone.

Roderick and Olive wanted me to be with them but it was a twelve mile tramp or $5.00 expense on the stage so I did not go. I am feeling real well and have had a quiet day of rest and reading; the weekly *Oregonian* (2 copies)

came opportunely in one of which was the Presidents message which I have enjoyed greatly. *[page missing…]*

[Ezra's 70th birthday came four days after Christmas. Meanwhile, the Tacoma Ledger *on December 23 reported: "Mrs. Ezra Meeker will spend Christmas in Seattle with her daughter, Mrs. E.S. Osborn."]*

[Partial letters]

[Olive] was here yesterday and day before but home today. She was doing some shopping. Wilfred is walking everywhere but is yet backward about talking & he has five teeth I think she said.

And now my own dear dear wife I must close this letter and go to bed; my robe is very light covering but just as warm as several heavy blankets would be.

Loved as ever
Husband

not necessary as I can go to White Horse by stage after the river freezes up and the road is smooth and I think of doing so and manufacture some sliced potatoes and dried eggs. There will be a regular line of stages with hotels to stop in so that a person can ride all the way and stop in a house every night and have three warm meals a day besides.

I want to be with you on that golden wedding day *[May 13, 1901]* and then we can make our new wedding trip in here.

This leaves two comforts, two shawls and a heavy double blanket under me besides the heavy canvass that forms the bottom of my bed. I am only about seven feet from the stove and have a good tall glass lamp with a large burner that sits at the head of my bed for reading purposes. I now have a moveable closet in the store room so that I do not need to expose myself to the cold at anytime. My bowels are very regular and appetite good, and health ✳

Good Samaritan Hospital.
McBride Museum #3769, Yukon Archives

ENDINGS, 1901

[Ezra advertised almost daily in the Klondike Nugget. *The advertisements mostly were brief—one line long—providing samples of the products carried by the Log Cabin Grocery, and occasionally indicating delivery and commission services or other information. The last two advertisements (below) indicate a product that Ezra had a little trouble maintaining in stock.]*

Fresh carrots and turnips at Meeker's
Fresh Cabbage at Meeker's
Celery and cabbage at Meeker's
Fresh parsnips, carrots, beets, turnips Meeker
Ten varieties fresh vegetables at Meeker's
Meeker delivers fresh vegetables up the creeks
New Century apples $10 at Meeker's
Eastern Washington new Timothy hay at Meeker's
Hay and Grain at Meeker's
Good stock large eggs See Meeker
Chechako Eggs by the case-Meeker
Eggs 75 cents at Meeker's
Up-river frozen fresh eggs at Meeker's
Eggs by the case at Meeker's
Full line family groceries at Meeker's
Goods sold on commission at Meeker's
Pop corn popped at Meeker's
Fresh Eastern oysters at Meeker's
Sweet Potatoes at Meeker's
$1 reward for sweet potato thief: Meeker
$10 reward for sweet potato thief: Meeker

LOG CABIN GROCERY
E. MEEKER
Manufacturer of
Granulated and Sliced Potatoes, Granulated Eggs,
Dried Cabbage, Parsnips, Squash, Turnips, Etc.
Dawson, Y.T.

January 15th 1901

Dear Wife:

I have just received your letter of December 28th which arrived in Dawson yesterday—pretty good time as you see.

We are all well but it is now very very cold 74 degrees below zero. We do not notice any change in our cabin store and warehouse though I kept a fire all night. *[The* Klondike Nugget *reported an official temperature of 64.5 degrees below zero, but noted the common thermometer at the newspaper office reached 74 degrees below zero and promptly froze.]*

We have just had a nice short visit from Roderick and have heard all about Wilfred. Roderick seems to be happy and cheerful.

In fact almost everybody here is in good spirits which seems to be "catching." We have now a jolly set of lady customers who seem to enjoy their shopping experience. Notwithstanding the extreme cold yesterday a good many ladies were out.

I tell you it begins to look as though I will not get out on the ice and leave the business here. We will not make much on our potato shipment but our business will pay and I conclude I had better stay and take care of it. If I do not get out you had better come in here when the river opens next summer. I will write more this evening before mailing.

Husband

LOG CABIN GROCERY
E. MEEKER
Manufacturer of
Granulated and Sliced Potatoes, Granulated Eggs,
Dried Cabbage, Parsnips, Squash, Turnips, Etc.
Dawson, Y.T.

January 31st, 1901

Dear Wife:

Our boy is dead. I dreaded to write you this, knowing the shock it would give you. To me my grief is no

Dawson City winter hearse.
Yukon Archives

more than it has been for my cup has been full for the two weeks since Fred's fall. He had been kind to me and diligent in his habits and I had come to lean upon him as like a staff but all at once it snapped and was gone. I can not truthfully say, but there was a feeling of relief when the end came. I never before experienced such a feeling of utter despair for I could not look upon Fred's life other than as a blank. I did all I could to save him from his besetting sin and came to know him more intimately than ever before his many manly virtues. Poor boy, no wonder of your tenderest regard for him over all that has been born to us.

The end came peacefully but I was not present until a few moments later. Clara, Olie and Mrs. Brown were there but he was not conscious for an hour or two before and seemed like as if he had dropped off to sleep. He did not suffer much. The doctors now say that it was not pneumonia, but a deeper seated lung trouble, like consumption. Fred's lungs had not troubled him in this climate any more or in fact as much as at home although he had spells of coughing like at home. It was wonderful how strong he was up to the very last of his work in the store.

Now, my dear wife I know your grief will be great but you must remember that time is the great healer of our sorrows and that our duty lies to the living and the future instead of the dead and the past. You must not think that I have fallen into an unhappy strain of thought or that I will lead an unhappy life for I have not. We have <u>so</u> much to be thankful for; so many many blessings vouchsafed to us that I feel more like saying, "oh let us be joyful" and fulfill our mission in life, to live for each other and for others as well as for ourselves.

My dear wife, now you <u>must</u> not let your fears for my safety prey upon your mind for this is not a place dangerous to good health or devoid of opportunities for healthful living. My health continues good and my rest at night refreshing. We have a very equable temperature in our store and pure air while we do not have the convenience of our home yet I have things so arranged that we live comfortable.

Clara and Olie are here with me and happy little Wilfred is the busy body in all parts of the store mixing up things generally. He is the happiest child I ever saw. Just now as I write he is out in front of the counter walking

Fred's final resting place—Hillside Cemetery, Dawson City, 1901.
University of Washington #1209, Yukon Archives

the floor with his bottle in his hand elevated so he can get a little milk at times. He is a dear little boy.

I send money order to Cady that is payable at Seattle for fifty dollars for you and she will draw the money and send it to you. As the mail will close tonight, I will write a little more this evening and so send you the sad news.

[Fred's obituary appeared in at least three northern newspapers—the Klondike Nugget *(January 31, 1901), the* Yukon Sun *(February 2, 1901), and Skagway's* Daily Alaskan *(February 19, 1901). Many decades later, Wilfred McDonald added more details in his September 17, 1971, letter to the Dawson City Museum.*

Fred took ill sometime in mid-January 1901. On January 26, he was admitted to the Good Samaritan Hospital with a Dr. McDonald attending. Pneumonia developed and he died on January 30, 1901. Ezra's sad letter to Eliza Jane states that Clara, Olie, and Mrs. Brown were with Fred

when he succumbed and that he long suffered from coughing spells. Perhaps Fred actually died from consumption.

Fred's funeral was held the next day at 2 P.M. in the Presbyterian Church with Dr. Grant presiding. At the conclusion of the service, the black-cloth covered coffin was loaded onto a horse-drawn hearse sleigh and taken to Dawson City's Hillside Cemetery for burial. (According to Laura Berton in I Married the Klondike *[1961], graves were dug in the summer and left open in anticipation of winter burials when no excavation could be done due to the frozen ground.) On March 5, Ezra paid Greene's mortuary $165.00 in gold dust for the funeral expenses and burial.*

In his 1971 letter, Wilfred noted that the wooden headboard had succumbed to the ravages of time; he could no longer find the grave. Neither the Dawson City Museum or City Hall records identify the location; thus the grave today is unmarked and its precise place is unknown.]

Greene's mortuary handled Fred Meeker's funeral arrangements.
Anton Vogee #79, Yukon Archives

LOG CABIN GROCERY
E. MEEKER
Manufacturer of
Granulated and Sliced Potatoes, Granulated Eggs,
Dried Cabbage, Parsnips, Squash, Turnips, Etc.
Dawson, Y.T.

February 3rd, 1901

Dear Wife:

This evening I do truly feel lonely and lonesome. This will doubtless disappear tomorrow when business is resumed. Yesterday we had a very very busy day which run our sales up to $424.00. Wilfred has been with us for four days and has cast a flood of cheerfulness over us all. He is a lovely child, so good natured and <u>so</u> busy. He was the busiest one about the store but he would get mixed and never could get things into place to suit him as he would move them from time to time first one place and then another. When evening comes Olie would put him to bed and he would lay there for hours kicking up his heels, talking to himself or singing baby songs until finally he would drop off to sleep. His health is now the best it ever

has been and he is growing in weight rapidly. Clara went home on the morning stage and Olie and Roderick on the afternoon trip so now I am really alone except the help in the store. I felt almost compelled to discharge Mr. Houck while Fred was sick and employed a man of the name of John Fletcher an englishman who is far away better than Mr. Houck. In some respects he reminds me of Kendal; then I have another young man by the name of Moore from Kent as a helper but I do not think he will develop much. Mrs. Brown is again here and cooks for us and takes care of the house but is all the time looking out for a place where she can get better wages.

If our business continues to increase in the next two months as it has within the last sixty days I doubt if three of us can take care of the customers as fast as they come. We are getting quite a family trade on account of our fresh vegetables.

I do not feel in the mood to write you much for my mind is on Fred but I thought I would not write you of him now. My dear wife, may God bless you till we can be reunited again. Your

Husband

Feb. 22nd, 1901

Dear Wife

I felt in cheerful mood today and so during a lull in business this afternoon thought to write you a gossipy letter—have just been interrupted and sold a sack of oats for $10.00—but first to say that I am well.

The sun is shining brightly and now the days are of good length. Its broad day light at 7 O'clock when I get up in the morning and from now on we will have all the daylight we need. The weather too is pleasant though cold but there is not a breath of air stirring. We have had a prolonged cold snap but now everybody feels that the "backbone" of winter is broken.

Our business is not as good as it was the first of the month, but I think that is the case all over town and that we are holding our own with the balance. I have good help in the store so that I am entirely relieved from any of the heavy work about the warehouse or store. In fact I have plenty to occupy my time with the care of the accounts and buying and incidental business always connected with such work—I have again been interrupted, this time for about two hours with quite a spurt of trade and so now it is nearly supper time and I am in a mood to do good justice to a supper. I bought us a good sized mush pot and so now Mrs. Brown makes the mush at night. Latterly I have been keeping a slow fire all night and so the mush cooks all night and is simply delicious in mornings. Then when we have some left over she fries it for the evening meal. Both the boys that are with me like the corn meal mush the best and so we do not use the oat meal at all. This diet is especially good for me and builds me up in strength and good feeling. If you conclude to come in next summer I think we ought to have some more carpet. I would like to have some potted plants for our window. Your part of the room would face upon the street with a large window and a recess in it 15 inches wide that will give ample room for plants of various kinds. The windows (for there are two of them) are about six feet high so that there would be room for quite a vine. Some rose cuttings or small rooted rose bush—a monthly would be nice. The market next year will be well supplied with early garden stuff such as lettuce, radishes and the like which I expect we will have to sell. Preparations are being made for some substantial buildings to go up next season. One not far from here 50 x 100 feet will be of bricks with stone foundation. Large quantities of stone is now delivered for the foundation and the pile is getting bigger every day—I must quit now.

23rd I thought I would write you a continued story for the next Wednesday's mail and so this morning while Mrs. Brown is getting breakfast I am off here behind the counter where our gold scales are and which is near the window, a writing to my sweet heart.

I am usually up in the night for a short time, but last night I slept until morning and was not out of bed at all until after seven O'clock. We had some trade last night late—after 9 O'clock and also some company—Mr. Campbel, part owner of the mine where Clara is working—and so after our customers left we had a cup of cocoa and cake, but I did not eat any cake but drank some cocoa and so it came about that I did not go to bed until after ten O'clock.

Roderick was talking to me yesterday over the telephone. I always ask him "how is that Wilfred" and invariably get the same answer "Oh he's just fine." Roderick thinks there never was quite such a boy before—<u>Breakfast</u>

LOG CABIN GROCERY
E. MEEKER
Manufacturer of
Granulated and Sliced Potatoes, Granulated Eggs, Dried Cabbage, Parsnips, Squash, Turnips, Etc.
Dawson, Y.T.

February 25th, 1901

And now my dear I am just so happy that I don't know just how to behave myself. A big mail is in and sure enough the first dash there came a letter from you into our box and also one from Cadies *[daughter Carrie Osborne]*. This comes at the close of a very busy day for we have had the largest days trade of any day since I opened this place—over six hundred dollars. It does make me happy to think that I can do something to help us and to have an opportunity to provide something for the future. If our business would hold up like today for six months I could go home with quite a lump sum—anyway it <u>is</u> encouraging. But along with this comes some conditions not so promising as the price of potatoes continues low and the final outcome from our shipment is problematical though I can see that we will not make an actual loss even if we do not make a profit.

STOCKING THE LOG CABIN GROCERY

Reconstructing Meeker's business dealings during his Klondike years must be ascertained from his personal letters because very little of the business correspondence has survived.

What quantity of freight did Ezra ship north? He provides the exact totals of the two 1898 shipments and for the first shipment of 1900. Reasonable estimates can be made regarding the other two shipments. For 1899, it can be assumed that Ezra sent north at least as much freight as in September of the previous year. The September 1900 shipment sent by Marion Meeker was probably smaller as funds were tight. The chart below illustrates the best estimate as to the amount of food products shipped during Ezra's time in the north.

Year (Month)	Amount
1898 (June)	30,000 lbs. (Ezra arrived in Dawson City with 18,000 lbs.)
1898 (September)	40,000 lbs.
1899 (October)	40,000 lbs. *[estimate]*
1900 (June)	61,000 lbs. (shipped in 932 crates weighing 65 lbs. each.)
1900 (September)	30,000 lbs. *[estimate]* (sent by Marion)
Total	201,000 lbs. (100 tons)

(These figures, of course, do not include any shipments sent north to Dawson City after Marion relieved Ezra at the Log Cabin Grocery in March/April 1901.)

Packaging

Much of what was shipped north was canned and evaporated (dehydrated) food, with processing done by family members and employees in the old Puyallup light factory building, located about a block from the Meeker home. Soup vegetables were packed in 4.75" square, 9" tall, cans with threaded tops, manufactured by a Seattle company. Larger 25 pound capacity cans, made by the Puyallup Hardware Company, were primarily used for evaporated potatoes. The cans were packed into wooden boxes or crates for shipping. Each fully packed box weighed 65 pounds.

Fresh eggs needed special packing. While on the Chilkoot trail in April 1898, Ezra had sent Eliza Jane advice he gained from an experienced supplier: "Pack the eggs in a double weight case, that is, have the case more substantial than the ordinary case; then pack as usual in the paper holders but take nice rolled oats and pack in each layer, being sure to have them well filled around the outside row. He says to have the case tin lined; what would be better would be to solder on a top after filling and make it entirely waterproof. He said all the eggs packed that way and kept dry arrived in good order and sold for $4.00 a dozen while those poorly packed or become wet or, I think he said those packed in saw dust or bran did not keep; the rolled oats he says is 'springy' and protects the eggs and is salable after having served its purpose in packing."

Fresh potatoes were individually wrapped in paper and put in sacks. These needed to be kept at a cool, but not freezing, temperature. Ezra took great care in constructing a cold room at the back of the Log Cabin Grocery to ensure a proper temperature to prevent wintertime spoilage. It can be assumed the same care was taken with onions and other fresh vegetables.

The freight was handled a number of times before reaching the docks at Skagway or Dyea. The packaged foodstuff was loaded onto wagons in Puyallup and transported to the local train depot, transferred to railroad cars, and shipped to Tacoma. Here it was unloaded and then put aboard a steamship bound north. At the Alaskan docks, of course, the freight was transferred again, for Ezra's handling thereafter. Over 3,000 freight packages were shipped between 1898 and 1900.

Supply and Demand: 1898 prices per pound

	Dyea	Lake Bennett	Dawson City
Potatoes	10¢	25¢	60¢
Onions	50¢	65¢	$1
Soup Vegetables	27¢	40¢	50¢

Products Mentioned in Correspondence and Advertising

Soup vegetables and potatoes were the main foods shipped north, but these two staples were supplemented by a wide variety of other provisions that were advertised in Dawson City newspapers. Meeker promoted "Ten varieties fresh vegetables," including potatoes.

Meeker sold fresh whole potatoes, evaporated potatoes (sliced, then dried with heat to remove moisture), granulated potatoes (evaporated potatoes ground into a rough grain), and potato meal (ground evaporated potatoes sifted several times into a white powder similar to corn meal). Meeker referred to all of his potato products as "Sure Enough Potatoes." He called his granulated (dehydrated) eggs "Chechako Eggs."

In addition, he sold hay and grain. In an experiment not repeated, Roderick followed Ezra to Skagway in September 1898 with 500 live chickens. The two then transported the chickens to Dawson City where they sold for $5 each. Chickens required much attention in getting them to their destination safely. Despite the profit gained, it apparently was not worth the trouble.

The following were available for purchase when in stock—

Beets
Cabbage, fresh and evaporated
Carrots
Celery
Onions
Parsnips
Squash
Sweet potatoes
Turnips
New Century apples

Eastern Washington new Timothy hay
Fresh eggs
Chechako Eggs
Up-river frozen fresh eggs
Pop corn
Fresh Eastern oysters
Lemons
Pickles
Sauerkraut

I know that I will get another letter from you tonight as you mentioned having written one the day before the one I received. It is now after 10 O'clock and Mrs. Brown has gone to bed and Mr. Fletcher is just getting ready so that I will be up all "by my lone," which I do not mind. I have a splendid steady electric light to write by and which is on a long cord so I can move the light to the head of my bed to read by when I go to bed—but I dont read long at a time as you know.

My dear, you can scarcely realize how thankful I am that you can have Miss Graham with you. Caddie wrote me about your going home together. You must tell her how I feel about it. I would hardly know how I could stay here were it not that you have such a good companion; in this time of our bereavement, how much we have to be thankful for and look forward to.

26th I have just received your letters of 9th in which you say you and Caddie were writing at the same table before breakfast. I also have received one from her—the second one from each of you in this mail so I do not now feel so much "by my lone" when I know I have such faithful correspondents. My health is so good and my sleep so refreshing that I begin to wonder how long will this frame work continue to wear—well no matter, we both have had a long lease of life and surely no reason to complain but all the same I <u>do</u> want to be with you again.

Husband

LOG CABIN GROCERY
E. MEEKER
Manufacturer of
Granulated and Sliced Potatoes, Granulated Eggs,
Dried Cabbage, Parsnips, Squash, Turnips, Etc.
Dawson, Y.T.

March 17th, 1901

Dear Wife:

I have had two letters from you by the last mail. You may be sure I was pleased to get them. I am well and hearty and so let us be thankful for the many blessings we enjoy even if we cant have everything just as we want it.

Wilfred was here again last week for two nights. Olie came down with him. At night—Olie would undress him and put him in my bed and he would play by the hour and seemingly not care whether anyone noticed

him or not; finally would lay down outside the covers (it was warm) and drum with his feet against the wall, sing a sort of baby song and finally go off to sleep for the whole night. As Uncle Usual would say "he's a good one."

Won't yet talk to me through the telephone when he is home though I can frequently hear his voice "eh" "bye bye" and the like but after awhile he will get over his timidity and then we can talk over the phone at any time we choose.

Our last weeks business was not so good as the week before but yesterday was a good day. Potatoes remain cheap and I begin to fear will remain so till the end of the season. I think I will arrange here for the freights on shipments for the summer and if I do will send out for Marion to buy and ship and later on we can conclude what best to do. I fully agree with you that we ought to be together.

I wrote an article not long since for one of the papers here about the care of vegetables, eggs etc. for the Dawson market in winter. The manager of one of the big companies sent for me yesterday with a view evidently of some future business. The waste here has been enormous in their warm storage houses and cost also very heavy for fuel, night and day and two firemen. I pointed out how all this could be avoided and in fact have demonstrated it by the operation in our warehouse by the condition of our stock of potatoes kept all winter substantially without artificial heat without wilting or rotting or deteriorating in quality at all. It is a revelation to these people and will revolutionize the preservation of vegetables here in winter. I have no doubt but there has been 150 tons of potatoes, onions and the like lost here last winter by improper care. Then added to that is the very large item of cost of fuel, wages of firemen and of men to assort the vegetables made necessary by some of them rotting and sprouting, the whole amounting to a good sized fortune. One hundred thousand dollars in my opinion would not cover the loss that has occurred that might have been avoided besides the question of good healthful vegetables that might have been had. I am to have another conference with this gentleman this week and am not without hope some business may come out of it as I pointed out how necessary it was to make shipments of suitable stocks as well as to be prepared to keep them properly. If I did make some arrangement I would hope that it would result in my going out in August to select the shipment for september to store for the winter. Now you wont call me vain will you, when I write you what follows will you? Businessmen here look upon me as authority on this subject. Another large firm has offered to take up our freight bills next summer if we ship. One firm that has large warehouse room have long ago sent their eggs and apples over to me to care for and pay us $8.00 a ton a month as they acknowledge they can't do it in their warehouse as I can. I had to refuse a dozen people who wanted to store with me when it come to be known about the condition of our stocks—how it was keeping. I could have had enough to store to fill our warehouse several times over. Now all this is gratifying but the main thing with me is whether I can turn this to profit to ourselves. I hope I can; maybe it may be in the buying to ship here, but more likely in the keeping here or perhaps both; there is certainly a very great field this kind of work for some one who understands it.

March 19th Am well, busy, happy.

Husband

LOG CABIN GROCERY
E. MEEKER
Manufacturer of
Granulated and Sliced Potatoes, Granulated Eggs,
Dried Cabbage, Parsnips, Squash, Turnips, Etc.
Dawson, Y.T.

March 17th, 1901

Dear Caddie *[Osborne]*

Last week I passed you by in my letters home but write mother a good long one which I "spect" she may on the sly show you, though I know she dont like to have "sweet heart" talk made too public. You tell her next time not to forget one page of her letter but after all as I get two letters from her by last mail I ought not complain and in fact do not complain.

Your letter of 28th came in yesterday and I read it twice before I slept, the second time like one would take their desert at a meal—just for the pleasure of it. I suppose I do shock you by persistently referring to our "old dear home" as the "cabin." Sure, it was a home in the truest sense of the word as you write; dear to me, dear to us all, presided over as it was presided over by that Queenly "Mamma" and full of that family love that fairly filled the house—there now, I have called it a house this time—the old cabin—what have I said—I should have said the house. Well, cabin or house or whatever we may call it the precious memory of it will be the same. *[Ezra is refer-*

ring to the log cabin in Puyallup where the family resided from 1862 until 1889, when they moved into their nearly completed new mansion.]

I deeply regret that I can not be home on our golden wedding anniversary *[Ezra would change his mind about this in only a few weeks]*, but so it is and so we must make the most of it and turn our thoughts to the future rewards. Of course, as I have written, if she can not come here then I wont stay but cant in any event now get away until the summer season's business is over. It is yet problematical as to what the out come of this years business will be as the market here have been overstocked and declining and if it continues till the end of the closed season may cut off most, if not all expected gain. My present plan is to try make some shipments when navigation opens, by the regular steamer line for the summer trade though all this may be changed by later developments.

Mrs. Brown has gotten a place on Eldorado a mile beyond where Clara is and will leave me in the morning and Mr. Foster, who is now with me (not our Foster of ye olden times) will be married tomorrow. I will expect to break up my regular housekeeping and take some of my meals out; I will always though have my breakfast of brown toast and coffee at home as also probably my evening meal. Otherwise my habits will not be changed as I will continue to live in the store building, go to bed early, have a short spell of reading by the electric light which hangs at the head of my bed, and have a good nights rest, a morning bath before breakfast and a good appetite for breakfast.

We now have perfect weather and long days with bright sunshine—neither too cold to be uncomfortable nor warm enough to make it "sloppy" under foot. However we soon will need to change over foot wear from felt shoes to leather and our headgear from the fur cap to the more genteel hat—in fact I have already bought the hat and worn it some.

That "Wilfred" has been down to Dawson twice and both times stayed over night and worked mighty busy in the store during his wakeful hours. He was his own boss behind the counter and was an expert in tearing down but not much of a hand at replacing things. He would play by the hour all "by his lone" but I didn't say dont except by way of covering up the beans, sugar, rice and the like but he had free access to the nail box and plenty of small cans to handle—he <u>is</u> a great boy.

Well I must stop and write to that mother else she may be jealous if you get a letter and she dont, so I know you will excuse me for not writing more; I hope though you will not pattern after me and cut your letters short.

Father

Dawson
April 4 *[1901]*

Dear Caddie *[Osborne]*

I am just writing to ask you to send me in some belladona plasters. My back hurts and they always help me but they cost 75 cents here and as they don't last long they are expensive. You can put 3 or 4 in a letter & they will come. I have moved into a larger cabin but took cold in moving and have the rheumatism awful & have such a nervous hurting in *[page missing...]* he *[Marion Meeker, just arrived]* will stay all summer. He thinks I have a nice place & is pleased to see them so good to me. He sold his wheel *[perhaps a mining device]* for double what he gave for it so thinks he is in luck. He said Mary *[Marion's wife]* would be glad to know he was with me & I am glad to know he is doing well. I have 18 men now & find it rather hard work this year. I find I am not as strong. When Marion just came in he said he thought mother ought to come in. But yesterday he said Clara you are right. This is no place for mother. I don't want to see her come in. So you see we all feel very much opposed to her coming. Ollie said the last time I saw her "mercy can't we do something to prevent mother coming." Father must go out. I feel I can't say enough on the subject.

Lovingly
Clara *[Meeker]*

John P. Hartman, Jr.
Attorney
Burke Building
Seattle, Washington

April 22, 1901

My Dear Mrs. *[Eliza Jane]* Meeker:
I have just this moment received a cipher message from Mr. *[Ezra]* Meeker at Dawson, which being

Marion Meeker, in 1890. He started north in March 1901. *Ezra Meeker Historical Society, Puyallup*

translated, omitting the business portion, contains the following:
"Expect to be home about the beginning of next month for Golden Wedding. Notify all parties. All are well."
I am very happy to be able to give this information to you and send it by the very first possible post. I have telephoned Mrs. Osborne.

Sincerely yours.
John P. Hartman

Seattle
April 25th 1901

Dear Mother
We do heartily rejoice at the news of Father's return in May. It seems almost too good to be true and now if he only will stay we will be happy. Marion, Clara and Olie all are anxious to have him stay home and are implicitly of the opinion that it's no place for you to winter. We will try our persuasive powers and keep him if it's possible. I send Clara's last letter received today.
We are wanting to put out a lot of holly for future use for profit. Have you any seed or cutting we could get? We think we will put out all the upper part of our orchard alternately into rows between the rows of fruit trees. Let us know if there will be a chance to get the cuttings. I hope you can come down in time to meet Father here. I am to go across the lake in half an hour to see about some work being done there. We are feeling well. I am much better the Dr. thinks today but still need to go twice a week for tests.
Have some new glasses and they are pretty but do not know how they fit yet.

Love to you both
Caddie

[In April 1901, the winter stages left Dawson City for Whitehorse at 6 A.M. on Wednesdays and Saturdays, an approximately 300 mile trip taking 5 days. The Yukon River, then fast thawing, was used as part of the road. Once the ice broke up, however, all traffic ceased until the river cleared of ice and the water level rose enough to accommodate steamboat travel.

Lower LeBarge Hotel on the Dawson City-Whitehorse winter stage route.
H.C. Barley #4930, Yukon Archives

When Ezra quickly decided to leave Dawson City that spring, time was of the essence in going out before the thawing river closed down stage travel to Whitehorse. Ezra likely departed Dawson City at 6 A.M., Wednesday, April 24. Once at Whitehorse, he would have taken the White Pass train for Skagway (8 A.M.–4:30 P.M. daily except Sunday), and from there, a steamer to Seattle. Ezra arrived in Puyallup early in May.

Nearly two months earlier, the Tacoma Ledger of March 17, 1901, had reported in its Puyallup column that "Marion Meeker left Sunday evening for Dawson, where he will assist his father E. Meeker." Marion, age 49 and Ezra's oldest son, was the last family member to arrive in the Klondike. It did not take Marion long to get into the mining business. He took out a Free Miner's Certificate, No. 82145. On May 21, 1901, Marion staked a bench claim above Bonanza Creek in Lovett Gulch and registered claim No. 37729 the next day in Dawson City with R. Hardway, the mining recorder. Marion's main purpose in going north, however, was to relieve his father in operating the grocery business, freeing Ezra to go home.

Fourteen months after Marion's arrival, Dawson City land records show that Marion Meeker and Roderick McDonald bought the Log Cabin Grocery property for $3,000 in June 1902, from John W. Little and Charles F. Nelson (from whom Ezra had been renting).

Nearly 1½ years afterward, in November 1903, Marion and Roderick sold out to Henry F. Abraham for $2,000. The 1903 Dawson City Tax Roll No. 1514 listed the land value of the property at $1,400 and the building at $500; Roderick paid the $35.50 taxes. (Wilfred McDonald's 1971 letter explained that his father did not have control of the property and that in putting his name on the tax rolls, he was simply acting as an agent for the Meekers.) Marion was living in Puyallup by 1903, leaving Roderick to clean up affairs in Dawson City. Business prospects had declined after the height of the great rush and Marion saw no future for himself in Dawson City.]

[The last Yukon letter preserved in the Meeker Papers dates from October 15, 1901, when Marion wrote to Robert Wilson, the Meeker family real estate agent and accountant. It concerned property in southern California on which Marion and his family formerly lived. They had moved to Poway, California, in 1889, just outside of San Diego. His daughter Grace was born there. By 1892, the family had returned to Puyallup. In 1908, they moved permanently to southern California—first to Redlands, then San Bernardino. Marion's autumn 1901 letter referred to the Poway or San Diego property.]

LOG CABIN GROCERY
E. MEEKER
Manufacturer of
Granulated and Sliced Potatoes, Granulated Eggs,
Dried Cabbage, Parsnips, Squash, Turnips, Etc.
Dawson, Y.T.

October 15, 1901

Robert Wilson
Puyallup

Dear Bob

I wrote you twice since I came up here but have no reply. I now write you to have you consult with Mrs. Meeker *[Marion's wife Mary]* about the sale of the California property and to look after the taxes which will fall delinquent about the last of November.

Write the tax collector at San Diego and find out the amount and don't let them go delinquent. The property is assessed to Mrs. Anna W. Cox *[Mary's sister]* and Mrs. Meeker has the description which you can get from the title deeds.

Don't delay about this matter.

How do we stand on the lumber deal and did you finally sell off all the lumber?

Mrs. Meeker has a deed of the California property which has never been recorded. She will explain to you. If Mrs. Cox can give a 800 or title now this deed need not be used. You can decide the best course to pursue. I am well and hearty. Let me hear from you.

M J Meeker ✳

POSTSCRIPT

In *The Busy Life of Eighty-Five Years of Ezra Meeker* (1916), Ezra noted: "I came out over the rotten ice of the Yukon in April of 1901 to stay, and to vow I never wanted to see another mine, or visit another mining company. Small wonder, you may say, when I write, that in two weeks time after arriving home I was able to, and did celebrate our golden wedding with the wife of fifty years and enjoyed the joys of a welcome home even if I did not have my pockets filled with gold."

Ezra, indeed, never looked back. He spent the next few years deeply involved in Washington State Historical Society activities, writing *Pioneer Reminiscences of Puget Sound* (1905), running a pioneer exhibit at the 1905 Lewis and Clark Centennial Exposition in Portland, and planning his Old Oregon Trail Monument Expedition.

The crusade to mark and preserve the Oregon Trail, and to honor the memory of the pioneers who had traveled on it, became the central focus of Meeker's life from 1906 until his death in 1928, just short of his 98th birthday. It propelled him onto the national stage. He retraced and mapped the trail, campaigned for a national highway to follow the route, lobbied congress for funds, met with three presidents, and founded a preservation organization that still inspires efforts today to recognize and preserve the trails of the Westward Migration.

Ezra Meeker as the nation came to know him, retracing the Oregon Trail by ox team and covered wagon. In April 1910, he stands by a commemorative marker at Meacham, Oregon.
Dennis Larsen collection

Fred Meeker's story, of course, was much shorter. Fred was 34 years old in the fall of 1897 when his father sent him north to explore the Stikine River route to the Klondike. He died shortly after his 38th birthday. It seems rather unfair of Ezra to write, "I could not look upon Fred's life other than as a blank," for throughout his life, Fred usually did Ezra's bidding. The demands on him came early, but Fred always seemed to handle them capably.

When Ezra decided to experiment with growing sugar beets in the Puyallup valley in 1885, he needed a chemist. Fred was dispatched to study chemistry at the University of California, Berkeley. After completing the classes, Fred was employed at the Alvarado sugar beet factory in California. He sent regular reports to his father regarding how the experimental beets Ezra sent him were doing (not well). When the hop lice infestation swept through the Puyallup valley, Fred was sent to London to search for a solution. When gold was discovered in the north in 1897, Fred was dispatched to reconnoiter. He seemed always at his father's beck and call.

It is unknown when Fred's alcohol difficulties began. A number of Fred's letters are preserved in the Meeker collection, some dating back to his time at Berkeley. Fred's letters seem quite personable and gave no hint of any problems. It is only in Ezra's letters to Eliza Jane that Fred's dark side is exposed.

Perhaps Fred's alcoholism provides a simple explanation for much of his behavior. In 1897, Fred did not show up in the Kootenay mines until days after he was expected. He provided no real explanation for his tardiness. When Ezra asked Fred to join him in sailing down the Yukon River in June 1898, Fred just could not get his affairs in order to meet Ezra's schedule. This declaration came despite the fact that Fred and Clara had shut down their Skagway restaurant months earlier. NWMP records indicate that Fred, along with J.R. Pesterfield of Tillamook, Oregon, entered Yukon Territory via Chilkoot Pass and Lake Bennett on July 21, 1898, and floated down the Yukon in boat No. 14309, about a month behind Ezra.

When reaching Dawson City, Fred chose to go out to the mines rather than stay in town and work for

Ezra. He resided in a cabin on Little Skookum gulch in partnership with Pesterfield. Ezra reported that Fred did little work that winter beyond looking for a mining claim to buy. There is no evidence that Fred accompanied Ezra on his trips home. Fred went to his father only when alcohol finally seemed to overwhelm him.

The Meeker women needed to be a self-sufficient lot. Ezra only returned to Puyallup for three limited periods, just months or weeks at a time, totaling no more than nine months out of the three years of his northern venture. During his absences, Eliza Jane mostly remained at their Puyallup home. She produced granulated eggs and obviously was involved in other food manufacturing aspects of the family business.

Local newspapers reported her visits to daughter Caddie and family in Seattle, and Ezra's letters note her friend and companion, Katherine Graham, who eventually became a live-in caretaker at the mansion. Unfortunately, none of Eliza Jane's letters survive in the Meeker Papers, but Ezra's replies to her letters hint that the separation did not sit well with Eliza Jane. Ezra constantly urged her not to be lonely.

Clara Misamore Meeker faced a similar situation; her husband also was often gone. She and Fred married on March 14, 1886, in Portland, Oregon, at her brother Milton's home. Clara and Fred's letters suggest that Portland was where she stayed during much of his absences.

Clara, however, often was not content to simply take care of the home fires, waiting for Fred's return. In 1890, for example, she accompanied Fred to London on hop business.

In 1897, when Fred left for the Kootenay mines, she stayed in Portland only for a time. In April, she invited Eliza Jane to come down for a visit, while fretting about the danger to the Meeker men, working in thawing snow in British Columbia. On June 11, Fred wrote his sister Caddie, saying he expected Clara to stay in Portland until September, when he would return for the hop trade. But on July 1, Ezra wrote that Clara was with him in Spokane and they were proceeding to Nelson, British Columbia.

Ezra and Eliza Jane—likely at their Golden Wedding Anniversary, May 13, 1901. *Ezra Meeker Historical Society, Puyallup*

By September, Clara was back in Portland at 91 Park Street, and Fred was off on the Stikine River reconnaissance. For Clara, her situation often was not easy. On October 25, for example, she wrote: "My rent was due yesterday. I did not pay it because I had to eat."

She did not sit by idly; Clara took an active role in planning the Meekers' upcoming Klondike ventures. She conferred with her brother, Milton Misamore, recently returned from the north. Milton was building Yukon sleds to sell to would-be stampeders, giving lectures to the Portland Chamber of Commerce, and had written a letter about the Yukon that was widely publicized in the press. He worked on a plan similar to Ezra's initial scheme to build boats for the Yukon trade. Discerning what she learned, Clara sent word to Puyallup about the type of boat that would be suitable. She interacted with Paris Packard, also recently returned from the Yukon, and sent on what she gleaned to Ezra.

Clara wanted to go north, too. On September 21, she wrote Ezra: "Did Fred tell you I have fully made up my mind to go with him in the spring. I should like a job on a boat—on the river fine but—I am young & get something to do for a year or two." Clara was then 39 years old.

She did find employment in the north. At first, she cooked in the Skagway restaurant she and Fred opened. By the end of May 1898, she was working the telephones at the Chilkoot tramway office, making $40.00 a month plus meals. By July 21, she was alone again after Fred departed for Dawson City.

On August 23, Ezra reported that Clara was cooking for the tramway company for $75.00 dollars a month: "She thinks the Tram will shut down last of October in which case she will lose the job and will then go back."

What Clara did in the winter of 1898 and the spring of 1899 remains unknown, but she chose a destiny in the north, proceeding to the Klondike. It appears she spent many months on Eldorado Creek, cooking for workers at Campbell's mine, while presumably living with Fred. On September 9, 1900, Ezra reported she came to see him after Fred had gone off on another drinking binge. Clara announced she was not going back to him. Yet four months later, she was there at the hospital when Fred died.

Clara and the McDonalds stayed with Ezra for a few days after Fred's death. On February 3, Clara took the morning stage back to Grand Forks and her cabin. The last documentation for Clara in the Yukon was her April 4, 1901, letter to Caddie, when strongly stating her opinion that Eliza Jane must not come north and that Ezra should return to Puyallup.

Seven years later, in a letter of October 28, 1908, Ezra mentioned that Clara would be working in his pioneer exhibit at the Alaska-Yukon-Pacific Exposition, held in Seattle from June 1 to October 16, 1909. In November 1909, Clara, with Caddie's help in co-signing, leased property near the Puyallup fair grounds, where she tried to make a living operating a boarding house.

On March 13, 1910, Ezra wrote from Vancouver, Washington, to his Puyallup friend and business associate, Charles Hood. At the time, Ezra was beginning his second Oregon Trail Expedition and was aboard a train bound for The Dalles. "Just as I was leaving Puyallup Mrs. Osborne spoke to me about Clara. Her boarding house business near the Fair grounds is not prospering—things are dead out there. Clara would make a good clerk in the Post Office, or for that matter in the store; she is both competent and honest; I wish you and George would put your heads together to help her help herself."

Ezra wrote an additional letter on April 18, 1910, to George Edgerton, another Puyallup friend and businessman, asking him to consider giving Clara employment in Edgerton's office. These efforts failed. Caddie noted on June 23, however, that Clara had a housekeeping job for the summer with the "Putnam" family and then another in the fall with the "Lathrops." In 1913, Clara was working at the Staghurst Hotel in Bellingham, apparently as a cook.

On March 13, 1913, Clara wrote Ezra: "In regard to the letters of Fred's and mine, I have been trying so many years to have them destroyed that perhaps they were, but if not they are in a 5 gallon coal oil can somewhere in the house. Several years ago I wrote Bob Wilson to go & destroy them, then when Caddie was going to rent the house, I asked her to look for them & burn them. So now I hope you will hunt around in the attic & if you find them, burn all of them." (Today, the letters indeed are gone; Clara must have got her wish.)

In 1915 at San Francisco's Panama-Pacific International Exposition, Ezra arranged with a Mr. Reid for Clara to work for $60.00 a month. She sailed south on the *Congress* on February 2 and took a housekeeping room with her niece, Bertha Templeton, for the duration of the exposition. Ezra wrote Caddie on February 7: "Clara, well what shall I say. She arrived mad all over; rough trip." A bit latter Ezra wrote: "Clara visited me at the building yesterday. Strong Clara and its just as well, and I think better that we are to live apart."

In 1919–20, Clara was working at a telephone exchange somewhere in Seattle. Here the trail seems to end. It can be surmised that she returned to Portland to be near her brother Milton or sister Susan, for she died there on October 18, 1922.

Roderick McDonald stayed on in the north, working for the North American Transportation & Trading Company. From 1900 to 1904, he served as manager of the NATT store at Bonanza, Grand Forks. Olive, however, returned to Washington with Wilfred in September 1902, taking a month of medical treatments in Tacoma. Ezra tried his hand at caring for Wilfred alone that month, since Eliza Jane was in California with their daughter Ella, visiting friends. As late as September 1902, Ezra still wrote about sending potato shipments, presumably to Roderick and Marion in the Yukon.

For reasons unknown, Olive extended her stay in Washington for at least a year, living at the Puyallup mansion during this time. Roderick made a short visit south in late spring 1903. The exact date of Olive's return to Dawson City is unclear. Correspondence indicates she was in Puyallup as late as November 1903 but definitely back in Dawson City by July 1, 1904.

Olive and Roderick with Wilfred outside their Dawson City home (Lot 10, Block J, of the Dominion Government Survey No. 4). Years later, in 1918, Wilfred sold the lot and house for $200; the structure was razed for the lumber.
Roderick McDonald 82/409, #1, Yukon Archives

Roderick, Olive, and Wilfred at Eagle, Alaska, probably during a summer visit, 1914.
Ezra Meeker Historical Society, Puyallup

Roderick next managed the NATT's Dawson City store from 1904 until May 1908, when he was transferred to Eagle, Alaska. The 1910 census lists Olive and Wilfred along with Roderick at Eagle. In July 1910, Roderick was transferred back to Dawson City and put in charge of the dry goods department. In 1912, the NATT shut their stores.

He next managed the Northern Commercial Company store at Forty Mile, a remote station not far downstream from Dawson City, from July 4, 1912, to July 31, 1915, when the post closed. In a June 5, 1915, letter, Roderick informed Ezra that he was preparing to move to Wiseman, Alaska, and run a company station on the Koyukuk River. Olive was to stay in Dawson City near doctors, due to her poor health, and Wilfred would attend school there. Then abruptly, plans changed; Roderick penciled a P.S. that he was to be the cashier at the Dawson City store.

Around this time, A.S. Miller of Dawson City visited Penticton, British Columbia. In a letter published in a Dawson City newspaper, Miller described the virtues of the Okanagan valley sufficiently enough to draw several long-time Yukoners south (among them, Judge Craig, E.W. Mutch, W.R. King, Wm. Dobie). While still residing in the Yukon, the McDonalds decided to buy a fruit farm in Penticton.

Due to Olive having injured her ankle, in early summer 1918 they proceeded to Vancouver, B.C., so she could receive medical attention. After Olive's treatment they moved permanently to Penticton, becoming orchardists, growing apples and peaches. In a letter to Ezra, Wilfred described the farm as being two miles outside of the city.

Roderick's reminiscences eventually appeared in the *Penticton Herald*, December 17, 1936, shortly after Olive had died on December 12. Roderick passed away on June 2, 1943. They are buried in the old section of Lakeview Cemetery, overlooking the Okanagan Lake locality that became their final home.

Wilfred, of course, attended schools in Dawson City and Eagle, apparently receiving a first class education judging from the quality of his writing. He and Ezra corresponded often over the years.

In August 1916, 17-year-old Wilfred went to work for the Bank of British North America in Dawson City. He remained employed there until August 1918, when he left for Vancouver to join the Canadian Army. As the Russian civil war continued at the conclusion of World War I, he was shipped with the Allied intervention to Vladivostok. By August 1919, Wilfred was in Penticton.

In 1936, he was employed in Shanghai, China, as the district passenger agent with the Robert Dollar Steamship Company, and by 1943, served as a Lt. Commander in the U.S. Navy.

Wilfred, the little boy who so delighted Ezra, lived to see the birth of his own great grandchild in 1989. Wilfred passed away in Seattle on June 2, 1991, at the age of 92.

One key aspect of Meeker's Klondike adventure remains to be unraveled. What made him quit the north in April 1901? Meeker himself offered two explanations for the abrupt return to Puyallup, but there is likely a third reason not specifically mentioned.

He suggested in *The Busy Life of Eighty-Five Years of Ezra Meeker* and other publications that it was mining losses that chased him out of the Yukon. Those losses, however, occurred in late 1899; yet Ezra remained in the north into 1901.

In a document titled "Tribute to My Wife," Ezra offered an additional explanation. "As the time approached for our golden wedding anniversary the attraction became too strong to resist and so I left my business in Dawson, Yukon Territory, came out over the ice of the Yukon River and arrived in good season. If not as ardent a lover, certainly as admiring as before when we first plighted our faith fifty years before."

But he had this to say in a letter to Caddie just one month before leaving Dawson City for good: "I deeply regret that I can not be home on our golden wedding anniversary, but so it is and so we must make the most of it and turn our thoughts to the future rewards."

Indeed, in February and into March 1901, Ezra and Eliza Jane seemed to be making plans for her to join him in Dawson City that summer, despite the opposition of their children. Ezra suggested that if Eliza Jane could not come north, then he would return to Puyallup after

the summer's trade. Thus, up to this time, it seems that neither mining losses, the upcoming golden wedding anniversary, or even the death of Fred had broke Ezra's determination to remain in the Yukon.

So what changed his mind? It must have been a compelling reason because Ezra departed during the spring breakup of the Yukon River, a difficult and dangerous period for travelling. A report in the March 28, 1901, *Klondike Nugget* demonstrated how hazardous it could be at that time of year—the Whitehorse stage broke through the Yukon ice and it took a supreme effort to extract it from a potential watery grave. Nevertheless, Ezra departed, "over the rotten ice" as he described it, within several weeks of this reported incident.

On the very day Ezra wrote Caddie saying he would not be coming home for his golden anniversary, the *Tacoma Ledger* of March 17, 1901, reported in its Puyallup column: "Marion Meeker left Sunday evening for Dawson, where he will assist his father E. Meeker."

The apparent purpose of Marion's trip north was to take over management of the Log Cabin Grocery so his father could go home. Was this simply an act of kindness on Marion's part—a gift to his mother? Marion originally expected to stay in Dawson City only through the spring and summer of 1901, but instead stayed two years, leaving his own family behind in Puyallup.

It could be supposed that Marion, who along with John Hartman was running the Puyallup end of the vegetable business, was simply trading roles with his father for a time. However, there appears to be considerably more to the story. In a coded telegram to Hartman, Ezra had sent word he was coming home. Hartman immediately delivered the news to Eliza Jane in his brief April 22, 1901, letter (see Chapter 7).

Why did Ezra send a coded message to Hartman, instead of sending a telegram directly to Eliza Jane? An argument can be made that Ezra had received a warning, either sent by Hartman or delivered in person by Marion (or both), that creditors were threatening the Puyallup house and property, and Ezra needed to come home at once to deal with the matter.

Who were these creditors? The International Mine Development Company that Ezra and his partners created in 1896 had sold considerable stock to a number of wealthy people, from Puyallup all the way to Scotland. After he departed down the Yukon in June 1898, there is no further mention of the company or its stockholders in Ezra's correspondence to Eliza Jane. He obviously dealt separately with business matters—this correspondence never made it into the Meeker Papers. In any case, Ezra

Modern-day view of Dawson City, looking up the Yukon River valley, July 2007.
P. Ziobron

was hard pressed to even scrape up spare income to send home to Eliza Jane. Surely the stockholders never made a penny on their investments, and no doubt a number of them were unhappy.

There also was the matter of leftover obligations from the Puyallup bank business of 1895 and the secured creditors who discovered their loans were not so secure after all. They had not been paid. Furthermore, there is correspondence in the Meeker collection, written as late as 1907 from the London & San Francisco Bank, suggesting that Meeker still owed money, perhaps dating back to the 1896 foreclosure of his hop farms.

Thus, by the end of Meeker's stay in the Yukon, there was a long list of potential creditors who likely felt Ezra owed them money. The Puyallup property was the main asset in the Meekers' possession in 1901 and it appears somebody was after it.

This view is supported by the following. In his tribute to Eliza Jane, apparently first presented at the anniversary celebration and later revised after her death, Ezra claimed that their home belonged to Eliza Jane, not him, and that it had been built from her design and with her money. "Residents of Puyallup are all proud of the beautiful home and surroundings of what they call with pride the Meeker Homestead that yet adorn the city. It is remarked by strangers as a monument to the builder. The wife built that house from her own plan with her own funds. The government gave the wife half of the donation claim: this in time was sold and other property bought which in time, together with the proceeds of a life insurance policy supplied $20,000 to build a residence."

But in 1901, a good lawyer could make a case that Eliza Jane's house and the land it stood on actually belonged to both of them, not just to Eliza Jane. This

The Meeker Mansion today, headquarters of the Ezra Meeker Historical Society, Puyallup, and listed in the National Register of Historic Places. *D. Larsen*

was remedied two months after Ezra returned. On July 3, 1901, Eliza Jane sold the mansion and property to their middle daughter, Carrie Osborne, for $10,000.

Next, on November 11, 1901, Ezra and Eliza Jane signed a statement claiming the mansion and land were the separate and personal property of Eliza Jane when she sold it to Carrie. This statement was filed with the sale papers. Carrie's husband, Eben Osborne, providently was a title attorney in Seattle, and he no doubt made sure the title was free and clear when transferred to his wife, Carrie. Ezra could now rest easy. The mansion was safely in his daughter's hands and removed from the reach of any possible creditors.

Mention of the Osborne contract appears in a number of the Meeker letters. Although the actual contract has not been found, its terms can be deduced from the correspondence. The contract stipulated that Ezra and Eliza

Jane would be allowed to live in the Puyallup home until their deaths, and would receive lifetime payments of $50.00 a month. Eben and Carrie would be responsible for taxes and general upkeep of the property.

From Carrie's point of view, it seemed like a good arrangement all around. She was assured her parents were guaranteed a home until their deaths, and protection from creditors. As Ezra and Eliza Jane were likely nearing the end of their lives, Carrie and her husband would in time become the owners of valuable property, worth well more than the $10,000 purchase price (a decade earlier, it had cost $25,000 to build and furnish the mansion).

The fly in the ointment was Ezra. He lived another 27 years. Eben, for one, came to regret the financial aspects of the deal, as evidenced by a response prompted by Ezra's request for a 100 percent cost of living adjustment in the contract.

March 27, 1912

Dear Father

...If I was able to pay you regularly $50 a month I would gladly do it. I am not hoarding up money so that all that I need to do is to draw checks—I owe today my bank $1500 & will have to ask them for $1000 line credit. My salary here is $200 a month & I am not sure of getting anything else in the way of dividends before the last of the year if then. $200 a month is not enough to pay my home absolute expenses. You are perhaps not aware that aside from my contribution to you of $50 per month I have to pay general special taxes besides repairs & c. on account of the Puyallup place of over $50 a month. In other words your account costs me more than $100 a month & you would if you could squeeze more out of me. I owe you a moral obligation, but no greater than your other children owe you of caring for you. I have been assuming this entire burden myself. I will ask you whether or not I have dealt other than honorably with you & whether or not I am not doing more than my share. To say that my business relationship with you has been extremely hard on me does not begin to express it...

Very truly
E.S. Osborne

On April 9, 1912, Eben apologized for his outburst, but ruefully noted the following: "I want to carry out every promise even though financially it has cost me more than $22,000."

Ezra had walked away from his Puyallup home after Eliza Jane's death in 1909. He never lived there again. The Osbornes finally sold the mansion in 1915 for $8,000 and other goods and considerations. They too, like Ezra in the Yukon, found much of their accumulation swept away, "slick as a mitten." ✻

REFERENCES

ARCHIVAL SOURCES

Ezra Meeker Historical Society, Puyallup.

Ezra Meeker, "Miscellaneous Folder," Dawson City Museum and Historical Society.

Meeker Papers, Letters, Folders 17–19, Box 4, Washington State Historical Society Research Center, Tacoma.

Mollett, William, MSS 273, 2000/7R, Textual Records, Yukon Archives, Whitehorse.

North-West Mounted Police Records, Dawson City Museum and Historical Society.

"Record Book for Placer Mining Claims," Creek Book, Gov. 130, Eureka and Tribs (page 246), Yukon Archives, Whitehorse.

_____. Creek Book, Gov. 418, Folio #37729, Yukon Archives, Whitehorse.

CENSUS AND GENEALOGICAL RECORDS

Tacoma-Pierce County Genealogical Society. *Pierce County, Washington, Auditor's Census 1889, 2 Vols.* Tacoma, 2003.

_____. *Pierce County, Washington, Auditor's Census 1892.* Tacoma, 2003.

United States Census. 1880, 1900, 1910, and 1920.

Washington Territorial Census.

Yukon Genealogy Gold Rush Data Base www.yukongenealogy.com/content/database_search.htm

MANUSCRIPTS, BOOKS, AND ARTICLES

Backhouse, Frances. *Women of the Klondike.* Vancouver/Toronto: Whitecap Books, 1995, rev. ed. 2000.

Becker, Ethel Anderson. *Klondike '98: E.A. Hegg's Gold Rush Album.* Portland: Binfords and Mort, 1967.

Berton, Laura Beatrice. *I Married the Klondike.* Madeira Park, British Columbia: Harbour, 1961.

Berton, Pierre. *The Klondike Fever: The Life and Death of the Last Great Gold Rush.* New York: Alfred A. Knopf, 1958.

Bonney, W.P. *History of Pierce County, Washington, Vol. 2.* Chicago: Pioneer Historical Publishing, 1927.

DeArmond, Bob. "This Month in Northland History." *Alaska Sportsman*, May 1968.

Ferrell, Ed. *Biographies of Alaska-Yukon Pioneers, 1850–1950.* Westminster, Maryland: Heritage, 1994.

Green, Frank L. *Ezra Meeker, Pioneer: A Guide to the Ezra Meeker Papers in the Library of the Washington State Historical Society.* Tacoma: Washington State Historical Society, 1969.

Gurcke, Karl. "Klondike Gold Rush Era Telephone Companies." (Draft) Klondike Gold Rush National Historical Park, 2007.

Hunt, Herbert. *Washington, West of the Cascades.* Chicago/Seattle/Tacoma: S.J. Clarke, 1917.

Keigley, Ken. "Summary of Meeker Land Transactions." (Unpublished) 2005.

Krefting, E.T., and Marshall Hunt. "The Story of Ezra Meeker," *Puyallup Press*, September 21, 1939.

Mayer, Melanie J. *Klondike Women: True Tales of the 1897–1898 Gold Rush.* Athens: Swallow Press/Ohio University Press, 1989.

McDonald, Roderick (reminiscences). *Penticton Herald*, December 17, 1936.

Meeker, Ezra. *The Busy Life of Eighty-Five Years of Ezra Meeker.* Indianapolis: Wm. B. Burford, 1916.

_____. *Hop Culture in the United States.* Puyallup: E. Meeker, 1883.

_____. *Pioneer Reminiscences of Puget Sound.* Seattle: Lowman and Hanford, 1905.

_____. *Ventures and Adventures of Ezra Meeker.* Seattle: Rainier, 1909.

_____, and Howard R. Driggs (rev. and ed.). *Ox-Team Days on the Oregon Trail.* Yonkers-on-Hudson, New York: World, 1922.

Morgan, Murray. *One Man's Gold Rush: A Klondike Album.* Seattle and London: University of Washington Press, 1967.

Norris, Frank; ed. by Karl Gurcke. "The Chilkoot Tramways." Klondike Gold Rush National Historical Park, 1990.

Satterfield, Archie. *Chilkoot Pass: Then and Now.* Anchorage: Alaska Northwest, 1973, rev. ed. 1974.

Shape, William. *Faith of Fools: A Journal of the Klondike Gold Rush.* Pullman: Washington State University Press, 1998.

Spencer, Lloyd S, and Lancaster Pollard. *A History of the State of Washington, Vols. 2–3.* New York: American Historical Society, 1937.

Washington Northwest Frontier Family and Personal History, Vol. 3. New York: Lewis, 1957.

NEWSPAPERS

Daily Alaskan (Skagway)
Dyea Trail
Klondike Nugget (Dawson City)
Morning Oregonian (Portland)
Penticton Herald
Puyallup Press
Puyallup Valley Tribune
Seattle Daily Times
Seattle Post-Intelligencer
Skagway News
Tacoma Daily News
Tacoma Ledger
Tacoma News Tribune
Yukon Sun (Dawson City)

INDEX

LETTER DATES AND TEXT PAGES